Echoes

From

Women Of The Alamo

GALE HAMILTON SHIFFRIN

Echoes

From

Women Of The Alamo

LAURENCE PARENT

BY
GALE HAMILTON SHIFFRIN

Echoes From Women of the Alamo
By Gale Hamilton Shiffrin

Published by

AW PRESS

Printed in the United States of America
by Clarke Printing Company
a division of the Mail-Well Corporation
San Antonio, Texas

ISBN.0-9676709-0
ISBN.0-9676709-1

Cover design by Gale Hamilton Shiffrin and Carlos Duran.

Echoes From Women Of The Alamo

Table Of Contents

Part I
Echoes From Women Of The 1836 Battle Of The Alamo

Part II

Echoes From Women Of
"The Second Battle Of The Alamo"

Illustrations

Acknowledgements

Because this book was written about women and directed mainly toward women readers I decided at the outset it would be best if I sought help and advice from women only. I felt that women would understand best what I was trying to say about these women of the Alamo. And so when I began I called on women only. I soon had to accept it is not safe to say things like "never" and "only." I have had to call on a number of men to help me, too, from time to time.

First and foremost was my husband, Ben. He has been a great help to me in many ways. But, most of all, I am indebted to him for his support, no matter what, plus the patience of a saint to listen to me talk about these Alamo women endlessly.

I did call on women to be readers of the manuscript, however. Cathy Herpich, a former Director of the DRT Library at the Alamo for her knowledge of the subject and her advice on many pertinent areas was invaluable help. Also, Marianna Jones, a former President of the San Antonio Conservation Society and professional librarian; and Constance Jones, a DRT member, a retired Professor of Mathematics and a Commander, USNR. The essential index was provided by the expertise of editor and publisher, Alice Evett-Geron. All of these women were of immeasurable help, each in her own way with her own particular skill.

After due consideration, I did add a male reader. My friend and neighbor, attorney Damon Ball, was called on for a legal opinion in certain areas. Not only did he give me legal advice but he also offered some helpful suggestions on content arrangement and form.

Another gentleman who did not read for me but one whose work I turned to frequently for information on Adina De Zavala was Dr. L. Robert Ables. I talked to him soon after I began my research on her and asked if I might quote him extensively since he was the only person who had written much about her. He answered, "Be my guest, I have been trying to get the word out for years." I accepted his offer and I am indebted to him for a great deal of information on that often overlooked Alamo woman.

Many others, both men and women, were very helpful, also. I mention here only those I called on most repeatedly: Martha Utterback and Elaine Davis, of the DRT Library; Linda Peterson and Janis Olsen, of the Center for American History at the University of Texas in Austin; Tom Shelton, of the Institute of Texan Cultures; and Jo Myler, of the San Antonio Main Library. Further, when the time came to print the book, I asked author George Nelson for his recommendation and he helpfully advised me to turn to Ralph Pais, Earl Lowry and Carlos Duran of Clarke Printing Co. Their assistance was always most cooperative and generous.

There is one more person without whom I could never have completed this project and that is my typist, Clarice Baggett. She has been almost as anxious to see this book happen as I have, and no one could have been more patient and understanding about my continual re-writes. I can never repay her fully for her faithful and efficient service.

To these and all of the friends and my family who continually encouraged me and wished me well throughout my long pursuit of this goal, I am most grateful.

Gale Hamilton Shiffrin

Introduction

Some of today's trend toward revision ("re-writing"?) of history seems to be to destroy some who preceded us who are dead and can offer no defense.

I recall a conference of professional historians and students of history where every report, one after the other, seemed intent on slandering the makers of the past as well as the recorders of it. Finally, an eminent historian in the group, who had not made a presentation but had served on a panel, rose and made a very brief statement. The primary message of her remarks was that it was exceedingly unprofessional and unethical for those present, or indeed anyone, to diminish and destroy those who had come before us, for as she put it we stand on the shoulders of our predecessors. All that we know is based on the accounts of those who have recorded things as they saw them, either as eyewitnesses, or as the reporters of written accounts from information available to them.

Because it was men who fought and died at the Battle of the Alamo, much has been written about them. But, very little has been said about the women of the Alamo. Women at the Battle of the Alamo? Yes, several, as well as some children. Their story has been known for some time now, but surprisingly, many people are still unaware of it.

The material in this book is not new but some of it is frequently overlooked or scattered information. It is not intended to be a strictly historical account, but it is a collection in one source for easy access and easy reading of the life-story of some of the better known women who were there during those fateful thirteen days of the Battle of the Alamo. And it also includes two other women who came to its defense later under battle conditions of an entirely different nature.

These are the life-stories of women, whom I felt should be viewed, not just as people who happened to be involved in historical events, but viewed as real women with human faults, and with redeeming features as well. I have tried to record the accounts as I perceived them from written material that was available to me. I have attempted to be as factual as possible where there were recorded facts, and have interjected personal opinion where it seemed appropriate, when there was no written record or firm evidence available. I have tried to reveal them simply as human beings with the flaws and the virtues that are present in all of us. None were perfect and none were totally imperfect. Until we are faced with the same circumstances with which each of these women were faced, we should be very cautious in our judgment of them.

Adina De Zavala, one of the women of the Alamo, once said: "History is written about men, by men, for men." I, as a woman, wanted to write history about some of the women who contributed to two very special events at this special place in the history of Texas. And, in this sense then, it is written primarily for women.

Gale Hamilton Shiffrin

Echoes From Women Of The Alamo

Foreword

For the next sixty-five years after the Battle of the Alamo ended on March 6, 1836, recorded history told of only two survivors of that world famous conflict—a lone young woman and her infant daughter. No others had ever been heard of by the general public until November of 1901 when the research of Miss Adina De Zavala, granddaughter of the first Vice-President of the Interim Government of the Republic of Texas, suddenly brought to light the story of another survivor. A seventy-three year old man named Enrique Esparza claimed in his interview with Miss De Zavala that he, as an eight-year-old boy, had been present in the Alamo with his family and had survived the battle with his mother and his brothers and sister. In time his story was followed by those of still more survivors. Over the years Alamo historians and researchers have learned more about these others, which included several women and children as well as one or two young black men who were non-combatants. But, surprisingly, many people today are still unaware of those others and their stories.

Most of the proven survivors were women and children, and though later accounts would list them by name, seldom was anything ever said about them. Who were these women? Where did they come from and why were they there? And what ever happened to them?

My curiosity as to what happened to those who lived to tell their tales was stimulated initially by a museum exhibit I saw in 1986 entitled "Remembering the Alamo." It was a very comprehensive exhibit which, of course, included a display of those two who were thought originally to be the only female survivors, Susanna Dickinson and her little fifteen month old daughter Angelina who became known as the "Babe of the Alamo." In the museum exhibit their story was covered in a brief account attached to a picture of each that told of their presence in the Alamo during the battle and the immediate after-math, with little else except for a statement at the end which said: "Both of these women became prostitutes."

I had never in my life heard that and I frankly did not believe it. Certainly I didn't want to believe it. Not only had I never heard this, but no one else I questioned at that time had either. I have found some repetition of this statement in various forms since then in my research including an 1869 newspaper account of Angelina's death, portions of which I quote from later. One self-styled historian and local sometime newspaper columnist, known for his sensational exaggerations and misrepresentations, paraphrased this newspaper article, the one and only account in print of Angelina's later life and death, in lurid detail in one of his columns published as recently as 1992. The damage done by out-of-context writing, such as that column and the museum exhib-it, is like ripples on a pond which grow wider and wider and cannot be interrupted. It is repeated over and over again until finally it is accepted as fact.

Other than this one newspaper account concerning Angelina, and the claims about Susanna later made by a husband, Peter Bellows, seeking a divorce from her, I found no documented written evidence referring to either of them as prostitutes. I found only sketchy legends and rumors repeated by writers over the years. This kind of evidence does not warrant a blanket statement such as that made by the muse-um without some kind of an explanation of circumstances.

Of course, as the old saying goes, where there is smoke there is usually fire, but it seems the very least we could do is give these women a fair trial before we hang them. It was the statement at the museum that prompted my search initially to find out if the claim made really was true and just what actually had become of these two women.

What happened to them after the smoke from the battle and the funeral pyres that followed had drifted away and disappeared into the mists of history? What had life ultimately held for these two who had witnessed one of the world's most stirring and immortal dramas?

And of almost equal curiosity, what were they doing there in the first place? Where had they come from that brought them into the path of this historical moment in time? My memory from earlier history lessons from my elementary school years did not include that.

What I found in the exploration and unfolding of the life stories of Susanna and Angelina Dickinson led me to wonder as well what had happened to the others who survived that momentous battle. As I searched for their stories, details of another battle which later surrounded this famous landmark, the Alamo, began to intrigue me. This one became known as "The Second Battle of the Alamo," and it took on a life of its own. My research then expanded to include not only the stories of the women of the actual Battle of The Alamo, but, also, those of the two women who were the major contestants in that second battle.

This book is the result of my search for a better understanding of all those women. Unfortunately very little documented information is available on several of them and therefore some of the women who claimed to have been there are not included. Of those who are included, one or two have briefer stories than others, and where extensive information was available, their story expanded.

Part I is concerned with those survivors who were present during the thirteen day siege and the actual "Battle of the Alamo" which occurred on March 6, 1836, and lasted no more than an estimated ninety minutes. The major portion has been devoted to Susanna Dickinson and her daughter, Angelina, not only because there is more information available on them than the others, but in the hope of balancing the overemphasis of some of the sensational claims made about these two tragic survivors.

Part II concerns the two principal women in the "Second Battle of the Alamo" which began in the early 1900's, and sad to say is still being waged by some to this day.

These are "echoes" then from some of the "women of the Alamo."

~ ~ ~

PART I

ECHOES

FROM

WOMEN

OF THE

1836 BATTLE OF THE ALAMO

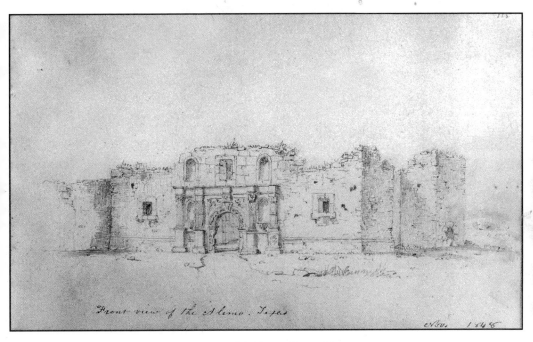

Front view of the Alamo. Texas

Nov. 1848

THE ALAMO, 1848 BY SETH EASTMAN
(Collection of the McNay Art Museum, San Antonio, Gift of the Pearl Brewing Company.)

YOUNG SUSANNA DICKINSON
(Adina De Zavala Papers, CNO1230, Center for American History,
University of Texas at Austin.)

Chapter One

Susanna and Angelina Dickinson

— Tragic Survivors —

As a native born Texan I have been familiar with the story of the Alamo all my life. And even though I had no forebears there, as a fourth generation Texan I have always felt something of a personal involvement in the stirring story of how these men never surrendered, even though their position was virtually hopeless; knowing finally that no help was coming, or if it did that it would be too little too late; of how they all died, with no survivors left to tell the tale; of how (as people were reminded for years in heroic terms) "Thermopylae Had Her Messenger of Defeat, The Alamo Had None". All of this never failed to move me. Eventually, the obvious question arose in my mind though—if they all died and there was no one left to tell the grim tale, how did the world come to know of some of the things that reportedly happened?

From what I recall of my early school years, the history text books did not include the Alamo survivors we know of today. Nothing was said about several women and children, as well as two black men who were released because "Mexico did not allow slavery". And as for no survivors and "no messenger of defeat", that glorious sounding phrase always seemed somehow contradictory, because, in fact, we were taught that there were two survivors—a woman named Susanna Dickinson and her little girl Angelina, the "Babe of the Alamo." Every school child was told of how these two miraculously survived that terrible battle, and we may have been told how they got out of the mass of carnage and confusion that followed, but those details were an anticlimax to the real story and they didn't stay with me even if told. I probably assumed they

3

returned to their home, wherever that was, and went on to live out normal lives.

Actually, that was far from the case, but I never gave that matter much thought, not as a school child nor even later. It was not until one day in the spring of 1986, when I saw what was for me at least a very startling statement in a museum exhibit in San Antonio called "Remembering the Alamo," that I gave the fate of those two survivors any further thought.

The display case covered all of the Alamo survivors and included a picture where available and a small information card on each. The pictures of Susanna and Angelina Dickinson were both familiar to me by then as was the text of the card, which included nothing noteworthy or new, until I got to the final line which read: "Both of these women became prostitutes."

Well, that really got my attention, which was exactly what was intended, of course. What an anticlimax to even such a brief view of the story of two who had witnessed that hallowed and noble event!

More than anything though, I was surprised that a major museum would use such a shock-value statement that was so out of context and without explanation even in an understandably limited space, especially about these two women who had endured and survived such a traumatic and historic moment in time and who, until now as far as I knew, had continued to live ordinary lives and been allowed to rest in peace afterward. The statement in the exhibit, however, could lead one to believe they had lived out their days in the pursuit of "the world's oldest profession."

Since I, and no one else I spoke to had ever heard this before, I decided to register an objection to the inclusion of such a statement and, more important, to find out about the basis for it. I finally reached the person responsible and I told him I did not think the statement was appropriate in this kind of exhibit nor even relevant. What did that have to do with "Remembering the Alamo"?

4

Further, I wanted to know on what evidence he based this statement.

Not surprisingly, he was unmoved by my objections to its use to begin with, and as for the validity of it, he said something like 'it was all a matter of record' or 'it's a fact'. Whose record? I asked. Whose fact? Regardless of its appropriateness or validity, though, I asked him how he thought the descendants of these two women would feel seeing a statement such as this in a major museum exhibit? I asked if, in fact, he knew of any descendants. He said he understood there was "some woman named Nitschke in Austin who kept things going." He could not, or would not, tell me how to reach that "woman up in Austin," and since it really was not my "battle" it seemed the best thing to do was to let the matter drop at that time.

But this incident with such seeming unfairness along with what came across as an overbearing and somewhat arrogant attitude of the exhibitor continued to bother me. And I thought, one day I would like to go up to Austin and meet this "woman named Nitschke" and hear her story. Unfortunately, I waited too late. Mrs. Nitschke died before I got around to doing that. I never knew she was Susanna Dickinson's great-granddaughter until I came across her death notice in my research some time later.

But the question about these two Dickinson women and what happened to them afterward kept haunting me. I wanted to know more about them and, of course, whether or not the "prostitute" statement was true. Who was Susanna Dickinson and where did she come from and what happened to her and her daughter after the battle? What I found out about them proved to be quite a story.

Susanna Arabella Dickinson, nee Wilkerson, was born in the Blue Grass country of Hardeman County, Tennessee in 1814. When she was 15 years old, she married Almeron Dickinson. Originally from Pennsylvania, Dickinson had served in the U.S. Army Artillery for a time where he acquired the skills of a blacksmith and gunsmith.

Family legend says that Almeron Dickinson had been court-ing young Susanna Wilkerson and they had had a lovers' quarrel that interrupted the romance. Dickinson was nearing thirty years of age by then and apparently had decided it was time to settle down to married life, and so after the break-up with Susanna, he had turned his attention to one of her friends who lived on a neighbor-ing farm. This new romance progressed rapidly and before long the two were to be married. Now, instead of becoming a bride, Susanna had been asked and had agreed to serve as a bridesmaid in the wed-ding of one of her friends to her own former suitor.

As arranged, Almeron came on horseback to the Wilkerson's farm to escort Susanna to the bride's home. What hap-pened on that ride is open to speculation, but the romance between Susanna and Almeron seems to have been rekindled. Apparently she wasn't going to let him get away this time. Instead of going to the home of her friend, the intended bride, Susanna Wilkerson and Almeron Dickinson eloped and were married at the Hardeman County seat of Bolivar, Tennessee on May 24, 1829.[1] A few months after their marriage they migrated to Texas and started a new adventurous life on the frontier.

They arrived in Texas and settled in the Green DeWitt Colony on February 20, 1831, in the town of Gonzales. In addition to property in Gonzales, Almeron Dickinson received under the law a Mexican headright grant of one league of land located in what is now Caldwell County. This land grant of 4,428 acres was to sustain a destitute Susanna several years later.

How did the newlywed Texans fare in Gonzales? Being born of second generation pioneers, they settled down to frontier life readily. Susanna had been taught to sew a neat stitch and cook a good meal, including a peach cobbler for which she later became famous. Even though cooking, sewing, and housekeeping were no problem for her, to the end of her 69 years of life she never mastered the very important skills of reading and writing. She never even learned to write her own name. Just a neat "X," as it was described was her only signature even on official documents. This was not unusual, however, for women in rural, frontier America at that time. Almeron on the other hand was said to be literate and he wrote a fine hand. There are examples in the records of his hand-written testimonials. His biography shows he was a Mason, a skilled gunsmith, farrier (blacksmith) and a farmer. From all accounts he was highly regarded by his fellow citizens as a most responsible, reliable man with a "strong sense of duty and a capacity for leadership."

On December 14, 1834, five years after their marriage, Susanna and Almeron welcomed into their life their first and only child, a little girl they named Angelina Elizabeth. Their new life on the Texas frontier had now settled into a very stable and promising future.

In September of the next year, 1835, however, things took a different turn. The first shot of the Texas Revolution was fired in Gonzales and Almeron Dickinson was involved since he was the most experienced artillery man in the community. After the encounter in October 1835 known as the "Come and Take It" episode, which involved a cannon assigned to them by the Mexican government to use for their own protection, some of the Gonzales group went to San Antonio to lend support in the "Siege of Bexar."

While Almeron Dickinson was away in San Antonio on this mission, his home was broken into by a band of robbers and Susanna feared for her life. Launcelot Smither, later a courier from the Alamo, had been left by the Army under Stephen F. Austin's order to protect the citizens of Gonzales while the men were away in San Antonio. In attempting to protect Susanna and her baby, who had been living in their home alone in Almeron's absence, he was severely beaten. He described this incident in very graphic terms, albeit with very little literary skill, in letters he wrote to Stephen F.

Austin who had gone to San Antonio as the Commander-in-Chief of the Army. The letters describe the deplorable condition of things in Gonzales with most of the men away. The first letter dated November 4, 1835 and headed "Gonzelas" [sic], reads in part, just as Smither wrote it:

> "Dear Sir—you have placed me at this place to attend to such matters as directed . . . all sober and honest men in this place knows that I have attended to them day and night—the companes that is coming has broken open allmost Evry house . . . and stole 100 dollars . . . of Miller—and Treated the wimon of this place worse than all the comanshee nation could have done—and dragged me out of the house and nearly beat me to death becos I was in the house of Mr. Dickerson . . . I have no doubt the would have kild if I had not bean there—there is no authority nor people to punish such people—and if the army dosnot protect the people at this place it must bee Intirely abanded by the Inhabtants . . ."[2]

A second letter dated November 5, 1835, from Smither to Austin tells of more problems in Gonzales:

> "Dear Sir I regret to bee compeld to address you on such a savage and hostile Conduct as was comitd by some of the troops that . . . come into the place on yesterday after being guilty of all the bad conduct and language that Sivelize beeing could put up with—after Night . . . nombers of the men broke open all most Every house in town and Robed all they could lay ther hands on—and such Insults wire never offerd to american women before . . . thire is no tribe of savages or Mexicans that would be guilty of such conduct—after 9 or 10 o'clock . . . finding the mob in town Mrs. Dickerson ho had been drivin from her house cald on me to go and stay in her house to protect her person and property.
> After goind to Bead thiy Entered the house twice by bursting Evry door and window and coming in crowds and dragd me into the Streats and beat my head to a poultice and would have kild me in the most torturing manner for no caws on earth but that I was in this house—I used Evey

means to pasefy them but the wild savage would have adherd with more humilty—I Refur you to Evey sober and honable man in this place what my conduct has been as Regards using Every means day and night to ade and assist Evey man that has past this place—and If the authority of this army does not take some steps to stop such conduct the wild savages would be preferable to the Insults of such Canebols . . ."[3]

These letters, as recorded in Jenkins' *The Papers of the Texas Revolution*, are clear indication that life in Gonzales for Susanna and Angelina without Almeron was not only unsatisfactory but was not even safe.

It was upon learning of this brutal incident that Captain Dickinson made arrangements to go back to Gonzales and get his wife and child and bring them to the Músquiz house on Main Plaza in San Antonio where he had been invited to stay. Had he not gone back to get them at that time, Susanna and Angelina, in all probability, would have been spared the battle at the Alamo, and their place in history would have been quite different.

Ramón Músquiz was Governor of the Texas Province and as a fellow Mason he and Dickinson had become friends earlier. Upon their arrival in San Antonio, Susanna and Angelina were established at the Músquiz residence on Main Plaza. There during those weeks just prior to the battle, Susanna cooked for boarders who came in support of the Texian troops at Bexar, including David Crockett who boarded at the Músquiz house when he arrived in San Antonio prior to going to the Alamo fortress. She did their wash as well as cooked for them. Life at the Músquiz home was a haven for the Dickinson family, even though it was short-lived. The story of those days, prior to the battle and after the battle itself, were recorded by Dr. John Sutherland in his account of "The Fall of the Alamo," after an interview later with Susanna and others.[4]

While Susanna managed the household affairs for her own

small family and the boarders who had been taken into the Músquiz home, Almeron worked on the Alamo artillery in preparation for the expected attack by the Mexican army. At noon on February 23rd of 1836, the fateful moment arrived. The bell in the belfry of San Fernando Church in the center of town began to clang furiously. The Mexican army had been sighted! The frightened citizens who had ranches in the countryside began to make hurried preparations to flee, while others took shelter as best they could.

When the alarm sounded, Almeron Dickinson was at the Alamo working on the artillery for the fortress. Mounting his horse he rode at a fast gallop to the Músquiz home and without even dismounting he called out to his wife, "Give me the baby; jump up behind me and ask no questions."[5] They rode full speed down the "Alameda" and then inside the Alamo mission compound walls where they were to spend the most memorable thirteen days of their lives.

The story of the fateful days from February 23rd to March 6th of 1836 has been told by many throughout the years, and Susanna would be called upon for years to come to tell her version of it. The Mexican army under General Antonio López de Santa Anna laid siege to the Alamo which was defended by 189 (claimed number as of this writing) Texians, all of whom fought to the death. This and all the drama and horror that surrounded that supreme price for freedom need no retelling here. But, what happened to Susanna and the other surviving non-combatants during those thirteen days and then what happened to them afterward?

Susanna Dickinson was to describe the scene over and over upon repeated requests as to what happened and who she remembered seeing there. For the remainder of her life it was never possible to put those scenes of horror and fright and the faces and names of the men who perished there completely to rest. She was called up as a witness, time and again, to testify as to whether some particular individual was present at the battle, usually in connection with a petition for compensation by his heirs for his service and death there. The ultimate irony of this was that she never was able to get proper compensation for her own little daughter and herself in spite of repeated petitions of her own plus those of others on her behalf.

Along with these testimonials for which she was called upon officially, there were the memories of events that had surrounded her and her own family that she told. One of the stories concerned her little fifteen-month-old Angelina which had a final ending that neither Angelina nor Susanna lived to see. It was the story of the cat's-eye ring which William Barret Travis, who commanded the Alamo, placed on a cord and put around the little toddler's neck.

As he watched this little child playing nearby on the last day before the final fury of the battle, Travis no doubt was reminded of his own two small children—Charles, who was seven years old by then, and five-year-old Susan Isabella, whom he had never really known, as she was born after he left Alabama for Texas. He had written a note from the Alamo on the 3rd of March, just two days before this last day, to the David Ayers family who were caring for Charles at their home near Washington-on-the-Brazos, the temporary capitol of the newly-declared Republic of Texas:

> "Take care of my little boy. If the country should be saved, I may make him a splendid fortune; but if the country should be lost and I should perish, he will have nothing but the proud recollection that he is the son of a man who died for his country."[6]

Travis must have wished there was some way he could leave his cat's-eye ring to that little boy. Maybe he even hoped it would find its way to him one day. Unfortunately, that was not to be, but the ring did travel a long and circuitous route before coming to its incredible final destination back in the Alamo one-hundred and nineteen years later. The amazing story of the journey of the ring is told in Chapter Two of this book.

Prior to the fall of the Alamo, Susanna had twelve days to observe and become acquainted with many of those who perished in the battle, as well as some of the other non-combatant women and children who survived. She came to know people she had never seen before, as well as to renew her friendship with some of her neighbors from Gonzales whom she knew well, for thirty-two of the men came in a group during the night of March 1st, eight days after the siege began. In later years she was to give testimony on behalf of many of these people.

The fateful days passed one after the other, filled with suspense and terror, but with periods of calm tension as well. And finally the morning of the thirteenth and last day arrived and terror reigned without ceasing. What must have seemed an eternity actually was little more than one hour. Toward the final moments of the battle she was to recall that her husband rushed into one of the few roofed rooms in the church ruins where she was crouching with Angelina and exclaimed, "The Mexicans are inside our walls! All is lost! If they spare you, take care of my child." And after embracing them and kissing them both he returned to his post and that was the last time she ever saw him.[7]

She was called upon to describe the final moments of horror and terror many times. The following quote is one of the testimonials attributed to an account she gave later:

> "The blood of noble men was seeping into the ground and the bodies of heroes were lying cold in death. The last man to fall was Walker. He had often fired the cannon at the enemy. Wounded, he rushed into the room where I crouched on my cot with my baby clasped in my arms and took refuge in a corner opposite me. The Alamo had fallen and the hordes of Santa Anna were pouring over its ramparts, through its trenches, through its vaults. The barbarous horde followed the ill-fated Walker and shot him first, then stuck

their bayonets in his body and lifted him up like a farmer does a bundle of fodder on his pitchfork. An officer rushed to stop them; then they dropped the body. They were all bloody, and crimson springs coursed in the yard. Some say they did this to Bowie's body, but it was the dead body of Walker they raised on their bayonets. He was the last to be killed and they were drunk with blood. I never saw my husband again after he went from me with his gun in his hand to die for his country. I feared for my fate but was saved by an English Colonel in the Mexican army. Through the intervention of Almonte I was permitted to leave the Alamo on horseback. Almonte said: "We are fighting men, not women." (N.B. Almonte was actually a Mexican army officer who had attended school for several years in New Orleans and had learned to speak English extremely well.)"[8]

In descriptions of the same scene later, Susanna told of how after the incredible noise of the battle ceased, a heavy, stifling silence settled over the stilled fortress. Waiting in terror for they knew not what, she huddled with her baby in the small, cold and musty room. After what seemed like forever, a voice called out from the doorway, "Is Mrs. Dickinson here?" This was what to her had been the English voice. Afraid to answer, but also afraid not to, she finally identified herself and was told to follow. As she left the church she fell in line behind the Mexican soldiers who had been brought to collect her. Suddenly she heard the whine of a bullet and felt sharp pain in the calf of her right leg as she walked through the courtyard.[9] Whether intentionally or accidentally she never knew, but she had been shot in the leg. This caused a wound which never completely healed and which was to trouble her for the rest of her life.

In her own words she later related: "I left the Alamo on horseback carrying my baby in my arms. I went first to the Músquiz house where I had lived before the Alamo siege."[10] Here she learned that her friend Señora Músquiz had personally interceded on her behalf for her release from the Alamo.

13

In complete shock, she must have been unable to comprehend fully that the nightmare was over, and that her husband Almeron was gone forever, along with all of the many other defenders with whom she had interacted just hours ago.

According to an interview with Susanna forty years later dated September 23, 1876, which is on file in the State Archives, we find: "After her removal to Músquiz, she expressed a wish to visit the scene of the carnage—(possibly hoping to find her husband's body?), but was informed by the people of the house that it would not be permitted as the enemy was then burning the dead bodies—and in confirmation thereof, she was shown a smoke in the direction of the Alamo."[11]

After several hours Susanna and the other survivors appeared before General Santa Anna to explain their presence at the Alamo. As she was interviewed before the Presidente and Commander-in-Chief he noticed her beautiful little Angelina, and just as Travis had been he was captivated by the coquettish and enchanting little girl. He reportedly asked to adopt her and take her back to Mexico City as his own, but Susanna was horrified at the thought of turning her daughter over to someone who was responsible for such carnage as she had just witnessed, including the death of the child's own father! Not only did she adamantly refuse but she was outspokenly critical of such a preposterous suggestion, according to the testimony of one of her granddaughters many years later.

Upon the conclusion of her interview with Santa Anna, she like the others was released, but unlike the others, she was given a special mission to fulfill—she was to carry the handwritten message of the "Fall of the Alamo" from General Santa Anna to General Sam Houston, who by now was in the town of Gonzales.

After being allowed a brief period of recuperation from the gunshot wound to her leg, she was sent on horseback on her mission. According to her own account, she was accompanied by a black servant named Ben who had served Colonel Almonte and

14

other senior Mexican army officers. Slowly they rode out from San Antonio toward Gonzales to the east. They had gone several miles and had come to an area near Salado Creek when out of the underbrush came another black man whom Susanna recognized from the Alamo as Travis' servant, Joe. He had been released by Santa Anna also, as proof that "Mexico did not tolerate slavery." Years later in interviews, Joe told the story of Susanna's journey to Gonzales along with his testimonial of the manner in which Colonel Travis died at the Alamo. Joe joined them, and the two men, one on horseback and one on foot, continued toward Gonzales with Susanna on her horse carrying Angelina in her arms.

It had just turned dark when the weary party arrived at the farm of Sarah and John Bruno some miles short of Gonzales. Susanna called out to the house and they came out to see who was there. They quickly helped the exhausted woman and her baby down from their horse and took them inside where they heard Susanna's tale of horror. She and Angelina were fed and they rested there for the night, but the two black men were uncertain of the situation and so they hid in the woods nearby.

According to the account of Marian Willard Griffith Nitschke, great-granddaughter of Susanna, they spent more than an overnight stop at the Brunos for as she stated "In a few days Mrs. Dickinson continued her journey to Gonzales." As soon as she had regained her strength apparently the Brunos set them all on their way to Gonzales with the message for General Houston.

In her own words Susanna was to testify later about all of this as follows:

> "I rode with my baby toward Gonzales. Out on the Salado (Creek) I met Colonel Travis' negro servant and he went with me. I was glad to see him." [After spending some time at the Brunos as related above, they continued to Gonzales.] "Several miles further out on the prairie we saw horsemen rapidly approaching. We thought they were

Indians and made the best preparation we could to defend ourselves. When they came nearer we saw they were white men. They proved to be "Deaf' Smith, Robert E. Handy and Captain Karnes who had been sent by General Sam Houston to ascertain the condition of the garrison in the Alamo. I told of it's [sic] fall and the terrible end. They went with me and the negroes to Gonzales."[12]

After the rest at the Brunos and she was sent on her way into town, Susanna reached General Houston accompanied by the three men named above. There she sobbed out her story "of the butchering and burning" and other details of the horrors she had witnessed. She told, " . . . of two who were pursued into her room and subjected in her presence to the most torturing death. They were even raised on the points of the enemy's lances, let down and raised again and again, whilst invoking as a favor, instantaneous death to their anguish, till they were at least [sic] too weak to speak, and then expired in convulsion."[13]

Houston read the letter which Susanna had delivered from Santa Anna and promptly ordered his troops to break camp and march to the east. When the word began to spread that the Alamo had fallen and that the Mexican army would be marching toward their village, the people in a panic began to pack what they could into their wagons and flee eastward in what became known as the "Runaway Scrape." General Houston ordered the town of Gonzales burned to the ground on their departure in order that it be of no use to the oncoming enemy. Susanna had no means of traveling on her own and the Brunos, whose home she had stopped in, mercifully took her back under their care. She was invited to travel with them to Mrs. Bruno's family home on Nash Creek near where the town of Houston is today. The Brunos stayed at the Nash Creek home for some time but eventually they returned to their farm in Gonzales and rebuilt their lives there and made that their permanent home.

Susanna had nothing in Gonzales to return to with Almeron

gone and her house destroyed. With no other place to go and no family to turn to, she elected to remain in the newly established town of Houston, which became her home for several years. Rumors and land speculations led everyone to believe that this would become the political center and capitol of the new Republic. And, in fact, it did. It won the vote ultimately by a narrow margin as the first capitol of the Republic of Texas, and was named for the hero of the moment, General Sam Houston, the larger-than-life person who symbolized the image of the new Republic. And so Susanna like others seeking assistance from this new Republic settled here at its seat of government to which they could appeal for help. The possibility of such help must have been her only hope for some means of support for herself and her infant daughter.

On October 18, 1836, a petition concerning support for Susanna on the basis of her husband's service and heroic death at the Alamo was referred to the appropriate newly elected committee of the Republic of Texas House of Representatives. After discussion and debate back and forth regarding this request and others like it that were bound to follow, the body of legislators ultimately voted to "table" the matter. In parliamentary language that was as good as saying the subject was dead. And so her hopes for governmental help faded, and how this survivor of the Alamo lived and where for the next several months remains a mystery.

Susanna was penniless. She had no income. She could not read nor write and there were no jobs for a woman of her situation except to cook for boarders and take in washing which is apparently what she did to sustain herself. She had known seven years of a contented and happy married life with Almeron Dickinson. Now, utterly alone, without any family here except for her baby Angelina, with no dependable income and no security, she ultimately entered into a series of three unfortunate marriages, seeking that security for which all human beings yearn.

The first of these marriages was to John Williams on 27

November 1837.[14] This was one year and eight months after the Alamo tragedy. This unfortunate marriage lasted only four months and Susanna was granted a divorce, one of the first in that area, on grounds "of indignities such that rendered her life intolerable with him; cruelty and barbarity which caused Susanna an abortion; and further, he abused and beat her child beyond endurance.[15] Certainly sufficient reason for divorce.

Nine months later, on December 20, 1838, twenty-four year old Susanna entered into her third marriage, this time to Francis P. Herring. The town of Houston had no water source at that time and her new husband's business was that of hauling water for sale from nearby Beauchamp Springs. Nothing is recorded of this marriage except that it ended after five years upon water carrier Herring's death when, according to one of his own relative's accounts, "He died of drink, not water."[16]

Again Susanna was a widow and what she did to sustain herself for the next four years is not clearly recorded, but from meager evidence available it appears she again operated a boarding house. There had been the petition, the first of many, made in October 1836, to the 1st Congressional Session held in Houston, as stated before, for a $500.00 donation to Susanna for her daughter but it had been turned down as were others later. Since the Republic had no funds for this, all such requests were turned down.

So, on December 15, 1847, once again she opted for marriage. Her fourth marriage was to Peter Bellows, or Bellis, as it is sometimes written, a Pennsylvania native 37 years of age.[17] Susanna by now was 33 with a 13-year-old daughter.

Some accounts seem to indicate the marriage was stable during the early years, others say otherwise. In any case, during this period Susanna was apparently supplementing the family income with boarders because one John Maynard Griffith, a farmer from nearby Montgomery County and sometime steamboat captain bringing bales of cotton to Houston, came to her boarding table. If

MATURE SUSANNA DICKINSON
(Daughters of the Republic of Texas Library.)

ANGELINA DICKINSON
(Daughters of the Republic of Texas Library.)

Susanna was having marital problems at this time, as some accounts suggested, she was having other problems of more immediate concern. Her "little angel," as stated later by Susanna's great-granddaughter, Marian Willard Griffith Nitschke, had grown up in an environment where she had received much attention and apparently little discipline, and she had gotten beyond her mother's control. Angelina was a pretty, black-haired, blue-eyed 16-year-old young lady now with a will of her own that was bent toward the pleasures of life.

John Maynard Griffith was almost ten years older than Angelina and had very strict ideas of morality and religion and Susanna selected this new boarder as the ideal husband for her daughter. They were married on July 8, 1851,[18] and set up housekeeping on John Griffith's farm in nearby Montgomery County. Two years later their first child was born, a son whom Angelina named Almeron Dickinson Griffith for her father whom she had never really known. Two years later, a daughter was born and she named her Susanna Arabella after her mother. Another son was born two years after that, and interestingly enough, he was named Joseph for the man who had become her mother's next and last husband. It seems significant to note that she did not name any of her children for her husband John Maynard Griffith nor any of his family.

The marriage between Angelina and John Griffith probably was doomed from the start though. Dr. Rufus C. Burleson, noted Baptist preacher, who later became an early President of Baylor (Baptist) University and served as such for twenty-five years, had married the couple in Houston. In the book *The Life and Writings of Rufus C. Burleson,* he said of this marriage:

> "Under the well-meant pious persuasions of her mother, she married a good, honest hard-working Baptist man from the country; I shuddered to see two such uncongenial spirits united in marriage. Marriage for money, for position, for convenience, or from parental persuasion, are often fearful

mistakes. Marriage should never be from anything but real love, springing from the heart, guided by the head and limited by conscience. When people marry where they do not love, they arc apt to love where they have not married. Soon the vivacious city girl got tired of her country home and her amiable plodding husband. Alienations, repinings and then divorce followed. The mother's heart bled over the ruin of her child's happiness." [19]

Probably the break-up of the marriage began following a party at the community of Cypress, as Mrs. Nitschke was to write later:

"At the Cypress "blowout", John Maynard Griffith lost his patience with Angelina and the homeward trip was a nightmare for her. With aching head and sore feet she listened to her husband pound at the evils of drinking and dancing. And so, they were divorced soon afterwards." [20]

After the divorce, Angelina's oldest child, Almeron Dickinson Griffith went to live with an uncle, Joshua Griffith, his father's brother, where he remained until grown. The two youngest children, Susanna and Joseph, went to live with their maternal grandmother, Susanna, who cared for them until they were grown and on their own.

Creed Taylor, was one of the original settlers who became a recorder of early Texas history, and possibly knew the Dickinsons in Gonzales before the Alamo battle. Later he had left Gonzales in the "Runaway Scrape" with his mother and settled in the Houston area. He may have kept in touch with Susanna and Angelina through the years, and was at the Cypress event mentioned above and saw Angelina. He or another chronicler like him wrote the following about her:

"Some two or three years later I again met the "Babe of the Alamo". She did not look so fresh and attractive as when

I first met her at the great fete at Cypress. Her greeting was less cordial, and shadows were lurking on the surface of the broad, open forehead. An anxious and at times a pained expression would creep over her face, and there was list-lessness and signs of langour [sic] perceptible in her eyes — and the rosy cheeks and lips were faded."[21]

After Angelina had married in 1851, Susanna apparently did begin to have serious trouble with her own marriage. In 1854, after seven years of marriage, Peter Bellows claimed she had left his bed and board for several months, then returned, only to leave again permanently soon thereafter.

Referring to the memoirs of *Dr. Rufus C. Burleson* again, he tells of Susanna "coming down the aisle with tears and penitential sobs" at one of his church services as early as 1849 (during the time of her marriage to Peter Bellows) to confess her lost condition and ask for forgiveness and guidance. Dr. Burleson says: "Later I visit-ed her at her house and wept and prayed with her. I found her a great bundle of untamed passions, devoted in her love and bitter in her hate." Again several years later in 1867 (while living in Austin and married to her last husband Joseph Hannig), she came to Dr. Burleson in penitence after a sermon preached there. She apparent-ly still felt she was guilty of some sin in her life that needed purg-ing. He states that over the years he came to hold her in high regard, with forgiveness and compassion. Regarding these accounts of Susanna and Angelina in *The Life and Writings of Dr. Rufus C. Burleson*, J. Frank Dobie says: "His word may be considered as good as any in Christendom."[22]

As for her husband's claim that she had left his bed and board in 1854, there is no documented record of this nor even of where she was during that time—only his claims. However, evi-dence is established that Susanna in fact did leave Houston in 1856 for the town of Lockhart in Caldwell County where the headright bounty land, granted to Almeron Dickinson when they came to

Texas in 1831, was located. This league of land of 4,428 acres along the San Marcos River had finally been awarded to Susanna by the Texas legislature. According to Dr. C. Richard King in an excerpt from the files of Mrs. Willard Griffith Nitschke as stated in his biography *Susanna Dickinson: Messenger of the Alamo:*

"On March 28, 1854, in Houston, Peter Bellows, Angelina Griffith and John M. Griffith, identified as heirs of Almeron Dickinson, appointed Susanna their "true and lawful agent and attorney" with power "to settle, sue for, demand and receive, be sued, compromise, receipt for, bargain, sell, make titles to, and do any and all things in and about the Estate of the said Almeron Dickinson". Using this power of attorney, Susanna on September 20, 1856, sold to John S. McKean the land "generally known as the Dickinson league—being the location of a grant made by the Mexican government to Ameiron[sic] Dickerson[sic] in his lifetime (as a Colonist in the Colony of Green DeWitt and one league in quantity)".[23]

From this evidence there can be no doubt that Susanna had left Bellows' bed and board in 1856 all right, but evidence shows she had gone to Lockhart for the specific purpose of selling her land, hoping no doubt to have an independent income of her own at long last. Documented records show she did just that and that after she had sold the Caldwell land grant on September 20, 1856, as shown in the previous quoted document, she purchased two lots in the town of Lockhart on October 10, 1856. She is then known to have left Houston permanently a few months later in 1857 and moved to Lockhart where she opened a boarding house. It appears that at last she was independent and on her own.

After Susanna's final departure, Peter Bellows filed for divorce under the claim that "she had taken up residence in a house of ill fame" and ". . . to committing adultery . . ."[24] Whether or not this was "a fact", as claimed by Peter Bellows and the museum exhibitor, I suppose only God and Susanna knew for sure then and only God knows now.

Personally, I cannot believe this troubled woman entered into the life of a prostitute with deliberateness and reckless abandon. There is no actual proof that she did, only the claim of her husband seeking divorce. If she did, it must have been as a result of despair, desperation and confusion, because whatever she did after leaving Bellows' 'bed and board' lasted only until she finally saw her way clear. History records that others in like circumstances have done just that.

In any case, the jury found the plaintiff Peter Bellows' petition, which had been filed in May of 1857, true and the divorce was granted on June 15, 1857,[25] ending another unhappy marriage for Susanna.

Once again Susanna opened a boarding house, this time in her own new home in Lockhart, as an immediate means of income. And on December 9, 1857, she married once more, this time to one of her boarders, Joseph Hannig. He was a man twenty years her junior, an immigrant from Germany described as a "tall, dignified man with a mustache," who was a cabinet maker. They were married at his Market Street residence in Lockhart,[26] soon after he had shown up at Susanna's boarding table.

E. A. Masur, a family member of Joseph Hannig's family who remembered "Aunt Sue" from his childhood days, stated later it was a pretty logical marriage even though the courtship was brief. Masur said, "Hannig was a pioneer blacksmith who really appreciated a good meal. When he sampled Susanna's cabbage, bacon and cornbread, he just up and married her."[27]

Soon thereafter in March of 1858 the Hannigs moved to Austin, Texas, where money from the sale of Susanna's land was used to set Joseph up in business in a cabinet shop on Pecan Street. Joseph Hannig prospered as a skilled cabinet maker. In fact, two of his pieces of furniture are in the Governor's Mansion today in

Austin, and one is in the French Legation Museum of that city, also. But, he became more than a successful cabinet maker. He was elected alderman, he had one of the largest furniture stores in Austin, he owned an undertaking business, and he invested extensively in real estate. In time he became one of the wealthiest men in Austin. When he died in 1890, he left an estate said to be valued at over $300,000.00, a substantial sum for that day.[28] In 1984, the city of Austin restored an area called "Hannig Row," where most of his business enterprises were once located.[29]

Susanna was an excellent cook and a good and devoted wife to Joseph Hannig. After her daughter's irresponsible abandonment of her children, Susanna took three of them to raise. The oldest child from Angelina's marriage to John Griffith was reared by his father's brother, Joshua Griffith, while the other two, little Susanna and Joseph, as well as the one child of Angelina's marriage to Oscar Holmes, little Sallie, were raised by their grandmother. She cared for them to their adulthood and she saw to their education in Catholic schools and convents. She also welcomed all of Joseph Hannig's nieces and nephews with their parents to frequent visits and stays in the Hannig home. According to Mr. B.J. Benefiel, a Hannig relative in Luling, Texas, the Hannigs' "Aunt Sue" and Uncle Joe were always very helpful to the Hannig family. They took Joseph's sister Josephine and her husband, Joseph Masur, and their four children in to live with them in Austin when they arrived in this country from Germany until they could find a place to settle.[30] Susanna was obviously a generous and warm-hearted woman. She made a good home for her husband, caring for her own family and her husband's and entertaining his friends as well. The Hannigs became a well respected and prominent family in Austin.

Her notoriety as the best, and for a long while, only , known female survivor of the Alamo, along with her infant daughter kept Susanna in the public eye for the remainder of her life. She was frequently interviewed by the press about her unique experience and status as the 'lone survivor' of the now world famous battle. One interview in 1878 with Charles W. Evers, editor of the *Wood County Sentinel of Ohio,* was highly complimentary of her as well as presenting a very clear picture of Susanna's character and personality:

> " . . . For one of the most pleasant incidents of my stay in Austin I am indebted to Col. Dupre, editor of the *Austin Statesman*, who kindly drove out with me two miles on a short visit to one of the most historic and to me interesting women of today. I refer to Mrs. Dickinson, now Mrs. J. W. Hannig, the only white survivor of the Alamo massacre, over forty years ago. We were made welcome at her beautiful home, which is on one of those commanding locations for which Austin is noted, overlooking the city and surrounding country. Mrs. Hannig is an intelligent woman of excellent memory, and is perhaps not far from 60 years of age, although but few grey [sic] hairs are yet noticeable on her head. [She was 64 years old at this time, only four years prior to her death.] She engaged readily in conversation about that dark episode in her history which robbed her of her husband and partially of her reason for a time. As she conversed she seemed at times to stop as if in a reverie or dream, and I fancied I saw almost a wild light dancing in her eyes for a moment, and it would not be strange, for her recital of the events of that awful day will excite the most stolid listener. If Mrs. Hannig was so inclined or if her circumstances required it (happily they do not) she could go on the lecture platform and draw crowded houses in any city in the United States . . ."[31]

What a wonderful picture of Susanna, survivor of the Alamo!

Susanna Dickinson returned only once to the Alamo after she had left it, as a "messenger of defeat." Forty-five years later in 1881 at age 66, just two years before her death and before any real sort of "historic restoration" at the Alamo had begun, she came back. But this time she came in the company of several dignitaries and two of her husband Joseph Hannig's nieces. *The San Antonio*

Express newspaper said of the visit:

> "The old lady recognized almost every stone. . . every
> corner. She said with tears in her eyes, "(it all) came back as
> vividly to memory as though . . . (it) . . . . . had been but yes-
> terday." She showed the reporter to where the couch had
> stood, and the window through which she peeped "to see
> the blood of noble men seeping into the ground, and the
> bodies of heroes lying cold in death." She pointed out the
> room where she saw the last man fall. "He was a man
> named Walker" she said, "who had often fired the cannon at
> the enemy." [32]

Susanna may have lost her way and partially lost her sense
of reason for a troubled period of her life, but she ultimately found
her niche. Susanna Arabella Wilkerson Dickinson Williams
Herring Bellows Hannig, and Joseph W. Hannig, her fifth and last
husband, enjoyed 26 years of happy married life. This is markedly
inconsistent with the image of a woman who would have been
inclined to pursue life in a "house of ill fame", or as "a prostitute"
as claimed by the museum exhibitor.

There is a vast difference in what a human being "who may
have been robbed of her husband and partially of her reason for a
time,"will do simply to survive or even just to seek happiness and
security, and the practice of the "world's oldest profession." It is
entirely possible that in times of despair and confusion, or more
precisely a need for survival, she may have pursued the lifestyle as
stated in the exhibit. The record before and after such possible period, however clearly indicates this woman was a respectable housewife and mother for the major portion of her life. The exhibitor at
the museum left the impression that she turned immediately to
prostitution as a way of life for the rest of her days. This simply was
not true and should not continue to be perpetuated by careless comment.

Regardless of what may have happened in the interim

before her marriage with Peter Bellows, when Joseph Hannig came into Susanna's life she must have been profoundly grateful and happy at long last to have someone to take care of her again in ways she couldn't seem to manage for herself. Her relationship with Joseph Hannig, with his orderly and purposeful sense of direction led her into a secure and contented life such as she had not known since the tragic loss of her first and only real previous husband, Almeron Dickinson.

Susanna died in 1883 at age 68, preceding Joseph in death by seven years. It must have been a mutually happy marriage, because Joseph Hannig, who had moved to San Antonio after Susanna's death and later re-married, requested in his will that upon his death he be buried beside Susanna.[33] And so he was. They are buried side by side, closer together than any other two graves in Austin's Oakwood Cemetery, it is said. Fortunately Susanna had finally found happiness and contentment in life again before the final peace of death.

And what about the other tragic survivor, the little 'babe of the Alamo'? What became of her? Sad to say, neither the same happiness in life nor even peace in death, ever came to Angelina. After she divorced her first husband, John Griffith, her search for excitement took her to Galveston, and later on to the colorful city of New Orleans.

In Galveston, it is said she lived with someone named James Britton in what was called "sin," for no documentation of a marriage between them has ever been established. Certainly, it was not an approved life style then, or now by most for that matter, according to the moral standards of many cultures. But since there are such things as "common-law marriages," this relationship with Britton in itself does not necessarily warrant being called "a prostitute" as the museum exhibit declared. My search for some verification of this statement turned up nothing more than the newspaper account of her death which stated "she had embraced the life of a courtezan [sic]". This same obituary among other seeming inaccuracies, identified her under the name of "Em. Britton" and stated "she married a Mr. Britton.[34]

Actually, according to all accounts, the relationship between Angelina and James Britton, whatever it may have been, ended at the outbreak of the Civil War when he left Galveston and returned to his home in Tennessee where he served in the Fourth Tennessee Regiment. Nothing more was ever recorded of him and it is possible he died in battle.

Quite some time after his departure, documented evidence shows Angelina moved to New Orleans where she married Oscar Holmes in 1864, and a daughter, whom she named Sallie, was born to them on September 6, 1865.[35] It was an unhappy marriage though which ended in divorce and nothing further is known of Holmes and not much that is authentic is known of Angelina either.

It was during these tumultuous years that Susanna, who by now was settled in Austin with Joseph Hannig, went to New Orleans to try to help her wayward daughter get control of her life, but she did not have the success she had hoped for. Eventually, with Angelina's consent, Susanna took her little granddaughter, Sallie, from the Catholic convent where Angelina had placed her and brought her back to Austin to live with her. Sallie Holmes remained in her grandmother's care until she was grown and married to Ben Berrera on August 21, 1883.[36]

As for Angelina, there is no record Susanna ever saw her again after she left her in New Orleans. Even though she may have given up on her daughter and probably lost contact with her, it must have been a terrible shock for Susanna to hear of her death and further to have her identified as someone named "Em. Britton," and back in Galveston. Susanna knew for a fact Angelina had subsequently married Oscar Holmes and she had their little daughter Sallie with her as living proof.

There are differing accounts of Angelina's death. Some say

she died in New Orleans, others say Galveston and that the grave there was washed away in the big 1900 flood of the latter city. According to Dr. C. Richard King's account of Susanna and Angelina:

> Sources differ on details concerning Angelina Elizabeth Griffith Holmes Britton's death. In a letter to L.W. Kemp, E. A. Masur of Lockhart [Related to them through Joseph Hannig.] says that "the Babe of the Alamo" died while visiting in New Orleans in 1870 and was buried there. The grave remains unmarked. An entirely different account was published in *Flake's Daily Bulletin*, published in Galveston on Wednesday, July 14, 1869:
>
> What a pure fancy that saying is that 'Death loves a shining mask.' We fancy a most practical fancy, and this is that death is no respector of person, but high and low, virtuous and vile, feel his inevitable grasp and fall before his breath. But 'shining mask' may have a different signification from the ones we have attached to it. It may have reference to the spirit more than the moral code as judged by the world, and while one's life may be like the corsair's name, 'linked with the one virtue and a thousand crimes', the one virtue may constitute the shining mask of the text and in the eyes of Heaven the soul thus styled may not be misnamed.
>
> But we intended to announce simply the death last evening of "*Em.* Britton," a name not unfamiliar to Texans, as being that of a woman connected forever with the struggle of the Republic at the Alamo, a Mrs. Robertson[35] and her only child, a daughter, were saved. This daughter was *Em.* Britton. "*Em.* was made quite a heroine because of her romantic fate in early life and we believe some grants of land were made to her. She grew up, was comely in face and person, and married a Mr. Britton. We do not know how it happened that they parted, nor is it necessary to know, but she embraced the life of a courtezan and so died last night.
>
> On Sunday, July 18, *Flake's Bulletin* mentioned in the mortuary report the name Emma Britton, aged 37, dead of uterus hemorrhage. Her place of birth was listed as Texas.[37]

While this obituary, written in the florid Victorian style of the time, seems to be an attempt to exonerate the unfortunate subject of questionable behavior, it makes other statements that raise a question as to its accuracy altogether.

In the first place, I could not make much sense out of 'Death loving a shining mask' and I looked for a source for the quotation. I could not find one but I did find a similar quote from an 18th century poet, Edward Young, in *Bartlett's Familiar Quotations* that did seem appropro: "Death loves a shining mark".[38] Quite a difference between "shining mask" and "shining mark". But, using the word "mark" would spoil the writer's point, wouldn't it? Another even more appropriate version is one from a later 19th century writer, Charles B. Fairbanks: "Slander, like death loves a shining mark."[39] So whether it was a typo error or a mistake on the part of the writer of the obituary we will never know, but shining mark seems more appropriate judging by the slander the poor girl suffered. One more minor point—the subject is reported as being 37 years of age. Angelina would have been only 34. These things, plus the use of the name "Em" as well as "Britton," along with the discrepancy of time and place of death as reported elsewhere, made me question the article all around.

Aside from this convoluted obituary and the differing accounts of the whereabouts and circumstances of the place of death and burial, the main question that kept coming back to me though was, why was Angelina Dickinson Griffith Holmes' death listed under the name "Em Britton" to begin with? As said earlier, as far as can be determined, there is no documented evidence of a legal marriage to James Britton, nor was she ever identified as "Em" or "Emma" anywhere else. Her relationship with Britton ended with his departure for the Civil War, and her marriage later to Oscar Holmes is documented. Even though that marriage ended in divorce, Holmes was still her legal name apparently. Why then would she go under the name of Britton, someone whom she had known before she became Holmes and whom she allegedly had never married? Could it be that in her fantasy she felt she still really was "Britton" or at least should be? And is it possible that Angelina herself chose to be known by that name because Jim Britton was the only real love in her life? And had she returned to Galveston because she fantasized he would some day return to her there? After all, according to the story that came to light later, it was to Jim Britton that she had given the ring which Colonel William Barret Travis had put on a string and placed around her neck when she was just a toddler at the Alamo.

By strange coincidence, according to the Travis legend, this was the ring given to him by a young lady named Rebecca Cummings as a token of her love and promise of marriage when he left for the Alamo. And just as Rebecca Cummings never saw William Barret Travis again after he left for the Alamo, so Angelina Dickinson never saw Jim Britton again after he left for the Civil War.

However, since Susanna never saw nor even heard from her daughter again as far as can be determined, it is possible that the woman identified as "Em Britton" was Angelina who may have returned to Galveston, and it is also possible that her life style could have been that of a "courtesan" as described. On the other hand, there is no documented proof that Angelina Dickinson and "Em" Britton were the same person at all. Again, only God knows now.

When dramatic incidents have resulted in catastrophe there is a tendency to engage in "what if" scenarios. Playing the "what if" game, what if Jim Britton had returned to Angelina after the Civil War ended, could there have been a secure place in life for her, too? Would he have been the anchor that would have given her life the stability she needed and no doubt longed for, as Joseph Hannig had been for Susanna?

This has been the story of what my exploration revealed of these two women of the Alamo, Susanna and Angelina Dickinson, who they were, where they had come from, and what happened to them afterward. And while I could not personally consider acceptable the "life style" that some have claimed about them, I can say, rather than be strictly judgmental, I have tempered my judgment with some compassion for each of them, considering the circumstances.

I find it very sad that Angelina's life took such a bad turn so early and continued in a downward spiral, ending finally in even sadder and hauntingly unproven and conflicting stories surrounding her death.

Wherever and however she died though, the tragedy of her once beautiful and captivating little girl, who had charmed Travis, and then the President of Mexico, General Santa Anna, so thoroughly he had asked to adopt her, who had married twice but walked away and left her own children, all of this must have driven Susanna almost out of her mind at times. She must have agonized over how things could have gone so wrong for her once vivacious and beautiful daughter. The void left by the tragic loss of her husband Almeron Dickinson along with the unending continual reminders, the series of failed marriages, and then later the sad life and ultimate loss of their only child, all of these heartaches must have been tragedies Susanna never was able to forget to the end of her days. These like the unreal horrors of the Battle of the Alamo were surely burned into her brain forever.

Reflecting on this woman who had experienced those unique and terrible moments of fame, one can't help but wonder when later in life she heard those ringing words, "Thermopylae had its messenger of defeat; the Alamo had none", if she might not have asked herself: "No messenger? What was I then"? No messenger indeed. As Dr. C. Richard King says in his biography of her, "Susanna Dickinson <u>was</u> the Messenger of the Alamo".

# # # # #

Earlier in this story of Susanna and Angelina, reference was made to a lady named Nitschke, whom the museum exhibitor referred to as "some woman up in Austin who kept things going." Who was this woman? And what was her relationship to these two survivors of the Alamo?

Marian Willard Griffith Nitschke was the granddaughter of Angelina and great-granddaughter of Susanna and Almeron Dickinson. She was married to Robert F. Nitschke, Jr. of Austin. He died in 1965. Willard (she was called by her middle name) Nitschke was a graduate of the University of Texas, a distinguished 41-year-career teacher of history at Austin High School in Austin, Texas, and a founder of the Austin Chapter of the Daughters of the Republic of Texas. She died in 1990 at the age of 92.

Mrs. Nitschke had no children of her own but she had several nieces and nephews. One of her nephews was a journalist named Charles Ramsdell, great-grandson of Angelina Dickinson and great-great-grandson of Susanna and Almeron Dickinson. He was the author of a well known book, *San Antonio, A Historical and Pictorial Guide* first published in 1959, familiar to many San Antonians. For several years it was considered the number one guidebook of the city. He was the son of Dr. Charles W. Ramsdell, Professor of History at the University of Texas at Austin, and Susanna Griffith Ramsdell, sister of Willard Griffith Nitschke. Willard Nitschke and her sister Susanna Ramsdell were two of the six children of the oldest child of Angelina, Almeron Dickinson Griffith, who was named for his grandfather who died at the Alamo.

One of Susanna's strongest supporters for many years was E.A. Masur, nephew of her husband Joseph Hannig. He was the youngest of the four children of the Joseph and Josephine Masur family referred to earlier, whom Susanna and Joseph Hannig had welcomed into their home upon their arrival from Germany until they found a permanent place to live. Masur remembered that stay and many other visits there as a young boy during the last ten years of Susanna's life. He spoke of "Aunt Sue" with great fondness in his later years. He felt her memory had been slighted in the Texas Centennial of 1936 when markers went up all over the state for what he considered far less significant cause, and he had worked tirelessly for over ten years for a marker to be placed on her grave. Sadly, he died several months before his campaign was successfully accomplished. Finally, as a result of his efforts on March 2nd, 1949, sixty six years after the death of Susanna Dickinson, the State of Texas put a white marble slab on her grave with the inscription: "Susanna Dickinson Hannig, Mother of the 'Babe of the Alamo.'"

Willard Nitschke spent much of her adult life trying to clear her great-grandmother's name and establish her reputation as a respectable woman who eventually found her place in life after years of misfortune and confusion. Like E.A. Masur she had campaigned for years for the State Legislature to recognize Susanna Dickinson, "the messenger of the Alamo," with another marker of some kind in the State Cemetery as well. Susanna's grave remained at Oakwood Cemetery because Willard's father, Almeron Dickinson Griffith, adamantly insisted it should. But Mrs. Nitschke's dream of a marker in the State Cemetery honoring Susanna was finally realized, appropriately enough on March 6, 1976, the 140th anniversary of the fall of the Alamo.

Dr. C. Richard King in his biography, *Susanna Dickinson: Messenger of the Alamo* described the event:

> Susanna's great-granddaughter, Mrs. R. F. Nitschke, Jr. upheld her father's wishes (to leave her remains undisturbed in Oakwood Cemetery), but she believed that the messenger of the Alamo deserved a monument in the state cemetery, so she campaigned for the State Legislature to recognize Susanna with a marker. Mrs. Nitschke's dreams were realized, and 140 years after Susanna Dickinson and her small child left a stilled Alamo to face Santa Anna, on

March 6, 1836, a granite marker shaped like the state of Texas was unveiled by A. Stasswender. A bronze plaque in the outline of the Alamo, superimposed on the granite, reads:

Susanna Dickinson

1814   Hannig   1883

Her name belongs to Texas history. She cast her lot with the immortal heroes of the Alamo. After its fall, with the "Babe" in her arms, she carried the news to Gen. Sam Houston at Gonzales.[40]

As Dr. King described it, "a chilling mist fell during dedication services" as various dignitaries spoke, including King who gave a brief account of the life of Susanna Dickinson. Mrs. Nitschke climaxed the event by telling of how her dreams became true at last with this monument to her great-grandmother after so many years of her impassioned pleas.

~ ~ ~ ~ ~ ~ ~ ~ ~

Once again indulging in a "what if" scenario: What if Almeron Dickinson had not gone to the Alamo as some of his neighbors did not? What if he and Susanna and their beautiful little daughter had remained an intact family in the town of Gonzales? He was, as was said, an outstanding citizen there with leadership potential and was held in very high regard by his fellowmen. He was also a man dedicated to his little family. His wife, Susanna, by all accounts, was devoted to him, and their "little angel," Angelina, was the apple of their eye. If the Alamo had not included them, what might life have been like for Susanna and Angelina?

Some people live through hard times without being destroyed by the experience. Others, once off the track, never seem to find their way back again. These two clearly got off the track. One recovered—one did not.

Susanna may have had deep regrets about some periods of her life, but her basic strength eventually emerged and she moved on to become a useful and respected citizen.

Unfortunately, her beautiful and willful daughter did not. From the moment she strayed from the path, she wandered farther and farther away, as though always seeking to escape the world she had been thrust into. The life-long attention she had had, and the lack of firm discipline, these combined with her own personal passions made it impossible for her to conform to the kind of life that proved to be her mother's salvation ultimately.

Unfortunately, Angelina may have adopted the lifestyle as claimed by the museum exhibitor and others. But, her mother, Susanna, did not in the final analysis and she should not continue to be labeled thus.

It is hard not to be judgmental of those whom we perceive as having missed the mark or who have done things differently from the way we might have done them. But, until we have walked in their pathway, under their circumstances, it is best to be very careful in judging. I have tried to do that in assessing the lives of these two "tragic survivors."

Regardless of how people may judge Susanna and Angelina Dickinson though, it should be remembered that there are those like Willard Nitschke whose heritage includes these two women. I believe they would like to see them recognized for just what they were—simply human beings, flawed though they may have been, who were merely fateful survivors of that historic and tragic moment in the history of Texas, "The Battle of the Alamo."

~ ~ ~ ~ ~ ~ ~

~ ~ ~  ~ ~ ~

Chapter Two

The Incredible Journey Of The Travis Ring

— From The Alamo And Back —

*T*he fact that a handful of women and children, found huddled in small corners of the old Alamo chapel, survived that bloody battle where all defenders died continues to be a surprise to a great many people and a matter of real wonderment. Beyond that, the hauntingly tragic story of the life of two of these survivors, the Alamo messenger to General Sam Houston, Susanna Dickinson and her little daughter, Angelina, still holds a special fascination. Not just the perilous 13 days they spent during that momentous event in history—that is certainly cause in itself for thoughtful reflection—but the turbulent years which followed that episode of terror were very unreal at times, and their lives were continually filled with more than their share of melancholy melodrama. The remainder of life for each of them was troubled with many ups and downs, before each finally knew peace, the daughter possibly through an early death and the mother through a tranquil and happy marriage at long last.

Their prominent place for so many years in the most dramatic ninety minutes in Texas history naturally caused many stories and legends to grow up around them. But one of the most unusual is that of the incredible journey of what is known as the "Travis Ring."

"Travis Ring"? It is surprising enough for most people to learn there were people who survived this "no prisoners taken" battle, but the thought of a small object such as a ring surviving such total destruction, and what is more, be there in the Alamo on display as proof today, is hard to believe. As I stood looking at it on one of my many trips there escorting visitors to the shrine, I hoped no one would ask me how it could possibly be there. The little card beside it at the time gave very sketchy information on that point. I vowed to research the matter to see if there was a more complete explanation. Was it found in the debris afterward, one might ask? Or, did some modern day archaeologist find it buried in the dirt during a latter day excavation searching for artifacts? No, but there is a story about the survival of this ring, that surfaced many years after the battle, that is almost more unreal.

There are unexplained gaps in this story, but that can be said about most of the legends and stories that have grown up about the Alamo. This is a story that some may doubt and some might even brand as a hoax, but recorded accounts disclose no evidence that it is anything other than what might have happened and allegedly did, incredible as it may sound.

~ ~ ~ ~ ~ ~ ~ ~ ~

It was the evening of the last day before the Alamo would fall at dawn of the next morning, the 6th day of March 1836. The continual sporadic firing on the old mission fortress had been going on for twelve days and nights and the tension had mounted daily. The men were near exhaustion. No reinforcements had come and there was little assurance that any would come at this point and yet hope never seemed to die.

During a lull in the Mexican bombardment, the Alamo commander, Colonel William Barret Travis, reportedly had gone to his quarters on the second floor of the old "long barrack." As he searched his mind for a possible solution to their desperate situation, he could look out on the compound and see the movement here and there from his slightly elevated vantage point.

Captain Almeron Dickinson, the chief artillery officer, was

out inspecting his guns located along the top of the old church walls. Dickinson had left his wife Susanna and their little fifteen-month-old daughter Angelina inside the walled area of the roofless church, along with the other women and children huddled about in little family groups. They had been camping there for the last twelve days and nights. There was growing fear and uncertainty among all of them.

Alone now in his quarters he was writing final communications in these few quiet moments. Poised there at a make-shift writing table, Travis sat staring down at an unusual ring on his hand. It was a hammered gold band set with a large dark stone which had a circle of light around the center of it. The stone in geological terms was known as a chrysoberl, but was commonly called a "cat's-eye" because it resembled one.

This ring was very special to "Buck" Travis. It represented a story filled with romance and sentimental dreams and promises of happy times for him. Now, as he stared into the hypnotic "cat's-eye," during what he may even have sensed was the last evening of his life, his mind was no doubt flooded with memories of the ring's symbolic meaning for him, as well as earlier significant events that led up to the time he received it.

His reverie took him back to his home in the state of Alabama, where eight years ago in the spring of 1828, he had married a young girl named Rosanna Cato. She was one of his students in the town of Claiborne where he taught school while studying law under Judge James Dellett, the foremost criminal lawyer in the state. A year later in 1829 a son was born to them whom they named Charles Edward. The marriage was reported to have been an unhappy one, though, and in time Travis had reason to believe his wife had been unfaithful to him.

In 1831, he had departed Alabama quite abruptly, leaving Rosanna with their little two-year-old son Charles and another child on the way. Some accounts claim he shot and killed a man involved with Rosanna. A written statement made several years later by a nephew said it was common family knowledge that "he killed a man on account of his wife." Someone else was indicted, however, and Travis was never charged.

In any case, he disappeared overnight, never to return to Alabama, having "G.T.T.," "Gone to Texas," as so many others did at that time, to start a new life.

There in 1834, three years later on this new frontier, he met and fell in love with a young woman named Rebecca Cummings. She was a daughter of one of the founding families in Stephen F. Austin's original colony, the "Old Three Hundred" at San Felipe de Austin.

One year later in 1835, his wife Rosanna Cato Travis came to Texas to try and persuade her husband to return to Alabama with her and their son Charles, who by now was six years old, and their little daughter Susan Isabella, who was now four. Rosanna was not successful in her plea for a reconciliation, however, and so she returned to Alabama with only Susan Isabella after having agreed to leave Charles in Texas with his father.

Unable at the time to care for him continually in his own quarters at San Felipe, Travis arranged for Charles to stay temporarily with the David Ayers family who lived nearby at Washington-on-the-Brazos. He was very devoted to his little boy though, and his visits were frequent and regular and he looked forward to the time he could make a home for him. On his way to the Alamo one of his last acts had been to stop and say good-bye to little Charles, and one of the last messages he sent from the Alamo was to the David Ayers family saying, "Take care of my little boy."

After the divorce of Rosanna and Travis was granted in the fall of 1835, Rebecca Cummings had agreed to marry him. Their pledge of love had been sealed with a gift to each other. He had given her a brooch and she had given him a lock of her hair and the hammered gold ring set with a dark "cat's eye" stone in it as the symbols of her promise.

It would be seven long years after Travis' untimely death at the Alamo before Rebecca Cummings would marry someone else in 1843, David Y. Portis, a lawyer and later Congressman from the San Felipe area.

Now, here in the Alamo, as he reflected on his life, clearly Travis must have sensed he would not live to continue wearing this ring which embodied his hopes for the future.

Suddenly, acting on his reputed sense of high drama, he removed the ring from his finger, knotted it onto a piece of string, and walked over to the old church ruins where little Angelina was playing innocently at her mother's feet. He placed the string necklace around her neck, explaining perhaps that he would not be needing it anymore. Why this particular little girl, though? Did she perhaps remind him of his own little girl Susan Isabella, whom he had never really had a chance to get to know?

As he relived the memories of the past in those final hours before the battle, no doubt he hoped and prayed that this child would survive this nightmare and possibly be able to carry this memento away with her as a sign of his final presence here. Perhaps she and her mother would live to tell the world the story in years to come. And just perhaps, he may have hoped they might some day pass the ring on to Rebecca Cummings or to his own little daughter or son whom he knew somehow he would never see again. Perhaps Angelina could be his link with his own children through this ring.

Having passed the ring on to this little girl, he could only trust it would eventually find its proper niche. He then turned his attention abruptly to the perilous hours he knew were ahead of him. And the outcome of that, of course, is history.

But, whatever became of that "cat's-eye" ring? Almost like a miracle, the gold band with its stone of dark chrysoberl, showing that central circle of light, suggestive of a cat's eye, seemed from that moment on to take on a life of its own. And today, after a very circuitous route, unbelievably it is back in the historic spot where its journey began.

The fact that such a small and vulnerable object survived the terrible turmoil and carnage of that horrendous event on March 6, 1836, is remarkable in itself. But then to be traceable through the tumultuous years of its new owner which followed, plus its trail beyond that, and now be back in the Alamo on exhibit today is incredible! What is its story?

That story of its life after the Alamo and return journey is a strange and convoluted one, indeed.

It is almost unbelievable in the first place that Susanna Dickinson's wayward daughter, who in later years lived such an erratic life, could have held on to a ring which had been placed around her neck on a string when she was just a toddler in the Alamo, until she was a grown woman. It seems impossible even with the help of her mother, because the mother also had an unstable period herself for a time. How did either of them manage to do that? And how did the ring ever find its way back to the Alamo after it later left Angelina? The first parts of that question will forever remain a mystery, but the second part has a reported answer.

Incredibly, the ring came back to the Alamo, not from a family descendant of Susanna or Angelina as might be expected, but as a gift from someone completely unrelated to them—a Houston attorney named Douglas W. McGregor.

The ring's journey from the Alamo began when it left there with Angelina Dickinson and her mother after the bloody battle. There were those many troubled years that followed the trauma of that event for them as told in Chapter One, describing how Angelina managed to grow into a beautiful, although undisciplined, young woman and at age 17 married John Maynard Griffith. The marriage, said to be doomed from the start, did last a few years and produced three children.

In time, the high-spirited young woman divorced her husband and left her children in her mother's care, seeking what proved to be ever elusive excitement and happiness elsewhere. She married again five years later, this time to Oscar Holmes and they had a daughter, who came under Susanna's care, also, when this marriage ended in divorce as well.

Between these two marriages Angelina is known to have had a lengthy "relationship" with a man named James Britton. Some accounts, say, in fact, that she was married to him, including the only known newspaper account of her death. There is no documentation of a legal marriage between them nor of her death but conceivably the marriage could have been what is termed a common-law marriage. In any case, according to the newspaper obituary she was known for a time by the name of Britton and it was from Jim Britton the ring later began the journey that brought it back to the Alamo.

Jim Britton reportedly said that Angelina had given him the "cat's-eye" ring that had been given to her by Colonel William Barret Travis at the Alamo. Wearing it when he left her upon the outbreak of the Civil War in 1860, Britton departed from Texas and returned to his home state of Tennessee to serve in the Confederate Army where he became a captain in the Fourth Tennessee Regiment. For some unrecorded reason, he allegedly gave the ring to a junior officer in his company, Lt. DeWitt Anderson, the younger brother of Paul F. Anderson, one of Britton's boyhood friends from Tennessee. Nothing more is recorded of Jim Britton after that and it is probable, as has been presumed, he was killed in battle. DeWitt Anderson is said to have worn the ring for the rest of his life and upon his death in 1902 in Marianna, Arkansas, the ring was passed on to his nephew, T.H. McGregor of Austin, Texas. He in turn gave it to his son, Douglas W. McGregor, a Houston attorney. Douglas McGregor returned it to the Alamo with the account of its circuitous journey.[1]

Assuming that each of the owners of this unusual ring, prior to Douglas McGregor, was made aware of its origin when he received it, one wonders why none of the others made an effort to return it to its famous source as an historic artifact.

The main reason may have been because there was no official museum or organization to receive such artifacts and be responsible for them for many years after the Battle itself. Even if it occurred to one of the earlier owners there was no official repository for such things.

It was not until 1889, fifty-three years after the Battle, when Miss Adina De Zavala of San Antonio met with a group of patriotic women whom she had interested in historical preservation, that a museum effort even began. These ladies called themselves the De Zavala Daughters and they made the first concerted effort to make the Alamo into a museum and shrine dedicated to those men who sacrificed their lives there.[2]

Even after that start, however, it was several years before organized effort brought the Alamo under central control resulting in improvements seen today. During the year of the Texas Centennial in 1936, which celebrated one hundred years of freedom from Mexico when Texas became an independent Republic, the Alamo chapel still had a dirt floor just as it had at the time of the Battle in 1836, and from the beginning during its years as part of the old Spanish Mission San Antonio de Valero. The floor was finally covered in 1937 with the stone flooring seen there today, and a real museum began to take shape.

The efforts which began in 1889 toward preservation of the Alamo and continued afterward through the years under the custodianship of the Daughters of the Republic of Texas, have resulted in the protection of this noble shrine and the creation of a true museum for the display of artifacts such as the "Travis Ring."

Though each person who came into possession of this ring may have been aware of its significance, it was Douglas McGregor, the final owner, who, knowing the full stirring story of the ring's origin and its place in history, returned it to its rightful resting place now that one finally existed. And so in 1955, one-hundred and nineteen years after its departure, the ring was returned to the Alamo in order that "future generations could see it and know its story."[3]

Today, the "cat's-eye" ring is on view in the Travis case at the shrine of the Alamo, watching the people walk through this hallowed spot in Texas history.

Throngs of visitors pass by it daily. Those who have heard the story, are eager to see it. But others, scarcely pause to give it more than a passing glance. Very little can be told on such a small card as the one beside it, and thus much of its story is lost for many.

Not only is the story of the ring's journey hard to believe, but it is also rather sad, just as so many things were that happened to the poor "Babe of the Alamo." But its final return miraculously brought the "Travis Ring" back to the very spot that William Barret Travis allegedly placed it on the little toddler, where it can rest in peace at last. Perhaps, just perhaps, it brought Angelina's restless spirit with it as well.

The survival of such a small, sentimental memento and its incredible journey is surely one of life's strange little miracles.

The "Travis Ring" is back where it belongs and its circle is closed at last.

~ ~ ~ ~ ~ ~ ~ ~

Chapter Three

Ana Esparza

"I will stay by your side . . ."

*F*or sixty-five years after it ended, published history in general, including Texas history textbooks, claimed that one lone woman, Susanna Dickinson, and her infant daughter, Angelina, were the only survivors of the 1836 Battle of the Alamo. But on November 10, 1901, a story appeared in the *San Antonio Light* newspaper that proved recorded history for all those years had been wrong.

ENRIQUE ESPARZA
(Adina De Zavala Papers; CNO9249, Center for American History, University of Texas at Austin.)

A dedicated and tireless researcher of the history of Texas, Miss Adina De Zavala, a native born Texan, was the first person to bring to the public in general the news of the discovery of a man named Enrique Esparza, by then 73 years old. He claimed to have been in the Alamo as a boy eight years of age at the time of the battle. He stated that his mother, he and three younger siblings, along with several other women and children were there, besides the Dickinson woman and her child.[1]

But why was this not known before? Why had it taken so long for this man to come forward with his story? This startling news came as a complete surprise to the general public, but, in fact, it was a matter that had long been common knowledge among the family members of those who claimed to be survivors and the Mexican community as a whole, because those other survivors were all Mexican-American. The reason given for not spreading the news of their survival is quite understandable for the time. For one thing, as they said, few other people outside their own community would have listened in all probability, and for another would not have believed them if they did listen.

Until about five years prior to Miss De Zavala's article, Esparza had lived in a farming community in nearby Atascosa County where he had moved some years after the battle. This small community was several miles from the town of San Antonio and limited communication means of the time provided little occasion or reason to discuss his Alamo experience outside the family and the community. There can be no doubt it was common knowledge there however, and elsewhere by Mexican-Americans in general.

As early as 1858, in an interrogation concerning a petition for inheritance rights as to whether or not Gregorio Esparza, father of Enrique and his two brothers, and husband of Ana, was at the Alamo, a citizen of the area, Gregorio Hernandez, is recorded as testifying:

> "It was as notoriously known among the Mexican Citizens of Bexar County that Gregorio Esparza was one of the Martyrs of the Alamo, as it is known and believed among the Americans that Bowie or Crockett was one . . ."[2]

Once his story in the *San Antonio Light* had caught public attention however, as a result of Miss De Zavala's story, the other San Antonio newspaper, the *Express*, carried their version of the story one year later on November 22, 1902, which gave further details of the battle as related by Esparza.[3]

Then five years later on May 12, 1907, a well known local journalist of the day, Charles Merritt Barnes, interviewed Enrique Esparza and an even fuller story appeared in the *San Antonio Express* and was copyrighted by Barnes and distributed to newspapers throughout the country.[4] Mr. Barnes made sure by frequent reminders and repetition of this story that he received credit for the "discovery" of another survivor of the Alamo. Evidence is clear, however, that it was Adina De Zavala who was the first person to "discover" and bring to the attention of the world the story of that other survivor, Enrique Esparza.

Years later, the story was told by a well known teacher of the day in San Antonio, Sarah S. King, who was a friend of Miss De Zavala's. No doubt it was Miss De Zavala who brought Enrique Esparza to the attention of Sarah King. Miss King co-authored a book in 1936 entitled *Rise of the Lone Star,* which included a chapter entitled "Esparza, The Boy of the Alamo Remembers." As principal of Bowie Elementary School in San Antonio, she had invited him some years before in the early 1900's, about the time Adina De Zavala discovered him, to come over and tell his story to her young pupils. She describes him as "an aged Mexican gentleman" by then. He entertained the children with a colorfully detailed story of his life before, during and after the Alamo, and at the end he closed with this statement:

> "I talk to few about the Alamo and the old days. Some believe me not; some know it all. I talk now and then to friends of understanding and sympathy."[5]

Thus, the Esparza story had been a long time in being brought to the public at large. Once uncovered, though, it was repeated over and over again and is still quoted today, with wide variations of details.

This book is not about the men or boys of the Alamo, however, and it is not my intention to just repeat the story of the life of Enrique Esparza. Instead it is to emphasize that part of his story which pertains to his mother, Ana Esparza, one of the women of the Alamo.

Who was this courageous woman who took herself and her four children into the Alamo to stay by the side of her husband to the death? And what became of her afterward?

The fact is, not even vital statistics of birth and death records are consistent in the sources I found. Further, none of the events in the life of Ana are recorded anywhere except in the accounts given by her son, Enrique. And so, we must call on his story for the story of his mother's life. Her story of necessity must be viewed through the eyes of her son, Enrique, plus a few later descendants. One of those descendants in particular, who was especially helpful in developing this account of Ana's life by making his files of family history available to me, was her great-great-grandson, Reynaldo "Ray" Esparza.

In the *San Antonio Express* article cited earlier, Enrique tells of how his father, Gregorio Esparza, belonged to the Benavides Company of the American Army, as he termed it. This company supported the Texas cause in upholding the Mexican Constitution of 1824 which they felt was being violated by Santa Anna and his Centralist government.

Upon learning of the approaching army of Santa Anna, many families began to move out of their houses in town. They left for their ranch homes for safety in the remote countryside and other places, out of the army's path. Esparza's friend, John W. Smith, had offered him a wagon and team with provisions to take his family out of San Antonio.

Quoting from Enrique Esparza's own words as they appeared in the *Express* news story on November 22, 1902, we learn:

"My father decided to take the offer and move the family to San Felipe. Everything was ready, when one morning, Mr. John Smith, who was godfather to my youngest brother, came to our house on North Flores Street, . . . and told my mother to tell my father, when he came, Santa Anna had come. When my father came, my mother asked him what he would do. You know the Americans had the Alamo, which had been fortified a few months before by General Cos.

"Well I'm going to the fort," my father said.

"Well, if Pop goes, I am going along and the whole family, too."[6]

"Enrique . . . recalled how his father and Smith hurried to the Alamo. All doors were barred, but they (the entire family) entered through a window."[7]

"There were a few other families who had gone in. A Mrs. Alsbury and her sister, a Mrs. Victoriana, and a family of several girls, two of whom I knew afterwards, Mrs. Dickson [sic], Mrs. Juana Melton, a Mexican woman who had married an American, also a woman named Concepción Losoya and her son, Juan, who was a little older than I.

"The first thing I remember about getting inside the fort was seeing Mrs. Melton making circles on the ground with an umbrella. I had seen very few umbrellas. "[8] . . .

"After the first day there was fighting. . . . But after about seven days fighting, there was an armistice of three days. . . . the interpreter, was a close friend of my father, and I heard him tell my father in the quarters that Santa Anna had offered to let the Americans go with their lives if they would surrender, but the Mexicans would be treated as rebels.

"During the armistice my father told my mother she had better take the children and go, while she could do so safely. But my mother said:

"No, if you're going to stay, so am I. I will stay by your side. If they kill one they will kill us all. . . ."

"The fighting began again and continued every day, and nearly every night. . . .

"On the last night my father was not out, but he and my

mother were sleeping . . . In the morning there was a great shooting and firing at the northwest corner of the fort, and I heard my mother say:

"Gregorio, the soldiers have jumped the wall. The fight's begun."

"He got up and picked up arms and went into the fight."[9]. .
. . .

"Enrique told how, when the Mexicans stormed the Alamo, his father, who manned a cannon, was struck down, shot in the chest and stabbed in the side by a sword. The mother, holding the baby sister, was kneeling beside the body. The three brothers were close to her. Enrique told how he clutched his mother's garments."[10]. . . . .

"We could hear the Mexican officers shouting to the men to jump over, and the men were fighting so close that we could hear them strike each other. It was so dark that we couldn't see anything, and the families that were in the quarters just huddled up in the corners. My mother's children were near her. Finally, they began shooting through the dark into the room where we were. . . . it was a miracle, but none of us children were touched.

"By daybreak the firing had almost stopped, and through the window we could see shadows of men moving around inside the fort. The Mexicans went from room to room looking for an American to kill. While it was still dark a man stepped into the room and pointed his bayonet at my mother's breast, demanding:

"Where's the money the Americans had?"

"If they had any", said my mother, "you may look for it."

"Then an officer stepped in and said:"

"What are you doing? The women and children are not to be hurt."

"The officer then told my mother to pick out her own family and get her belongings and the other women were given the same instructions. . . .

"The families with their baggage, were then sent under guard to the house of Don Ramón Músquiz, on Main Plaza."[11] . . .

"My mother, being familiar with the premises, began to

look about for food for herself and children, as well as her other comrades. While she was doing so Músquiz told her that it was dangerous for her to be moving about. and leaving the place and room in which she was under guard. She told him she did not care whether she was under guard or not, she was going to have something to eat for herself, and her children and her companions whom she intended to feed if Santa Anna did not feed his prisoners. Músquiz admonished her to silence and told her to be patient and he would get them some food from his own store."

"After urging my mother not to leave the room, Músquiz disappeared and went to his pantry, where he got quite a quantity of provisions and brought them to the room in which the prisoners (the women and children), some ten or dozen in number, were and distributed the food among them. There was some coffee as well as bread and meat. I recollect that I ate heartily, but my mother ate very sparingly."[12]

"At 3 o'clock we went before Santa Anna. . . . He had a great stack of silver money on a table before him, and a pile of blankets. One by one the women were sent into a side room to make their declaration, and on coming out were given $2.00 and a blanket. While my mother was waiting her turn Mrs. Melton, who had never recognized my mother as an acquaintance, and who was considered an aristocrat, sent her brother, Juan Losoya, across the room to my mother to ask the favor that nothing be said to the president about her marriage with an American.

"My mother told Juan to tell her not to be afraid." . . . [13]

"My mother was next called before the dictator. When she appeared before him, my baby sister pressed closely to her bosom, I with my brothers followed her into his presence. My brother was clinging to her skirt, but I stood to one side and behind her. I watched every move and listened to every word spoken. Santa Anna asked her name. She gave it. He then asked:

"Where is your husband?" She answered, sobbing:

"He's dead at the Alamo."

"Santa Anna next asked where the other members of the family were. She replied a brother of my father's, she was informed, was in his (Santa Anna's) army. This was true.

My father had a brother whose name was Francisco Esparza, who joined the forces of Santa Anna. It was this brother who appeared before Santa Anna later and asked permission to search among the slain for my father's corpse. The permission was given. My uncle found my father's body and had it buried in Campo Santo where Milam Square is now. I did not get a chance to see it before it was buried there as the burials, as all others incident to the battle, was a very hurried one. It is probable that my father was the only one who fought on the side of the Constitutionalists and against the forces of the dictator, whose body was buried first without having been burned.

"Santa Anna released my mother. He gave her a blanket and two silver dollars as he dismissed her. . . . After our release we went back to our home and my mother wept for many days and nights."[14] . . .

The question has been raised could Enrique, a child of such young age, really remember all he claimed. His age at the time of the battle is recorded variously as eight, ten or twelve years. I found no reference to an actual birth record so the reader must make a choice as to what his actual age was. Regardless of eight, ten or twelve, Enrique Esparza himself is quoted as saying years later:

"You ask me if I remember it. I tell you yes. It is burned into my brain and indelibly seared there. Neither age nor infirmity could make me forget."[15]

Frequent quotes from contemporary San Antonio historians and self-proclaimed "authorities" say in their opinion Enrique could not have absorbed and remembered so many details as he described of his Alamo experience. Perhaps. Of course Ana's son was told by her through the years that followed what she recalled, which admittedly could have colored what he told in later years as his own recollections.

However, as for young children's capability of remembering horribly traumatic experiences, almost everyone alive has heard a story of some personal experience of this nature by someone. Few are so severe as Enrique Esparza's but all are very frightening and absolutely unforgettable to the child. As an example of one such experience, an account in Texas history is told about Mrs. Rebecca J. Fisher who became the second woman to be elected president of the DRT. The account was written by a Lt. Hannum and entitled, "A Thrilling Adventure of Mrs. Rebecca J. Fisher" and published in Austin, Texas on March 15, 1906. This was just about the same time Enrique was telling his story. Mrs. Fisher states in her own words:

> "I was seven years of age when my parents were mur-
> dered. Fifty-nine years have passed since then, and yet my
> heart grows faint as that awful time passes in review. It is
> indelibly stamped upon memory's pages and photographed
> so deeply upon my heart that time with all its changes can
> never erase it."[16]

Her parents, Mary (Barbour) and Johnson Gilliland, were attacked and killed by a Comanche Indian raiding party as Rebecca and her younger brother, William, watched in horror. The two terrified children were then taken captive by the Indians. Fortunately, they were soon rescued by General Albert Sidney Johnston and his detachment of Texas soldiers. The two children were raised by an aunt in Galveston, and Rebecca grew to young adulthood and married Orceneth Fisher, a Methodist minister. She went on to become one of the founding members of the DRT and serve as its state president the last thirty-two years of her life. She was an influential spokesperson for that organization and state patriotism in general. She gave the opening prayer for several years when the Texas legislature convened.[17]

I have never heard of any doubts about the veracity of Mrs. Fisher's recollections as a seven year old child told later as a 66-year-old woman. Why then should we doubt the ability of a small Mexican-American boy of twelve, or possibly even eight, to remember an equally if not greater horrifying experience? And there are many other such stories that could be cited, no doubt. For me, the recollections of Enrique Esparza of his Alamo experience are quite believable.

When it was all over, what happened to Ana Esparza and her children, the widow and orphans of one of the heroes of the Alamo, a man who would go unheard of and unheralded for many years to come?

According to an account given by a great-granddaughter of Gregorio and Ana Esparza, Lena Olivares, who lives in Atascosa county on an original Esparza land grant site as of this writing:

"When Ana and the children came out of the Alamo, Ana was very sick with pneumonia."[18]

Family lore continues to describe the difficult days they went through. They were taken in by a cousin until Ana could regain her health. For awhile though it appeared the children would lose their mother as well as their father, so seriously ill was Ana. She did recover in time but only to face many hardships for the remainder of her life.

To be a woman in her circumstances would be difficult at any time, but in frontier Texas in 1836 it undoubtedly was an especially discouraging situation. What did she do to hold her family together?

Again we turn to the story of her oldest child, her son Enrique, now the "man of the family," for his recollections. According to Enrique, the family ultimately returned to their house on Flores Street, where they had lived prior to the battle. The widow Esparza had no money, no steady income and four small children to support, so what did they do to sustain themselves?

According to family legend, Ana worked for several years as a housemaid and young Enrique, who never had a childhood from that time on, worked as a stable boy for many years. An account of their life during those difficult days is described in a family history written in 1970 by Ana's descendant, Reynaldo "Ray" Esparza after years of personal research. He wrote the story of the Esparza family for his young children so they could have an appreciation of just who their forebears were. Two of the stories Ray Esparza related give us an insight into life for Ana and Enrique and her other children during those years of struggle after the battle.

> "A determined lady was Ana, and it took determination to survive those post-war years as a war widow with young children. All accounts of Ana that your Daddy (Ray) has heard has had to do with the sufferings that this family endured during the post-war years. One story has it that all Ana and her children had to eat was buggy meal. The method that Ana used to separate the bugs from the meal was explained to me by an old aunt. It seems that the meal was put in water in such a way that the bugs rose to the top. Don't try this though, I may be wrong. Another story has it that Enrique as a boy worked in a stable and with the boss's permission picked up grains of corn that were not eaten by the horses and with that corn they were able to supplement their diet. These are stories of privation for the Esparza family with hardly a drop of honor or glory for having survived thirteen days in the Alamo. Remember I said we should not brag about our family. We should instead be humbled. A story in a lighter vein is told about Ana and one only hopes that it happened in better times than those described above. Ana worked for a prominent lady who owned a buffalo throw rug. So badly did Ana want that throw rug that she offered to do the lady's wash for a year in return for the rug. Not a very prudent thing to do we would think now, but we must remember that Ana was a determined lady."[19]

Very little else about Ana seems to have been handed down in family lore and nothing is recorded officially. We can only hope her years following the devastating experience of the battle had some happy times as well as difficult ones. I could find no official record of the birth date of Ana Salazar Esparza nor the place of her burial. The date of death is recorded, however, as December 12, 1847,[20] and there is a possibility she was buried in the same Campo Santo area where her husband, Gregorio, was buried in the vicinity of present day Milam Park in downtown San Antonio. Some claim the bodies of those who had been buried there were removed to San Fernando Catholic Cemetery in later years when Santa Rosa Hospital was built and Milam Park established. No trace of the graves has ever been found at San Fernando Cemetery, however, as of the date of this writing.

Ana Esparza never received any benefits for her husband's service and death in the Alamo. His sacrifice went unnoticed and unrewarded until long after his death, and hers as well, leaving her with nothing but heartaches and hardships for the rest of her life. Eventually, after many years of claims submitted by the Esparza brothers, with cross-examination of witnesses, translated testimony to English and repeated rejections, long after the death of Ana, the surviving heirs of Gregorio Esparza and his three sons received land grants amounting to only a small percentage of their true rights. The little daughter who survived the battle had died in early childhood. The three brothers, Enrique, Manuel and Francisco, moved to Atascosa County and established farms on their bounty land there. They combined their farming with their business venture as "freighters" of cargo which they brought up by ox-carts from a coastal port to the San Antonio markets.

Francisco reportedly moved elsewhere later, but many of the Esparza descendants still live in Atascosa County where the other two brothers, Enrique and Manuel, established their families on their farm lands. Many descendants live in San Antonio, as well. Among them is the great-great-grandson, Reynaldo "Ray" Esparza, referred to earlier, who provided me with so much information from his own personal collection which included the family history he wrote for his children quoted from previously.

There is a poignant postscript to the Esparza story that comes from him, with which I would like to end Ana's story.

Ray Esparza was born in San Antonio, went to school there and after graduating from high school in the spring of 1941, he joined the U.S. Navy on December the 7th, "Pearl Harbor Day," the start of World War II. As his famous forebear had done, he, too, served in the defense of his country.

After the war ended, he returned to civilian life in San Antonio and soon entered a lifetime career as a U.S. Postal Service employee and worked at the Main Post Office Building on Alamo Plaza. The front portion of this building is on the actual site of the north wall of the Alamo fortress where many died during the battle, including William Barret Travis, according to tradition. It is also just a few hundred yards from the hallowed site where Ray Esparza's great-great-grandfather, Gregorio, sacrificed his life for the freedom of Texas. And within the now restored Alamo building called the shrine, in the southwest corner room to the right of the entrance doors, his great-great-grandmother, Ana Esparza, is believed to have gathered her children around her for protection during those thirteen fateful days.

Oftentimes on his lunch hour, Ray would walk across the Plaza and wander about near the spots where his forebears had played out their personal roles in the historic drama of that struggle for the freedom of Texas. He said to me one day in an interview, in a beautiful spirit of humility, he could not help but feel a surge of pride and even a sense of awe to know he came from some of those who had been there during that historic moment in time.

As a child in grammar school, Ray's homeroom teacher, with a wonderful insight of what teaching is all about, said to him one day, "You have a very famous name— 'Esparza'—in Texas history." What a way to stimulate an interest in history in a child! Well, that is exactly what it did and as Ray grew to adulthood he gradually learned a little here and a little there about his 'famous name' from any source he could. Of course, nothing was in the school textbooks at that time though, and so it was primarily from family stories, church records, archives, etc. that his "scrapbook" and collection of information began and grew.

In time, on one of those days at the U.S. Post Office on his lunch hour, Ray walked across Alamo Plaza, and bolstering up his courage, he went into the Daughters of the Republic of Texas Library next to the Alamo building, on a mission of inquiry into his past. He was greeted cordially by one of the librarians with the usual, "May I help you?" offer, and he replied with something like, "Well, yes ma'am. You see, I have an ancestor who died in the Battle of the Alamo and I was wondering if you have any information on him?" He said you could tell the lady didn't believe him at first but said she would be happy to look and see. After what was unquestionably a rather brief search, she returned with a folder. Upon opening it , he found one lone sheet of information. Needless to say, Ray was deflated, not to mention a little hurt. Undaunted, though, he pursued his search, and in time as his collection grew, he began to share what he found with the DRT Library. The Esparza file has grown considerably over the past several years since Ray's initial inquiry, and today happily there is perhaps as representative a collection there on this "hero of the Alamo," Gregorio Esparza, and his family as can be found anywhere.

Ray Esparza and his wife Nora have been of invaluable help to me in sorting out the story of Ana Esparza, stalwart survivor of the battle and heroine of the Alamo in her own right. Ray and Nora are the grandparents of little Emma Esparza pictured here.

A sixth generation descendant of her famous forebears of the Alamo, Emma's positive stance seems to embody the indomitable attitude of her courageous great-great-great-great-great-grandmother, who chose to stay by her husband to the end. Ana Esparza's spirit seems to shine through little Emma's eyes.

In that history of the Esparza family which Ray Esparza

wrote for his children, he describes so well the courage and character of Gregorio and Ana Esparza both:

EMMA LOUISE ESPARZA,
6th generation descendant of Ana Esparza.
(Picture courtesy of Ray Esparza Family.)

"Not much is known about Gregorio but . . . one statement is attributed to him. Enrique, his son, stated that he overheard James Bowie ask his father if he, Gregorio, wished to leave the Alamo during a temporary truce, and Gregorio replied, "No, I will stay and die fighting." Many millions of words are spoken by a man in his lifetime. It is indeed a memorial to be remembered solely for this last sentence. For it takes a special kind of man to say words like, "No, I will stay and die fighting." And it takes a special kind of woman to have said to her husband, "I will stay by your side and with our children, and die, too."[21]

A special kind of woman, indeed, is what Ana Esparza was—a real survivor in the truest sense of the word.

~ ~ ~ ~ ~ ~ ~ ~ ~

~ ~ ~  ~ ~ ~

Chapter Four
Juana Navarro Perez Alsbury
and Gertrudis Navarro
"I have neither money nor husband."

*T*his declaration reportedly was made by a terrified
Gertrudis Navarro, younger sister of Juana Navarro Perez Alsbury,
during the height of the intense fighting in the Alamo. A Mexican
soldier came to the rooms the two women were occupying along
the west side of the compound, and when Gertrudis opened the
door the soldier demanded, as he tore her shawl from around her
shoulders, "Your money and your husband!"[1]

Her reply of, "I have neither money nor husband," was
indeed true of her circumstances at the time, but ironically the same
could be said for her sister Juana's situation, also, much of the time,
particularly in the later years of her life. For while Juana had at least
two husbands during her lifetime, and some reports say she had a
third, she never seemed to have one when she needed one most and
she never seemed to have any money during those later years so she
claimed.

From an early substantial beginning as a member of two
highly respected and reportedly wealthy families, Juana Navarro's
life led her through many colorful, adventurous, and dramatic periods. However, that affluent and exciting life eventually grew into
one in which she was described as a lone widow, "getting old with
only one son . . . extremely poor with hardly the means of subsistence."[2] This was according to Juana Navarro Alsbury's own sworn
statement later in her petition to the State of Texas for compensation for her services rendered attending the sick and wounded at the
Alamo, and her husband's service at the Battle of San Jacinto and

imprisonment later.

Who were these Navarro sisters, how did they come to be in the Alamo at the time of the battle and what became of them afterward?

Juana and Gertrudis Navarro were the daughters of José Angel Navarro and Concepción Cervantes Navarro. José Angel Navarro was the brother of the famed Texas "tejano" patriot, José Antonio Navarro. The Navarro girls' father, José Angel, remained loyal to the Mexican dictator, Santa Anna, and his centralist government, whereas his older brother, José Antonio, supported Stephen F. Austin and the Anglo-American colonists in their idea for a self-governing state.[3] José Antonio Navarro was a leader in the Texas political scene until his death at age 76 in 1871.

The sister of José Angel and José Antonio, Josefa Navarro had married another well known citizen of San Antonio, Juan Martín Veramendi, who owned the locally famous "Veramendi Palace." The Veramendi Palace was the most luxurious and gracious home in the area at the time, along with the "Spanish Governor's Palace" located nearby. Both impressive dwellings had been built in the mid-to-late 1700's and both housed governors of the area at one time, hence the customary term "governor's palace."

Don Juan Martín Veramendi had come into possession of his large stone house in 1809 and it served as his home as well as a "Governor's Palace" when he was Governor of Coahuila and Texas in 1832 and 1833. Its spacious halls and rooms were the scene of social gatherings and stately governmental functions and meetings during the various regimes of Spain and Mexico.[4]

This historic landmark building stood on one of the oldest streets in San Antonio, "Calle de Soledad" between present day Houston and Commerce Streets. Surrounded in time by commercial growth, since it was at the center of the town that grew to be a large city, it eventually no longer served as a residence and over the years fell prey to a variety of commercial uses. It was finally abandoned altogether and deteriorated into an unsightly and unsafe ruin and ultimately was razed by the City in 1909.

The Navarro girls were nieces therefore of two prominent and distinguished San Antonians: Don José Antonio Navarro, their father's brother, and Don Juan Martín Veramendi, the husband of their aunt, Josefa Navarro, their father's sister. Both families were a strong influence in the girls' lives.

The home life of the Navarro sisters was interrupted at an early age for them, though, by the break-up of their family. As a result of this family separation of their parents, their father took the two girls to live with him. Apparently feeling he could not care for them properly, he eventually sent the girls to live with other family members. Juana became the godchild of her aunt, Doña Josefa Navarro Veramendi, and her husband, Don Juan, and they took her to live with them. According to some accounts both Juana and Gertrudis went to live with the Veramendis, but others say Gertrudis went to live with another family member. In any case, the Veramendis ultimately adopted Juana and raised her at the Veramendi Palace from a very young age, along with their own natural daughter, Ursula, and their other children and possibly Gertrudis, also.

Juana and her cousin Ursula considered themselves "sisters," as did others apparently, for after Ursula Veramendi married James Bowie he addressed Juana as "sister."[5] Jim Bowie was one of the living legends of the Alamo, who had led a colorful life before he ever came to San Antonio in 1828. He was famous for his fights, his "Bowie knife," his physical feats and his business acumen as well. He reportedly had made vast fortunes and, also, lost some. But for all his toughness and roughness he was said to have a smooth and gentle side as well, which perhaps was what made his marriage to Ursula Veramendi a success. He had charmed this reputedly beautiful young heiress even though her very Catholic and staunchly Mexican loyalist family had some misgivings about him initially. In a ceremony at San Antonio's San Fernando Cathedral the two were married on April 25, 1831,⁶ and the marriage was apparently a very happy one which produced two little daughters in very prompt order. And, thus, Jim Bowie joined the Veramendi family at the "Palace" and became a respected and influential citizen of San Antonio, also, and later, as fate would have it, he was to become the protector of Juana and Gertrudis Navarro.

But this happy idyll at the Veramendi Palace ended abruptly in 1833, when Ursula Veramendi Bowie and her two infant daughters, along with her parents, died in a cholera epidemic in Monclova, Mexico, where they had gone on a visit. The death of Ursula and their two little girls left Jim Bowie a bereft and grieving widower, according to all accounts, who never recovered from his tragic loss. His attachment to the Navarro sisters was genuine, no doubt, and his affection for them was returned by them in his final days at the Alamo especially.

One year after her adopted sister Ursula's marriage, a grownup young Juana Navarro, twenty years of age by now, also entered into matrimony. On May 1, 1832, Juana Navarro and Alejo Perez were married in the San Fernando church.⁷

Unfortunately, this marriage was cut short by an untimely death also, when after a brief time of less than three years, Juana's husband died and left her a young widow. The exact date of his death is unknown but is said to be some time in the latter part of 1834, before the birth of their son, Alejo de la Encarnacion. Alejo, Jr., as he always was known, was born on March 23, 1835 and baptized at San Fernando when he was eight days old.⁸ This child was in the Alamo later as an eleven-month-old toddler during the battle, as well as that other little toddler, fifteen-month-old Angelina Dickinson, who became famous as the Babe of the Alamo.

Juana Navarro Perez remained a widow caring for her young son alone for almost a year after her husband's death. Then in early January of 1836, about two months before the Battle of the Alamo, she married Dr. Horatio Alexander Alsbury, an early Texas colonist. Alsbury had come to Texas from Kentucky with several family members as part of Stephen F. Austin's "Old Three-Hundred," the original settlers brought to this new frontier by Austin. Horatio Alsbury had been an active participant in the Texas independence movement since his arrival in the area. In fact, he had very recently been in Mexico and knew of the plans for Santa Anna and the Centralist forces to launch an attack on the settlers in Texas. Shortly before the arrival of Santa Anna's army in San Antonio, Alsbury had left town, either on a military scouting mission as some accounts say, or as others have said, he went east in search of a safer place to take his new wife and her baby to wait out the imminent probability of a battle in San Antonio. Expecting to return before Santa Anna's army could reach the town, but fearing for the safety of his new family while he was away, Alsbury had asked Jim Bowie to see to the needs and protection of Juana, her baby and her sister, Gertrudis. Gertrudis was almost twenty years of age [9] and unmarried, and Horatio and Juana had taken her into their home. Since Bowie looked upon the two as his "sisters-in-law," he no doubt agreed without hesitation to be responsible for them.

There are differing accounts as to when and how Juana, her baby and her sister Gertrudis got into the Alamo, as well as when they left, in fact. Some sources say they went in with Bowie when he went in himself. Others say he sent for them later before actual hostilities began. One account even says Alsbury took them in before he left town. In any case, they were established within the walls of the old mission for some time before the battle started.

Bowie was a sick man, though, and the Navarro sisters reportedly attempted to nurse him and care for him. It is speculated he feared he had a contagious illness and he had himself removed from the part of the old mission/fort occupied by Juana and her baby and Gertrudis.

The rooms the Navarro sisters and little Alejo occupied at the Alamo had been the Indian family apartments during the mission period. They were located on the west side of the compound, in the northwest corner, near the site where Sam Maverick, one of San Antonio's leading citizens of the time, was to build his home later (now the corner of Houston and N. Alamo Streets). Bowie was moved to the east side of the compound and quartered on the second floor of the "long barrack," according to Susanna Dickinson and accounts of some others later, in what was called the "hospital." Differing accounts claim that he was quartered in the "low barracks," along the south wall and that he died there. There is no positive proof though of the exact location of the place where Jim Bowie was killed. Both second floor "hospital" and the "low barracks" are gone now, as well as the west wall apartments, but the lower floor of the "long barrack" still stands and is part of the Alamo historical complex today.

What actually happened to Juana and Gertrudis and baby Alejo while they were in the Alamo during the battle that raged around them?

Researchers and writers over the years have paraphrased, condensed, reworded and variously reported the actual eyewitness account given later to John S. Ford by Juana Alsbury herself. Ford recorded it in what he called his *Memoirs* which was published some forty years or so after the battle.

Ford's account of his interview with Juana Alsbury is best told in his own words which are quoted here just as he recorded them from his meeting with her:

"Mrs. Alsbury's Recollections Of The Alamo

Juana, the daughter of Angel Navarro and a niece of Colonel José Antonio Navarro, when very young was adopted by Governor Veramendi, who had married her father's sister. Señorita Juana married a Mexican gentleman, Don Alejo Perez, by whom she had a son, Alejo, who is a respectable citizen of San Antonio. The elder Perez died in 1834 and his widow married Dr. Horatio Alexander Alsbury early in 1836. It must be remembered that Colonel James Bowie married the daughter of Governor Veramendi, consequently his wife was the cousin and the adopted sister of Mrs. Alsbury. This accounts for her being in his charge and in the Alamo.

When the news of Santa Anna's approach at the head of a considerable force was verified in San Antonio, Dr. Alsbury proceeded to the Brazos River to procure means to remove his family, expecting to return before Santa Anna could reach the city. He failed to do so; and his wife went into the Alamo where her protector was, when the Mexican troops were near by. She was accompanied by her younger sister, Gertrudis. Colonel Bowie was very sick of typhoid fever. For that reason he thought it prudent to be removed from the part of the buildings occupied by Mrs. Alsbury. A couple of soldiers carried him away. On leaving he said: "Sister, do not be afraid. I leave you with Colonel Travis, Colonel Crockett, and other friends. They are gentlemen and will treat you kindly." He had himself brought back two or three times to see and talk with her. Their last interview took place three or four days before the fall of the Alamo. She never saw him again, either alive or dead.

She says she does not know who nursed him after he left the quarters she occupied and expresses no disbelief in the statement of Madam Candelaria. "There were people in the Alamo I did not see."

Mrs. Alsbury and her sister were in a building not far from where the residence of Colonel Sam Maverick was afterwards erected. It was considered quite a safe locality. They saw very little of the fighting. While the final struggle was progressing she peeped out and saw the surging columns of Santa Anna assaulting the Alamo on every side, as she believed. She could hear the noise of the conflict— the roar of the artillery, the rattle of the small arms, the shouts of the combatants, the groans of the dying, and the moans of the wounded. The firing approximated where she was and she realized the fact that the brave Texians had been overwhelmed by numbers. She asked her sister to go to the door and request the Mexican soldiers not to fire into the room, as it contained women only. Señorita Gertrudis opened the door, she was greeted in offensive language by the soldiers. Her shawl was torn from her shoulders and she rushed back into the room. During this period Mrs. Alsbury was standing with her one-year-old son strained to her bosom, supposing he would be motherless soon. The soldiers then demanded of Señorita Gertrudis: "Your money and your husband." She replied: "I have neither money nor husband." About this time a sick man ran up to Mrs. Alsbury and attempted to protect her. The soldiers bayoneted him at her side. She thinks his name was Mitchell.

After this tragic event a young Mexican, hotly pursued by soldiers, seized her by the arm and endeavored to keep her between himself and his assailants. His grasp was broken and four or five bayonets plunged into his body and nearly as many balls went through his lifeless corpse. The soldiers broke open her trunk and took her money and clothes, also the watch of Colonel Travis and other officers.

A Mexican officer appeared on the scene. He excitedly inquired, "How did you come here? What are you doing here any how? Where is the entrance to the fort?" He made her pass out of the room over a cannon standing nearby the door. He told her to remain there and he would have her sent to President Santa Anna. Another officer came up and asked: "What are you doing here?" She replied "An officer ordered us to remain here and he would have us sent to the President." "President the devil. Don't you see they are about to fire that cannon? Leave." They were moving when they heard a voice calling "Sister." "To my great relief Don Manuel Perez came to us. He said: 'Don't you know your own brother-in-law?' I answered: 'I am so excited and distressed that I scarcely know anything.'" Don Manuel placed them in charge of a colored woman belonging to Colonel

Bowie and the party reached the house of Don Angel Navarro in safety.

Mrs. Alsbury says to the best of her remembrance she heard firing at the Alamo till twelve o'clock that day.

She says the name of the girl Santa Anna deceived by false marriage was (left blank).

She describes Colonel Bowie as a tall, well made gentleman, of a very serious countenance, of few words, always to the point, and a warm friend. In his family he was affectionate, kind, and so acted as to secure the love and confidence of all."[10]

The Navarro sisters maintained to the last that they were in the Alamo during the entire battle and to the very end, as quoted in the foregoing Ford *Memoirs*. Other accounts, however, claim they left two days before the fall of the Alamo such as those cited by Dr. Amelia Williams, in her thesis "A Critical Study of the Alamo" written in 1931. This was perhaps the first, and for many years only, in-depth study of the battle of the Alamo. Under the section entitled, "The Survivors of the Massacre," Dr. Williams reports:

"But there is another story about these Navarro women. Frank Templeton in his *Margaret Ballentine, or the Fall of the Alamo,* 177: Mrs. James McKeever to Governor James Hogg, July 25, 1803 (State Library): also the application of Louise Alsbury for membership in the Daughters of the Texas Republic [sic], (Records of the Daughters of the Texas Republic) [sic], all say that the Navarro women left the Alamo on the night of March 4, under flag of truce from Santa Anna, at the request of their father, Angel Navarro."[11]

It should be remembered that Juana and Gertrudis' father Angel Navarro, was the member of the Navarro family who, after all, had remained steadfastly loyal to Santa Anna and his Centralist Government. It is quite conceivable such a request could have been made by Angel Navarro and granted by Santa Anna, and that the

Navarro women could have left under a flag of truce before the final battle.

As for testimonials of other survivors regarding the presence of the Navarro women at the time of the fall of the Alamo, Susanna Dickinson claimed that Mrs. Alsbury and her sister were not there at the end of the battle, that, in fact, "the two women were traitors who had escaped to the enemy and betrayed our situation about two days before the assault." [12] Dr. Williams adds a further testimonial on this from Susanna Dickinson's granddaughter, Susan Sterling: "Mrs. Dickinson (Morphis, *History of Texas,* 175) says that on "the night of the 4th of March a Mexican woman deserted us, and going over to the enemy informed them of our inferior numbers." Dr. Williams also says: "Mrs. Susan Sterling, the granddaughter of Mrs. Dickinson, told me that this Mexican woman was Mrs. Horace Alsbury, and that her grandmother, (Susanna Dickinson), would never stay in the same house with Mrs. Alsbury—not even for an hour—in post revolutionary days, because of this desertion. Mrs. Sterling lived in Austin, Texas, until August 1929, when she died at the age of 83." [13]

Dr. Williams had this and other commentaries first hand from the granddaughter and those of the grandson of Susanna Dickinson as she stated in her thesis:

> "Mr. A. D. Griffith, a grandson of Mrs. Dickenson [sic], now lives in Austin. (As of date of thesis, June, 1931.) Until August, 1929, his sister, Mrs. Susan Sterling, lived with him. She is now dead. It has been my privilege to visit these old people—both past eighty—and to hear from them the stories their grandmother was wont to tell them concerning the Alamo disaster. Mrs. Sterling spent most of her young life at her grandmother's home and could retell many of the stories that she heard from Mrs. Dickenson [sic]." [14]

On the other hand, Enrique Esparza, who was an eight-year-old boy there at the time told in an interview years later that he remembered seeing them there when the fighting was over and the handful of survivors were gathered together and taken to the Músquiz home to appear before General Santa Anna. Esparza recalled that the Navarro women were the first to be interviewed.[15] Some people have held however, that an eight year old child's observations reported years later, might be questionable.

In any case, Juana Navarro Alsbury, her baby, Alejo Perez, and her sister, Gertrudis Navarro, survived the battle somehow, somewhere, and all three of them lived for many long years afterward, no matter when they left nor under what circumstances.

The bloody massacre of the Battle of the Alamo left those survivors who had witnessed it with terrifying and horrible memories that would last a lifetime. When the turmoil of the aftermath was beginning to subside somewhat, Juana's husband finally returned to San Antonio after what must have seemed an eternity to her. She had not seen him since the battle began, when he had left supposedly to find a safe haven for her. He had been unable to return to her before the Battle of the Alamo began, but where had he been since it fell over two months ago? Surely this was a time when she must have felt she needed him most.

According to Juana's testimony later, he had been at the Battle of San Jacinto, that final conflict of the Texas Revolution in which General Santa Anna was captured by the Texans and Mexico was forced to concede defeat. This battle of April 21, 1836, was the decisive encounter which resulted in the establishment of the new Republic of Texas. Thus, Horatio Alsbury had been a participant in the Texas independence movement from beginning to end according to his claims.

Upon Alsbury's return to San Antonio, he and Juana settled into an apparently stable life on a Navarro ranch along Calaveras Creek a few miles southeast of San Antonio. Juana and each of her immediate family members had inherited a share of money, cattle, and ranch land from their father's estate upon his death.[16] Juana's ranch land became a permanent home for her and her husband, and, according to family accounts, it was her final resting place as well, when she died and was buried there many years later. There is no grave nor marker to be found there for her, however.

Horatio's younger brother, "Young Perry" Alsbury, followed in his brother's footsteps and moved to San Antonio after the Battle of San Jacinto, also. He, too, married a local girl, Mary Rodriguez, and they settled on a ranch nearby. They lived all their long lives there and were buried in the family cemetery on the ranch. A memorial state historical marker was placed on their gravesites in 1936, the Texas Centennial year which celebrated one-hundred years of Texas Independence.[17] The contributions of both of the Alsbury brothers helped to make that possible.

It was during the years of settled home life on the ranch for Juana and Horatio Alsbury, beginning in 1836, that Horatio began to establish himself in the community. In 1841 he served as City Clerk of San Fernando de Bejar, the village that was the forerunner of the city of San Antonio.[18]

The Alsbury's life on their ranch continued without unusual event until the following year of 1842, when Dr. Alsbury, along with a number of other men was captured while resisting the invasion of San Antonio by the Mexican Army under command of General Adrian Woll. This was not an all out attempt on the part of Mexico to reconquer Texas, but a show of force. Santa Anna was President of Mexico again, and he refused to relinquish what he felt was Mexico's inherent right of sovereignty. The captured men were all taken to Perote Castle Prison in Vera Cruz, Mexico, and Juana is said to have followed them in an attempt to get her husband out of prison. She was unable to accomplish this impossible feat, of course, and she reportedly stopped in Mexico at some point along the way to await him. He was released with several other prisoners after more than eighteen months and they returned to San Antonio.

Life resumed then for the Alsburys and continued as before

until 1846 when Horatio left again. He was bound for Mexico once more, not as a prisoner nor a Texas Scout, but as a member of the U.S. Army. Texas by now had joined the United States as a state of the Union and Dr. Alsbury accompanied the American troops across the Rio Grande River in the War Between the United States and Mexico. When her husband left this time, although she did not realize it Juana told him good-bye for the last time. She never saw Horatio Alexander Alsbury again. He was reported to have been killed somewhere in northern Mexico between Camargo and Saltillo sometime in 1846, 1847 or 1848. His remains were never found.

Life for Juana after the death of her husband seemed to travel on a steadily downhill course. Her subsequent testimonials requesting help from the State of Texas for subsistence paint a rather bleak and destitute picture.

Her petitions for compensation, dated February 15th, 1854, March 3rd, 1855, March 29th, 1855 and November 1st, 1857, identify her as the wife or widow of Dr. Horatio A. Alsbury, a woman now in great need. The petition of November 1st, 1857 describes especially well events regarding her life, her husband's contributions and her own destitute situation at the time of the petition. Parts of it are quoted below:

> ". . . Juana Navarro Alsbury . . . was in the Alamo at the time of its fall. She was then the wife of Dr. (Horatio) Alexander Alsbury . . . during the siege of the Alamo she was ever ready to render and did render all the services she could toward nursing and attending upon the sick and wounded . . . That all the property she had to wit her clothing, money, and jewels were seized and taken by the enemy—that subsequent to that time her husband the said Dr. Alsbury was taken prisoner . . . and confined in the Castle of Perote in Mexico over 18 months . . . he accompanied the American Army across the Rio Grande during the war between the United States and Mexico, and in the

year 1846, was killed by the Mexicans somewhere between Camargo and Saltillo . . . that she is now getting old with only one son. That she is extremely poor with hardly the means of subsistence—she therefore prays the honorable Legislature will . . . allow her some compensation for her losses . . . in this her time of necessity.

Juana Navarro Alsbury" [19]

The elaborately styled penmanship on this and at least one of the other petitions includes her name at the end as though it might be her signature. On closer inspection, however, it is apparent that the hand that wrote the name at the end, wrote the entire document, because the name as it appears in the early part of the petition, naming her as the petitioner, is written precisely like the one at the end. Moreover, the handwriting is different in the two petitions, including the "signature" name at the end of each.

Furthermore the petition dated March 3rd, 1855, has "her X mark" at the end in the middle of her name on the signature line as shown here:

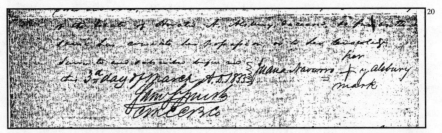

[20]

Further indication still of her inability to write is suggested in the will of her father wherein all witnesses to the will, including her sister Gertrudis, are listed as signers of the document in several places. In one instance her husband, Dr. Horatio Alexander Alsbury, is shown to have represented her by this statement:

". . . Alejandro Alsbury (as he was known in the Spanish speaking community) received the inheritance descending to Juana, his wife, under power of attorney dated January 5, 1837, which is presented for this purpose." [21]

Although Juana Navarro grew up in what would be considered luxury in a frontier situation of the time and place and came from apparently literate families, it would appear her training had not included the basic skills of reading and writing, if these petitions and documents are any indication. While young ladies of the day, were well schooled in social graces, oftentimes they were not trained in the basics of literacy.

Mary A. Maverick, an early Anglo settler of San Antonio, knew the Navarro girls and other ladies in her new hometown and she recorded the following in her *Memoirs:*

> Very few of the Mexican ladies could write but they dressed nicely and were graceful and gracious of manner.[22]

It was not unusual to find women everywhere at that time who could neither read nor write. It was especially true, however, on the far-flung frontiers in places where there were no schools of any kind, not even convents and very few home tutors. As pointed out in Chapter One, the best known of the women who survived the Alamo battle and the one most often quoted and called on to testify, Susanna Dickinson, never learned to read or write, not even her own name. A "neat X" was the only signature (mark) ever recorded for her.

In any case, regardless of who may have signed the petitions requesting aid for Juana Navarro Alsbury apparently the State finally heard her pleas and awarded compensation to her in 1857. Dr. Amelia Williams reports in her thesis:

> "Memorial No. 73, File 1, shows that in 1857 Mrs. Perez (Alsbury) applied for and received a pension for her services and her loss of money and jewels at the Alamo."[23]

The *San Antonio Light* newspaper in its story on her at the time of her death, also says:

"During the last few years of her life Mrs. Perez drew a special pension from the state of $100.00 per quarter."[24]

Juana Navarro Perez Alsbury, whose baptism is listed on the San Fernando Church Baptismal Records as December 28, 1812[25] (birth not recorded), died on July 23, 1888 at 78 years of age at her ranch home near San Antonio.

This is a photocopy of her son's original handwritten recording of the death of Juana Navarro Alsbury:[26]

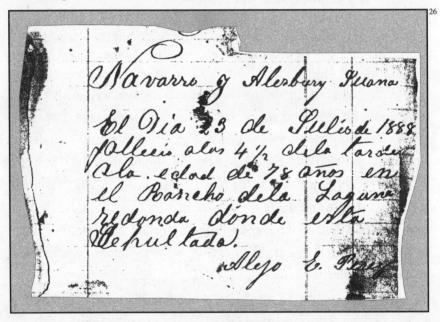

- Translation -
Juana Navarro y Alsbury
The 23rd day of July, 1888
died at 4:30 in the afternoon
at the age of 78 years
at the Rancho de la Laguna Redonda
where she is buried.
Alejo E. Perez

The handwritten record in Spanish of the death of Juana Navarro y Alsbury shown above is on a fragile fragment of paper from the personal ledger of her son, Alejo Perez, Jr. It was written by him at the time of her death in 1888 when he was fifty-three years old.

The recording of the death, written in this careful, old style penmanship, was found, with other notations, in a beautiful, old, chamois-suede ledger book which had been kept over a period of years by Alejo Perez, Jr., who was most definitely literate. The ledger was actually not merely a "ledger," it was something of a diary, for he had recorded not only certain of his financial accounts in it, but accounts of momentous events in his life as well, such as this account of his mother's death. It even included some poems written by one of his daughters.

The book was discovered in an old marble top dresser at the ranch many years after Alejo's death. It was given to one of his grandsons, George Perez, when some of the furnishings there were being divided among descendants upon the death of the last family member to occupy the old ranch house. Today, the fragile heirloom treasure, Alejo's recording of his mother's death, is framed and hangs on the wall of Juana's great-great granddaughter Dorothy Perez, to whom I am indebted for this reprint and many other family records.

At the beginning of this story of the Navarro sisters, it was said that some accounts state that Juana Alsbury had a third husband, whose name was said to be Perez, also. The earliest reference I found to this later marriage was in the *San Antonio Light* newspaper article published at the time of her death in 1888. The last paragraph of the article reads:

> . . . After Mrs. Alsbury's escape from the Alamo, Dr. Alsbury died and later she again married, and her husband's name was also Perez." [27]

The next reference I found was in the Amelia Williams thesis on the Alamo, written in 1931, in which she makes the statement:

"After the death of Dr. Alsbury . . . his wife married again, another Perez."[28]

This claim of Juana's marriage again to another Perez is frequently said in accounts written since then right up to the present day. As was stated earlier Dr. Williams' thesis was the first, most comprehensive in-depth study that had been made on the Battle of the Alamo at the time of its writing in 1931, and oftentimes what is written today is based on it, even though more recent research has revealed new information. However, I found no actual documentation for this marriage in Dr. Williams' paper—just the statement as it appears above.

Nor did I find any documentation elsewhere in Bexar County Records. A search of the Bexar County Archives and the San Antonio Catholic Chancery File of the San Fernando Marriage Records revealed no listing of such a marriage. Some of these early records are handwritten in old Spanish style and are very difficult to read. Fearing I may have missed the marriage listing, I consulted with the local descendant I have referred to frequently, who is known to have done extensive research on the family genealogy. Her response to my inquiry follows:

"In her Nov. 1, 1857 petition to the Texas Legislature, Juana implied that she was still a widow . . . She asked for compensation based on the loss of her husband, (Horace) Alexander Alsbury, in service to Texas. I have no information about her reported marriage to another Perez (cousin of her first husband) in later life."[29]

The only early references to this alleged remarriage I found were those in the 1888 newspaper article printed at the time of her death, and Dr. Williams' thesis written forty-three years later in

1931. Is it possible Dr. Williams based her statement on a newspaper article that may have been inaccurate, and writers have been repeating it ever since? Even Juana's own son, Alejo, recorded her name as "Juana Navarro y Alsbury" in his handwritten recording of her death in 1888, with no mention of the name Perez.

If there is no documentation that Juana Alsbury did remarry, then the statement should cease to be made. For one thing, it raises a possible question for some as to whether she was actually entitled to compensation if she was no longer a widow. I must confess the possibility of such misrepresentation is what sent me on a search for the "missing Perez," and as I say, I did not find him.

In the absence of documentation to the contrary, it would seem that the record should let her and her name as Juana Navarro y Alsbury rest in peace.

When I set out to research and write the story of Juana Navarro Perez Alsbury, I had not anticipated the conflicting accounts I found on seemingly trivial, yet important human interest matters, such as her literacy, a third husband or not, survivor benefit eligibility, and the like. After rewriting the immediate foregoing parts of her story endlessly, I finally reached the point where I had to say, 'I give up.' I really don't know the answers to these and other unsettled questions, because I could not get to the bottom line of the conflicting information, no matter where I went. And so, I leave them with the reader to puzzle over along with me.

There can be no doubt, however, that Juana Navarro Perez Alsbury was in the Alamo for at least part of the time of the battle if not all of it, and that she lived a long and sometimes exciting and colorful life with many ups and downs. She had two apparently happy, although rather brief marriages, each of which left her a widow at a young age. She had only one child, but his two marriages provided her with many grandchildren and great grandchildren to fill her last days. She may have been reduced to a frugal existence in her later years, but, she had known better days and she had some very rich memories.

Juana's son, Alejo Perez, Jr., that "other babe of the Alamo," had a number of business interests and a variety of occupations during his lifetime, including that of San Antonio policeman, the position in which he was serving at the time of his mother's death. And, like the rest of the family he, too, lived for many years. He died October 19, 1918, at the age of eighty-three, and is buried in San Fernando Cemetery #1 in San Antonio.[33] He was married twice and had four children by his first wife and seven by the second wife.[34] With many grandchildren from both families, he left a very large family heritage of memories.

And what about her younger sister who had survived the nightmare of the battle with her? Gertrudis had continued to live with Juana and Horatio for four years after the battle when in 1840 at the age of twenty-four she reportedly became engaged to be married to a recent newcomer from the United States named George Washington Cayce. Sad to say, though, the young man was killed quite unexpectedly in a skirmish called the "Council House Fight," which took place at the Council House, between a group of Comanche Indians and some citizens of San Antonio. Actually, Cayce was not intentionally involved in the disturbance. He just happened to be in the wrong place at the wrong time. Mary Adams Maverick, wife of one of San Antonio's early Texas patriots, Sam Maverick, records the incident in her *Memoirs:*

> "Young G. W. Cayce had called on us that morning, bringing an introductory letter from his father to Mr. Maverick, and placing some papers in his charge. He was a very pleasant and handsome young man and it was reported, came to marry Gertrudes [sic] Navarro, Mrs. Dr. Alsbruy's [sic] sister. He left our house when I did, I going to Mrs. Higgenbotham's, and he going to the Council Hall. He stood in front of the Court House, and was shot and instantly killed at the beginning of the fight, and fell by the side of Captain Caldwell. The brother of this young man

afterward told me he had left home with premonition of his death being near." [30]

The following year on July 26, 1841, Gertrudis Navarro was married to Miguel Cantú,[31] and apparently found happiness in a union that lasted a long lifetime for both and produced seven children.

Gertrudis Navarro Cantú, like her sister, had a long life, but considerably less eventful. She died in 1895 at the age of 79 years.[32] She and her husband, Miguel Cantú are said to have been buried on their ranch land, also, but there are no known gravesites there for them either. They had lived all their married life on their ranch surrounded by their many children and grandchildren. This ranch was located along the Salado Creek, near the community of Elmendorf, a few miles southeast of San Antonio.

GERTRUDIS NAVARRO CANTÚ
(Prints and Photographics Collection, CNO8198, Center
for American History, University of Texas at Austin.)

85

There are a great many descendants of these two sisters of the illustrious Navarro family living in San Antonio and vicinity today, and they continue to add to the story of the lives of Juana Navarro Perez Alsbury and Gertrudis Navarro Cantú, two of the women named as "Survivors of the Battle of the Alamo."

~ ~ ~ ~ ~ ~ ~ ~ ~ ~

Chapter Five
"Others"

*T*here were other women and children in the Alamo who survived the battle, in addition to those whose stories have been told in the previous chapters. However, there is little or no information on them, except for some very sketchy bits on one or two. They are known merely by name, and even those have not been agreed on by most historians with real finality. As Walter Lord, noted journalist and historical writer expressed it in his well-known book on the battle of the Alamo, *A Time To Stand,* "There were others, but the evidence is conflicting."[1]

Enrique Esparza, the eight-year-old boy (some time said to be eleven or twelve), an eye-witness who was there with his siblings and parents, listed many years later those others whom he recalled as being there. In his first public account of his Alamo experience, published when he was approximately eighty years old, he named them as: "Mrs. Concepcion Losoya, and her daughter and two sons, Vitona [sic - usually written as Victoria or Victoriana] de Salinas, and her three little daughters [two of whom Esparza says he knew later], and an old woman called Petra."[2] The first on the list, Concepcion Losoya, is identified in *The New Handbook of Texas* as the wife of Toribio Losoya, a Tejano defender who died in the Alamo. She and her children are said to have sought refuge in the mission compound.[3]

Until the newspaper article referred to earlier was published in 1901, history had said for over seventy years only one woman, Susanna Dickinson, and her child, Angelina, had escaped from the Alamo battle, but the statement by Enrique Esparza had thrown a whole new light on the subject. Once the story had appeared, others followed, and in another account published one year later, Esparza added Mrs. Juana Melton to his list of survivors.[4] She is said possibly to be Juana Losoya, who had married Eliel Melton, another defender who died in the battle.[5] In an account six years later, Esparza added still another name, a young girl, Trinidad Saucedo, "who was very beautiful."[6]

Esparza relates two little anecdotes about Mrs. Melton in the first of these later accounts which tend to verify his recollection of her presence there rather clearly. As recorded in Chapter Three on Esparza, he says when he first arrived at the Alamo, one of the first things he remembers seeing was Mrs. Melton with an umbrella, and in her state of nervous anxiety over the frightening situation, no doubt, she continually drew little circles with the tip of it in the dirt at her feet. This made a lasting impression on little Enrique, because as he said, he "had seen very few umbrellas."[7]

The other incident involving Mrs. Melton occurred after the battle was over while all the women were waiting with their children at the Músquiz home for their interview with Santa Anna. Even though Mrs. Melton knew his mother, she had never shown any recognition of Ana while they were in the Alamo, because, according to Enrique's statement, she was said "to be an aristocrat," and apparently considered herself socially superior to them. At this critical moment, however, Mrs. Melton seemed anxious to contact his mother, but still was reluctant to speak to her. Having no children of her own, she sent young Juan Losoya, said in some accounts to be her relative, over to ask a favor of Ana Esparza. She asked that Ana not mention to Generalissimo Santa Anna that she, Juana Losoya, now Mrs. Melton, had married an American, for fear of how she would be judged by the Presidente. Enrique says his mother assured her she had nothing to worry about from her or her family.[8]

It appears there is no actual documentation or further information on these other survivors named by Enrique Esparza, only this skimpy information cited here, which does identify some of them a little better than simply a name.

In an occasional account, others have been named or have

claimed that they themselves were there, but again there is no actual documentation on them. One noteworthy example of a self-proclaimed survivor is that of the famous, or infamous to be more exact, woman known as "Madam Candelaria." Since she is included in some accounts, a brief comment on her seems appropriate here, perhaps.

"Madam Candelaria's" name was not Candelaria at all, but was Andrea Castañon. She did not surface to the general public with her story of being in the Alamo as Jim Bowie's nurse until the late 1800's, fifty years or more after the battle ended. The first published account of her Alamo connection seems to have appeared in a book in 1890, written by a local book store owner, William Corner, who was something of a natural story teller and historical chronicler. His book, entitled *San Antonio de Bexar,* has been called the 'first guidebook of San Antonio,' and it is filled with a wealth of actual facts as well as some very colorful stories, such as the one on Candelaria, along with other entertaining information on 'the fastest growing city in the Southwest.' Along with collecting all these interesting tales on the early history of San Antonio, Mr. Corner can probably be credited with giving this woman, Madam Candelaria, the opportunity of a lifetime, which was, no doubt, just what she had been looking for—the chance to become really famous at last. She calculated her age to be 103 at the time of the interview with Corner, and in addition to describing in a dramatic reenactment how she was giving a drink of water to Bowie with one hand as she held his head with her other hand at the moment he was brutally killed, she told Corner many other colorful tales of all the varied experiences life had held for her.[9]

Some writers have recorded her story, which seems to be based primarily on Mr. Corner's account, as possibly factual, but most consider her simply a masterful liar, albeit a very imaginative one.

The 1901 article which appeared in the *San Antonio Light,* based on an article submitted to the newspaper by Miss Adina De Zavala, states:

Miss De Zavala and numerous other students of Texas history have contended all along that Madam Candelaria, the old woman who recently died, claiming to have been in the Alamo when it fell, was really not there. Miss De Zavala even says Madam Candelaria did not herself claim to have been in the Alamo at its fall until a few years before her death. Esparza says she was not there. She had been in it frequently before it fell, and was there immediately afterward, but was not present when the actual fall of the Alamo and massacre of its patriots-defenders occurred.[10]

Enrique Esparza says in the later 1907 account, "I do not remember seeing Madam Candelaria there. She may have been among the women and I may not have noticed her. She claimed to have been there and I shall not dispute her word."[11]

More recent writer Walter Lord summed his opinion up in one sentence, saying simply, "She was not there."[12]

There is no real proof to be found of "Madam Candelaria" being in the Alamo when it fell, and it appears to be nothing more than a dramatic fabrication of her imagination. Therefore, since it is not within the purpose of this book, the story of her long life, fascinating as it is, cannot be included here. There are several references that can be found if one wishes to read about her.

The purpose of Part I of this book was to tell the story of the life of some of the best known women who survived the Battle of the Alamo. Since no further information is available at this time on those others named by Esparza or other women who claimed to have been there, even though their presence has been accepted as fact by some, no stories of their lives are included. For them I hear no echoes. They are known by name only, simply as the "other" women who claimed to have survived the Battle of the Alamo. Perhaps their stories can be told at a future time.

~ ~ ~ ~ ~ ~ ~ ~ ~ ~

PART II

ECHOES

FROM

WOMEN

OF THE

"SECOND BATTLE OF THE ALAMO"

THE ALAMO BEER GARDEN SALOON AND RESTAURANT
(The Alamo, January 15th, 1888, Gift of Miss Isabel Wulff,
Daughters of the Republic of Texas Library,CN95.22.)

ADINA DE ZAVALA
(Adina De Zavala Papers, CN01738, Center for American History, University of Texas at Austin.)

Chapter Six
Adina De Zavala

"I did not surrender nor retreat . . ."

Adina De Zavala was an ardent and dedicated student of Texas history and a scholar of the subject in her own right. When she made the statement quoted above, without doubt she was inspired by the immortal words of the Alamo hero, William Barret Travis, in his stirring message written on February 24, 1836, the second day after the Alamo had come under attack.

Addressed "To the people of Texas & all Americans of the world", with bold strokes of his pen he wrote:

". . . I shall never surrender or retreat."[1]

Miss De Zavala echoed those words in her own statement to the public regarding her defense of the Alamo on February 10th, 1908. On that day she barricaded herself inside the old convento/long barracks building, known as the Hugo-Schmeltzer Building at that time, which was connected to the Alamo Chapel by a common corridor wall. There she remained for three days and nights to prevent its take-over and demolition by, as she termed it, "the enemy." This was unquestionably the most dramatic episode of what was a very long life filled with many colorful and dramatic moments.

The incident created an uproar in the press and directed national attention to the controversy raging within the DRT that became known as the "Second Battle for the Alamo." It was the climactic moment in a dispute that led to a split in the Daughters of the Republic of Texas that has never completely healed.

Shortly afterward, Adina De Zavala issued her printed, copyrighted explanation entitled "Statement by Miss De Zavala," in which she described this episode in the "second battle" as it had happened in her own words from her point of view, the opening line echoing Travis' words:

"I did not surrender nor retreat . . ."[2]

This bold thing she did, of barricading herself in that building, monumental as it might have appeared to be at the time, was a "mole-hill" compared to the mountain of achievements toward historic preservation she accomplished during her lifetime. But, it is still the one thing she is known for, almost exclusively.

From earliest childhood, to the last days of her 93 years of life, Adina De Zavala's thoughts were filled with the history of her native state of Texas. The preservation of its landmark sites became an obsession with her that increased with a passionate fervor as her life expanded and took shape.

This consuming pursuit continued even during periods of hospitalization, and almost up to her last breath and heartbeat in fact. Once when she lay in her hospital bed, her close friend Frances Donecker visited her and found papers she had been working on, pertaining to her life's mission, "the preservation of Texas history," strewn on a bedside table along with a small Texas flag.[3] Even though she was legally blind, and had been for almost two years, she had continued to work with her assistant up to the last few days of her life before slipping into a coma shortly before death came.

She seemed to have a conviction that, by some almost "divine right" her critics liked to say, she was put on this earth for the purpose of the preservation of Texas history, and she pursued that purpose with a zeal that more than once almost removed the object of her pursuit from her grasp. But this intrepid, and at times intractable, lady never gave up, no matter what opposition she faced. Almost prophetically she died on March 1st, 1955, just hours before the 119th anniversary of the Texas Declaration of Independence, a document that bore the signature of her grandfather and a date she had promoted to become a state holiday. A loyal

Texan to the end, even unto death!

Miss Winnie Allen, Archivist for the University of Texas, Mirabeau B. Lamar Library in Austin at the time, expressed it well in a letter of 15 March 1955 to authorities who were handling her estate:

All Texas is grieved over the loss of Miss Adina De Zavala. Her like will not be seen again . . .[4]

When the Senate of the State of Texas adjourned after a unanimous rising vote in her honor on March 22, 1955, less than one month after her death, they did so with the following Resolution:

SENATE RESOLUTION NO. 132
In Memory
of
Miss Adina De Zavala

WHEREAS, On the 1st day of March, 1955, our Heavenly Father in His infinite wisdom did call from her earthly home to join Him in His everlasting heavenly home, the beloved Adina De Zavala; and

WHEREAS, Adina De Zavala, who spent ninety-three glorious years in the service of her God and her fellowman, was a distinguished citizen of San Antonio, Texas and the grand-daughter of Lorenzo De Zavala, first Vice President of the Republic of Texas; and

WHEREAS, Adina De Zavala was the daughter of Augustine and Julia Tyrrell De Zavala and was born at the ancestral home of her grandfather, Zavala's Point opposite the San Jacinto battlefield. She received her early education from a private teacher at home, until she was old enough to attend the Ursuline Academy in San Antonio. Following her attendance there, she went to Sam Houston Normal College; and

WHEREAS, The single-minded devotion of Adina De Zavala to the preservation of the monuments of Texas history was unexampled, and with inspiring courage and matchless zeal she fought the first great battles against commercial encroachment on sites hallowed by Texas history; and

WHEREAS, Adina De Zavala was a living symbol of the great contribution made by Spanish speaking patriots to Texas Independence and played a major role in preserving the Alamo, along with the Spanish Governor's Palace, for posterity. Through the Texas Historical and Landmarks Society, which she founded, she placed permanent markers on some forty historic sites in Texas, many of which might otherwise have been forgotten; and

WHEREAS, Adina De Zavala through a life of devotion to Texas history, folk-lore and general civic and patriotic work, had perhaps, more than any one person in Texas, aroused in the general public a desire for a fuller knowledge of the history of the Lone Star State; and

WHEREAS, Adina De Zavala was the last surviving member of her distinguished family, her brother, Augustine De Zavala of Austin, having preceded her in death in 1952, now, therefore, be it

RESOLVED, by the Senate of Texas, that this Resolution be spread upon the Senate Journal as a memorial to Adina De Zavala for her work and aid in immortalizing Texas history for the ages; and, be it further

RESOLVED, That when the Senate adjourns today, it do so in memory of Adina De Zavala.

	Latimer	
	Kazen	
Aikin	Lane	Ratliff
Ashley	Lock	Roberts
Bracewell	Martin	Rogers of Childress
Colson	McDonald	Rogers of Travis
Corbin	Moffett	Secrest
Fly	Moore	Shireman
Fuller	Owen	Strauss
Hardeman	Parkhouse	Wagonseller
Hazlewood	Phillips	Weinert
Kelley		Willis

Ramsey, Lt. Governor

_____/S/ Ben Ramsey_____
President of the Senate
I hereby certify that the above
Resolution was adopted by the Senate
on March 22, 1955, by a rising vote.

__/S/ Loyce M. Bell__
Secretary of the Senate[5]

The above resolution is a fine tribute to Miss De Zavala and a concise summary of many of her achievements. But such a tribute, deserved as it is in every detail, cannot begin to convey the real spirit of the story of this remarkable woman's life – a story known by all too few Texans. The time is long overdue to correct that inexcusable omission.

What had life held for Adina De Zavala? What accomplishments had she achieved? What could have created such an unrelenting obsession to preserve the past, and where had she come from?

Adina Emilia De Zavala, born to Augustine and Julia Tyrrell De Zavala, on November 28, 1861, was the first of their six surviving children (three died in infancy). (Note: Adina De Zavala's middle name, Emilia, is occasionally misspelled. It is thought to be a variation of the name of her grandmother, Emily, and her aunt of the same name. The spelling used here is based on the standard form of names used by the Library of Congress, and the spelling of the name by the family as shown in *The New Handbook of Texas,* Vol. 6, p. 1146. The surname of De Zavala was more often spelled with a lower case "d" by the de Zavala family before her, including her grandfather, Lorenzo. For reasons of her own, which were not found in her papers, Miss Adina spelled the name with a capital "D". All references here to Lorenzo de Zavala are spelled with the lower case "d" and all references to Adina De Zavala are spelled with a capital "D", as she wrote it.)

The other surviving children were Florence, Mary, Zita, Thomas and Augustine, Jr. All of them preceded Adina in death and all are buried in the family plot in St. Mary's Cemetery in San Antonio, except Thomas who was buried in California where he had moved his family at an early date. They were the descendants of one of the founders of the Republic of Texas, Lorenzo de Zavala. Their illustrious grandfather was, among his many achievements, a signer of the Texas Declaration of Independence, a participant in the drafting of the Texas Constitution, and was elected by unanimous vote as the Vice President of the interim government of the new Republic of Texas.

No doubt many things contributed to Adina De Zavala's obsession with the preservation of Texas history, but probably none could have had a deeper and more profound effect on her than the influence of the life of her grandfather. Although he died long before she was born, her earliest memories were stories about him she heard from her grandmother, her parents, and important visitors who came to the family home at Zavala Point during her early childhood and the rest of her life. These stories about her grandfather and accounts of the formation of this new land called Texas must have awakened within Adina this lifelong passion that was expressed with such compelling and dynamic force to the end of her days.

Who was this grandfather who had such a powerful impact on Adina's life?

Lorenzo de Zavala was born in the village of Tecoh near Merida in the state of Yucatan, Mexico on October 3, 1789, while Mexico was still ruled by Spain. His Spanish ancestors, it is reported, were from a long line of titled inhabitants of Viscaya, Spain. When Spanish settlement of the "New World" began, members of the de Zavala family emigrated to the Yucatan peninsula before Lorenzo was born.

Lorenzo was exceptionally well educated and was described as a brilliant boy and young man. As a young adult he participated in community affairs and he rose to prominence readily in the local government. He showed early signs even as a young student of being a champion of the rights of the individual and an outspoken opponent of strong centralized governmental control. These were traits he never lost and they were carried over to his adult life and expressed in his participation in the movement for Mexico's independence from Spain. They were key to his direct involvement in the Texas Declaration of Independence from Mexico and establishment of the new Republic of Texas.

According to the genealogical and historical accounts of the family as described by Luther Robert Ables in his unpublished thesis, "The Work of Adina De Zavala," Lorenzo de Zavala possessed one of the most liberal minds and keen intellects of his time. Ables quotes from one source these descriptive words about de Zavala, that could easily be applied years later to his activist-inclined granddaughter, Adina:

> A completely restless and rebellious soul, from his early youth he was consumed with a desire for liberty . . .
> The life of Zavala explains his personality as a writer. He was a man of superior talent and culture, but he was enslaved by passion. He wrote while fighting, he fought while writing. . . .[6]

Because of his keen mind and ambitious desire toward greater progress for Mexico, he moved ahead in his political career very rapidly, rising to top level positions in the state of Yucatan first and then on to the national level in the national capitol at Mexico City. He was named as representative from Yucatan to the Spanish Cortés, a government body for the provinces which met in Spain. He was elected six times as representative from Yucatan to the legislature in Mexico City. He served as President of the Chamber of Deputies there and as such was the first to sign the federal constitution of Mexico when it was adopted in 1824 upon their independence from Spain. He held the office of governor of the State of Mexico twice, was Minister of the Treasury. Later, after a period of absence from Mexico, he returned and was named Minister to France.

Political unrest has plagued Mexico from its beginning as history records. Lorenzo de Zavala was there at the birth of the

Republic of Mexico and participated in the growth of the new nation from the start. Naturally he had made political enemies as well as friends along the way in his climb to the top, resulting ultimately in demands from his opponents for his resignation. Because of the continued political dissension, he did resign eventually and went to visit friends in the United States in Boston and New York City. His wife Teresa's poor health kept her in Merida where she remained with their young daughter, Manuela. Their young son, Lorenzo, Jr., was put in boarding school in the U.S.

Earlier during his years in government service in Mexico City, he had invested in real estate in the Mexican state of Texas. After arriving in New York City he joined the Galveston Bay and Texas Land Company, a New York and Boston based organization, and transferred his Texas land investments to that company. Their purpose was to recruit colonists for the Galveston Bay Company which covered the Houston-Galveston-Beaumont area of today and even a part of the rich East Texas oil fields that emerged later.

Soon after his departure from Mexico in 1830, de Zavala's first wife, Teresa Correa, died, leaving him with the responsibility of their two children, Lorenzo, Jr., and the older sister, Manuela. In the spring of 1831, he went to Europe to recruit colonists for the Galveston Bay Company. He left Lorenzo, Jr. in a private boarding school in Massachusetts and Manuela was cared for by family members in Merida.

He met a young woman in New York City named Emily West, a native of the state, who was born in Albany or possibly Brooklyn. They were married in New York City on November 12, 1831, at the Church of the Transfiguration.[7] They had three children from the marriage. Augustine, the father of Adina, was born January 1, 1832, in New York City[8]; Maria Emilia (Emily), was born February 2, 1834, in New York City[9]; and Ricardo was born May 26, 1835, in New York City.[10]

During Lorenzo de Zavala's off and on absences from

Mexico, changes were taking place in his homeland. One of those changes was the rise of a military man to the presidency whom de Zavala had admired earlier for his spectacular show of courage in the Mexican war for independence from Spain. His name was one that would become infamous later in Texas and in Mexico as well—Antonio Lopez de Santa Anna. Because of their earlier compatible relationship, Santa Anna invited de Zavala to return to Mexico and accept a post in his new government. Zavala accepted and returned with renewed hope for his country. His wife, Emily West de Zavala and young son, Augustine, and daughter Emily, soon joined him there. Ricardo, their youngest child had not yet been born. De Zavala had only been in his post a short time, however, when he received word he was to be minister to France. As it happened, he was beginning to be at odds with Santa Anna over the President's increasing tendency toward a strong central government. The assignment to France, rather than being an honor, was actually more of an imposed retirement from Mexico politics again.

He went to France but served in that post only one year. The relationship with Santa Anna grew more and more hostile and at the end of one year de Zavala gave up because of Santa Anna's now quite obvious position of self-declared dictatorship. Once more, Lorenzo de Zavala resigned from the service of Mexico and left his native land altogether, never to return. He took his family from France back to New York City for a brief time and then moved to Texas to the property he owned on Buffalo Bayou. There he established his permanent home, hoping to build a new life.

De Zavala rose to prominence in the government of his new homeland as he had in Mexico earlier. Texas was still a part of Mexico at the time of his arrival, of course, but the rumblings of a revolution for independence had already been heard.

He was regarded as one of the most learned and cosmopolitan gentlemen of the area, experienced in both national and international affairs and fluent in several languages. He became involved immediately in the forming of the new government by signing and participating in the drafting of a declaration of independence and a constitution for the newly declared Republic of Texas, as well as being elected ad interim Vice President.

De Zavala's experience and service in establishing the new Republic was invaluable and his position of leadership in its projected future looked bright indeed. After the capture of Santa Anna and the other Mexican prisoners following the Texas victory at the Battle of San Jacinto, however, things took a sudden and decided downward turn for him. He was very insistent that Texas return Santa Anna and the other prisoners to Mexico as the terms of the treaty specified. Others did not agree though, and de Zavala received a great deal of criticism for his position in the matter of the Mexican prisoners. Some unfair and unfounded doubts as to his loyalties began to arise among some citizens. He was unyielding, however, in his belief that Texas should live up to the treaty. In aligning himself with the revolutionary movement in Texas, he had put a price on his head both ways it seemed. He became a hero of the revolution against Mexico for some Texans, but not all as it turned out; and in Mexico he was considered a traitor to his own birth country. His situation in either country became an uncomfortable one to say the very least, sad to say.

Lorenzo de Zavala's efforts on behalf of the establishment of the new Republic of Texas, and the stress undergone later over the disagreement concerning the disposition of Santa Anna and the other captives, had taken a great toll on his already weakened health. His death was hastened by these circumstances, no doubt, but the immediate cause was the result of an unfortunate boating accident in the bay in front of the family home. He had taken his young son Augustine, out in a small boat and it capsized. It was the month of November and the water was icy cold, but he was able to put four year old Augustine onto the upturned bottom of the capsized boat and swim to shore, pushing the boat ahead of him. As a result of his exposure and his poor health in general, Lorenzo de Zavala developed pneumonia and died soon thereafter on November 15, 1836. He was only forty-seven years old. He was buried in the family plot on the estate at Zavala Point on Buffalo Bayou. Forty-six years later Emily West de Zavala was buried there beside him upon her death. In 1931 the State of Texas placed a marker at the gravesite.

Sometime during the 1930's Miss Adina had visited the area and had wanted to move the graves to a safer location in the San Jacinto battle ground site across on the mainland. However, another family member who had become heir to the estate, refused to allow it because, his father before him had given orders that the bodies should never be moved.[11] Miss Adina drew up a plat of the cemetery at the time locating each gravesite which was very fortuitous because it was used later as the guide in the solution to the problem that arose.

In 1964 much of the estate area, including the small cemetery plot, was to be submerged into Buffalo Bayou in the expansion plans for creating the Houston Ship Channel. There were intensive protests from the Texas Conservation Council, several historical societies, Latin-American groups and others in an effort to prevent what appeared to be, on the face of it, this incredibly crass act. But all to no avail.[12]

The fact is, there was an archaeological investigation conducted at the time to determine the feasibility of moving the graves, but it was found that not only was that impractical—it was impossible. Subsidence caused by removal of water from underground sources over the years for normal needs in the area, as well as erosion from the bay, had so undermined the graves that the remains of the bodies buried there and the caskets containing them had completely deteriorated. No traces of remains of any kind were found by archaeologists, according to Dr. Margaret Swett Henson.[13]

Before the area was submerged, the San Jacinto Parks

Commission moved the headstones to the San Jacinto Battleground State Historical Park across the bay where they were placed in an arrangement simulating the original small cemetery as Miss Adina had drawn them. The area, which is called De Zavala Plaza, is enclosed by a fence and has an appropriate marker identifying it. It is now under the control of the Texas State Parks and Wildlife Department.[14]

Lorenzo de Zavala had very nearly had a watery grave in the bay in 1836 upon his near fatal boating accident. Ironically, in 1964, one-hundred and twenty-eight years later, Buffalo Bayou claimed what may have remained of him after all. Mercifully, Miss Adina had been dead almost ten years by then and thus did not have to suffer the pain and indignity of it all. Had she been alive, need-less to say, it is doubtful she would have stood by and allowed it to happen without a protest of a kind that defies the imagination!

The stories of her grandfather filled her house of memories throughout her lifetime, but there was another quite unique family story that had no doubt always been of great interest and pride to her, also. It was one concerning her uncle, Lorenzo de Zavala, Jr. who was the son of de Zavala, Sr. by his first wife, Teresa Correa, and thus a half-brother to Adina's father, Augustine. Young 21 year old Lorenzo, Jr. served in the Texas army under General Sam Houston at the Battle of San Jacinto. Because of his fluency in Spanish and English and his knowledgeable and courtly manner, he had been called upon to act as interpreter for General Houston at that historic moment when Santa Anna was captured and brought before Sam Houston. [15] Quite a memorable occasion for him, no doubt, and one Adina must have reported on over the years with understandable pride.

After the death of Lorenzo de Zavala, just seven months after the battle, Lorenzo, Jr. in settling his father's estate remained at the family home at Zavala Point with his step-mother, Emily West de Zavala and her small children for a time. Some time around

1840 he returned to Merida, Mexico, possibly in an effort to reclaim some of the family land and fortune in that area and, as circumstances had it, he chose to remain there for the rest of his life. There is no indication that Adina ever met him personally, but she did correspond with him later.

In 1895, fifty-nine years after the Battle of San Jacinto, Lorenzo de Zavala, Jr., now almost eighty years old, wrote to his niece, Adina, from Merida describing that dramatic episode of his meeting with Santa Anna and Sam Houston under the gigantic oak tree on the San Jacinto battlefield. He had already written two letters previously in 1890 to the artist, H. A. McArdle, in response to that gentleman's request for an early photograph and a description of what he was wearing at that historic battle, in order that he might portray him correctly in the painting that he had been commissioned to do. A painting by H. A. McArdle entitled "The Battle of San Jacinto" hangs in the Texas Capitol. Another painting by a contemporary artist of the time, W. H. Huddle, entitled "The Surrender of Santa Anna," with what would appear to be young Lorenzo, Jr. as the interpreter between a wounded General Sam Houston seated on a blanket under the ancient oak and a much humbled Generalissimo/Presidente Lopez de Santa Anna before him, also hangs in the Texas Capitol Building in Austin. Reprints of these paintings were included in almost every Texas history textbook in use at times.

Copies of the three letters written by Lorenzo de Zavala, Jr. with his detailed descriptions of the event, were saved by Adina De Zavala and left in her personal papers filed at the Center for American History at the University of Texas at Austin. They reveal his personality very clearly, as well as tell the story of his life.[16]

Adina De Zavala grew up surrounded by stories of all this lore of her illustrious grandfather and others and tales of the early days of Texas. It is not surprising then that she had a keen understanding and a deep appreciation of what she perceived to be her special connection to the history of Texas from her earliest days. In years to come, filled with her recollections of all these things, and by natural inheritance, or "inspired imitation" as Robert Ables so aptly put it, she patterned her life's goals and endless endeavors after her famous grandfather. He was her role model, her guiding force. She was the tiny acorn cloaked in this diminutive, frail looking woman called Adina De Zavala from which grew a mighty oak,.

Of all the many things that would influence this Texas patriot, surely none could have had the impact that this grandfather she admired so had. But, what other influences came into her life? Where did her endless and tireless paths lead her? What was her early life like? And what were her other family origins?

Some members of what is referred to as the "Hispanic community" today occasionally make pointed reference to Adina De Zavala's ethnic origin. Because of her Spanish surname they lay claim to her as 'one of their own.' Miss Adina was very proud of her Spanish/Mexican heritage, but the fact is she was actually more of Irish and other ethnic origin than Spanish. Her paternal grandmother, Emily West's family genealogy included Anglo-Saxon forebears and possibly Walloon-Dutch,[17] but, in any case, none was Hispanic. And her mother, Julia Tyrrell, was of direct Irish descent, having been born in Ireland on May 24, 1842, at the family home near Dublin. Thus, Adina De Zavala was primarily Irish it would appear.

Julia Tyrrell De Zavala, Adina's mother, was the daughter of James and Julia Tyrrell, who had emigrated from Ireland to the U.S. when little Julia was a young child. The family came to Texas in 1855 and settled on Galveston Island. They were a devout Catholic family and Julia was educated at the Catholic Ursuline Academy for Girls in Galveston. While a student at the Academy she met her future husband, Augustine De Zavala, who was attending the nearby St. Mary's Catholic College for men.[18]

Augustine De Zavala and Julia Tyrrell were married on March 17, 1860, and for several years they lived at the Zavala estate which had been established by Augustine's father, Lorenzo, on Buffalo Bayou. Augustine built a one-and-a-half story cottage there at Zavala Point for his bride, and the first of their six children, Adina Emilia, was born there on November 28, 1861.[19]

Adina was a pretty little girl with fair skin and dark hair, but as her close friend of later years, Frances Donecker, said of her, "She was a small woman, about five feet three inches tall with soft brown hair, but the Spanish stopped at the blue eyes,"[20] which she possibly inherited from her Irish forebears.

Her blue eyes were a matter of comment by more than one writer who interviewed her. In an article which appeared in a popular magazine of the 1930's called *Holland's,* a well-known journalist of the day, Pearl Howard, described Miss Adina, who was 64 years old then, thus:

> Adina de [sic] Zavala is such a wisp of a person, so fragile looking, so ethereal, you are amazed to the point of disbelief when you learn of her constant patriotic activities. Her once black hair is dusted with silver. Her eyes are of that blue, which when gleaming with excitement or enthusiasm, seems black. Her skin, fine in texture, is delicately webbed about her mouth, her eyes. Her body in motion, reveals that restless energy which, on occasion, spares no one, least of all herself. Whatever she does she does with all her might.[21]

In another interview several years later in 1947 when she was 86 years old, Lois Johnson in an article in the *San Antonio Light* newspaper described her as having "blue eyes still sparkling with the determination to get things done." [22]

Not only was Adina De Zavala a pretty little girl, she was a very precocious one as well. Her first tutors were her mother and her grandmother, followed by family governesses. She often said in later years she did not remember when she could not read.

In the article by Pearl Howard from *Holland's* magazine,

Howard says of Miss Adina:

> She told me: "I could not remember when I could not
> read. My favorite story books were about history; myths
> came next. My sister and I produced 'plays'—always
> scenes from history. All children are impressed by
> pageantry. I am a firm believer in the value of exact science,
> object lessons.
>
> This is why I consider historic shrines of inestimable
> worth . . . If people—especially children—could actually
> see the door through which some noble man, or woman
> passed . . . they'll remember, they'll read everything they
> can find in print about that man or woman. Inevitably
> they'll be filled with high ideals, the desire to emulate."[23]

Not only does the article present a nice vignette of young
Adina and her sister play-acting historic roles, but it indirectly
describes so well her life-long efforts in later years to help other
children and grownups alike learn by doing the same kind of thing
with the real things.

The Augustine De Zavala family moved to Galveston
around 1866 and the cottage Augustine had built was put on a barge
and towed intact to the island! It was placed on a lot on West
Broadway across from St. Mary's College where Augustine had
attended school.[24] Once established in their home there, Adina and
her sisters attended Ursuline Academy as their mother had and the
boys attended the Catholic school their father had.

Adina's father had become the owner and captain of a boat
in service in the bay area, and during the Civil War years his boat
had served as a blockade runner and observation craft. His life had
been spent in the constant damp atmosphere of the coast which
eventually caused a rather severe condition of arthritis and disabling rheumatism. Upon the advice of his physician, the family
decided to move to a drier location and San Antonio was chosen as
their new home site. They purchased a ranch northwest of town on

what has become known as De Zavala Road and also established a home in town at 141 Taylor Street, just a few blocks from what would be Adina's most notable passion—the Alamo. Adina did not accompany the family in the move to San Antonio initially, but remained in Galveston as a boarding student at the Ursuline Academy for the next few years.

When Augustine and his family had moved to Galveston— cottage and all—his mother, Emily West de Zavala, had remained in the homestead on Zavala Point for several years. During this time her daughter, also named Emily, who was the younger sister of Augustine, and an aunt to Adina, married a Captain Thomas Jenkins. Emily de Zavala Jenkins died in 1857 in childbirth upon the birth of her only child, Catherine. Little Catherine's grand-mother, now in her mid-forties, took the infant under her care to raise at Zavala Point. In the late 1860's Emily de Zavala moved with young Catherine to Galveston where Augustine and his fami-ly were well established by then. Shortly after Emily and little Catherine left Zavala Point, the old homestead, which had been left in the care of some former servants, burned to the ground. Young Catherine Jenkins grew up and married William E. Hutchinson and they moved to Houston. Later Catherine brought her grandmother Emily there to live with her.[25]

Grandmother Emily came to San Antonio to visit Augustine and his family from time to time, but she would only stay for a very brief time according to Miss Adina. She always claimed she had to hurry back to Houston because "Kate" (Catherine) was all by her-self.[26] Emily de Zavala remained at the home of her granddaugh-ter, Catherine Jenkins Hutchinson, for the rest of her life. She died there on June 15, 1882. Her body was taken by boat to the De Zavala cemetery, not far from the old homestead site on Zavala Point, and buried there next to Lorenzo.[27] When the land was sub-merged to build the Houston ship channel years later any remains of the De Zavala family that may still have been there were auto-

"DE ZAVALA'S POINT"
(Adina De Zavala Papers, CN08529, Center for American History, University of Texas at Austin.)

matically "buried at sea".

Many years after Emily West de Zavala's death, Adina De Zavala wrote an article for the *San Antonio Express* newspaper describing her grandmother's visits to San Antonio and her garden at the old family homestead at Zavala Point. The article had accompanying pictures of garden nooks at Zavala Point and Emily de Zavala herself and the picket-fenced house and family cemetery. This article was published in 1934 around the time Miss Adina had visited the site and apparently tried unsuccessfully to move the bodies from the cemetery to the San Jacinto Battleground site across the Bay.

Although she was only a child at the time depicted in her article, her memories of the place were quite poignant and remarkably clear. She describes in some detail, as she remembered it, the beautiful garden of her grandmother whom she said was an ardent and knowledgeable botanist. On those visits to San Antonio, during her walks at the ranch on De Zavala Road, her grandmother would often collect and mount species of native wildflowers such as the Texas bluebonnet, the colorful Indian paintbrush, the wine cup, the Mexican firewheel (or gallardia), the Texas mountain laurel and others. Adina's recollections of the life and times and "Grandmother's Old Garden" at Zavala Point are a colorful glimpse into her early childhood and later periods of her life as well.[28]

YOUNG ADINA DE ZAVALA.
(Adina De Zavala Papers, CN08827, Center for American History, University of Texas at Austin.)

After Adina De Zavala joined her family in San Antonio in 1873, she attended the Ursuline Academy in that city. After completion of her high school level studies she enrolled in 1879 on the opening year of Sam Houston Normal Institute in Huntsville, Texas. She was 17 years of age.[29]

She pursued a teaching course of study at this school. It later became Sam Houston State Teachers' College and today is Sam Houston State University. Her studies there were followed

111

by an enrollment in a school of music in Chilicothe, Missouri.[30]

Following her preparation years of study, Miss Adina pursued a teaching career, first teaching in Terrell, Texas for two years, then in Austin, Texas.[31] Afterward, in 1886, she returned to San Antonio where she taught in several elementary schools of the city until 1907, a period of approximately twenty years in all.

During these years of teaching, she had not neglected her first consuming interest, the proliferation and preservation of Texas history. In 1889, she and some other women she had interested in this patriotic endeavor, met and formed a society which they called the "De Zavala Daughters" in honor of her grandfather. This group,

ADINA DE ZAVALA
Organizes the "De Zavala Daughters"
(Adina De Zavala Papers, CN10281, Center for American History,
University of Texas at Austin.)

insofar as is known, is the oldest society composed of women for patriotic purposes in the state of Texas, according to Robert Ables as taken from an article in the December 1919 edition of the *Interstate Index*.[32] This would mean the group predated the Daughters of the Republic of Texas (DRT), which was not formed until two years later.

In 1893 members of the De Zavala Daughters were invited to become affiliated with the newly founded DRT as the local San Antonio chapter. It was called the De Zavala Chapter and Miss Adina was named president. The Chapter announced early on its plan to place markers and plaques on historical sites and buildings in and around San Antonio. This goal was accomplished by an impressive number of them because of the many such sites in the area.

Among their various projects was the naming of public schools for prominent Texans. Until 1902, schools in Texas were designated by number. Miss Adina and the De Zavala chapter of the DRT introduced the idea of naming them for Texas heroes and statesmen, for as they said, "It would be much more meaningful, especially to school children". Today this is the practice statewide. They also made much of celebrating and commemorating events on those special days in Texas history, such as March 2nd, the day Texas declared its independence from Mexico; March 6th, "The Fall of the Alamo"; April 21st, "San Jacinto Day," when Texas won its final battle for independence at San Jacinto, and others. Ultimately, Miss Adina was instrumental in making some of these official state holidays.

The perilous state of ruin of all of the old Spanish Missions had always been of great concern to Miss Adina. Under her guidance the De Zavala Chapter, although always handicapped by lack of funds, began working to "save" the missions. This was an on going crusade for Miss Adina even after her later separation from the DRT.

These and many more of the efforts of Miss Adina and her co-workers in the cause of the preservation of historic sites and the promotion of Texas history in general enjoyed a great deal of success, but some disappointments and reversals were suffered as well. True to her nature, though, she was always undaunted and continued with characteristic determination on her course. She did not realize, however, that her course was headed for the monumental battle she was to encounter in her effort to protect from total destruction the "long barracks" building of the Alamo Mission/Fort complex.

This dramatic episode was to be the thing for which Miss Adina would be remembered best for the rest of her life as well as forever afterward. It was unquestionably one of her most significant contributions, for without her continued and determined efforts none of that historic structure would still be standing. However, as we have seen, it was not her introduction to the pursuit of the preservation of historic landmarks and the promotion of respect for the history of Texas; nor would it be her final act for those causes. The reservoir of experience she had been accumulating long before this would give her, a lone warrior, the courage and derring-do to take on the entire 'enemy' at that particular occasion of the so called "Second Battle for the Alamo," and the many other "battles" that would follow as well.

As circumstances would have it all around, though, the time had come for Miss Adina to leave the teaching field and devote herself to what some referred to as her 'self-appointed' cause. Her relationship with the San Antonio School District had begun and continued apparently for several years in a normal and amicable manner. As time went by, however, a series of episodes with the Board of Education, parents of a few students, her pay status and other things, led finally to her resignation from her teaching position in January of 1907. Her natural temperament had developed fully by then and it emerged with characteristic conviction.

She was a person of a quick tongue as well as a quick mind, impatient with what she perceived to be inaccuracies or inefficiency, plus one other lifelong trait. She was a great admirer of Davy

Crockett and a firm believer in the slogan attributed to him of, "Be sure you're right, then go ahead." The only problem was, she felt that she was always right, and many times she proved to be because she did her homework carefully. However, right or not, once she had decided what she was 'sure was right,' she went ahead full steam without compromise or regard for the consequences.

And so her career as a school teacher came to an end on the eve of the turning point in her life. It was probably foreordained though, for her real life's work truly lay in historic preservation and promotion of patriotic pride in Texas. As Dr. Robert Ables said, "She was determined that the people should not only read the history of Texas but have the opportunity to view it as well. The major portion of her life was spent in that endeavor and although she sometimes met failure she never deviated from her purpose . . ."[33], a trait she seemed to have inherited from her grandfather. This dedication to cause became a full time obsession with her and it left her with no time for other more 'ordinary pursuits' such as a teaching career.

Also, the decision to resign at that particular time undoubtedly was predicated to a considerable degree by the stress of the trouble she had had during the past two years with the Daughters of the Republic of Texas concerning the Alamo. There was simply not enough time for both the Alamo controversy and a teaching career. Teaching had to go.

For as far back as she could remember, she had been interested in preservation of all historic sites throughout the state, and that included a wide variety of places and things. High on the list were all of the old Spanish missions which were some of the oldest historic sites throughout the state. This included the five missions in her home city of San Antonio, of course, the oldest of which was Mission San Antonio de Valero, better known as the Alamo, the name acquired from its later use.

Mission San Antonio de Valero had undergone many changes since the mission period ended in 1793, as each succeeding group had occupied it. Detailed coverage of these changes with illustrations can be found in Chapter Eight. The summary here is a more general account.

After its mission life had ended, it became known as the Alamo and was occupied by a continuous group of soldiers, up to, through and after the famous battle that occurred there. First the soldiers of Spain occupied it, next Mexico, then those of the Republic of Texas, and, lastly the U. S. Army. Little by little the buildings around the compound had deteriorated after each occupant vacated it until only two were left. When the U. S. Army moved in, all that remained was the old convento/"long barracks" and the ruins of the church.

When Texas joined the Union the U. S. Army leased these two buildings from the Catholic Church and completely renovated them. They added a wooden exterior covering and a gabled roof to the old "long barracks" and took the ruins of the church building next to it and finished it off as it appears today. It had never been anything but an incomplete roofless shell, even during its mission days. Because of faulty architectural design and inferior building methods, it had collapsed midway during construction and had never been finished. Neither building bore any resemblance to its prior appearance after the U. S. Army's restorations and remodeling.

The U. S. army moved out of the Alamo buildings in 1876 and the Church leased the Chapel to the State of Texas just as the Army had rebuilt it. The State eventually bought the Chapel and the "long barracks" was sold to a businessman, Mr. Honoré Grenet. He promptly converted the old building into a unique and enormous emporium full of dozens and dozens of items of every description, from "dry goods" and clothing, to china, novelties, hardware and every kind of "general store" merchandise imaginable, including domestic and "fine imported liquors." The exterior of the building was faced with a wooden covering and, painted and re-done to resemble a military fortress complete with corner watch towers and cannons "pointing in every direction" sitting on top of the flat portions of the roof. The building had lost all resemblance to what it may have looked like at the time of the battle, but it was Mr. Grenet's idea of what a fortress should look like. He had great respect for the heroes of the Alamo and a portion of the building was even set up with a display on the battle to honor those who had lost their lives there.

Grenet died after only two years of occupancy and his magnificent emporium closed its doors for lack of anyone to carry on his business. According to Miss De Zavala, he had publicly announced his intention of eventually devoting the entire building to the purpose of a museum for the Alamo and dedicating it to the memory of the Texas heroes as a gift to the people. "The sudden death of Mr. Grenet before title to the property was executed to the public deprived the people of this benefaction." [34]

The building was bought by another merchandising business, the Hugo-Schmeltzer Company. After only a few years they moved their business to a new building on Houston Street and used this one as a warehouse to store their goods, including their liquor stock, and they put this building up for sale.

Miss Adina and the group she had led earlier as the "De Zavala Daughters", and now as the De Zavala Chapter of the DRT, had been trying for a number of years to protect the property which adjoined the Alamo Chapel. The Chapel itself was already secure, although markedly altered from its appearance during the battle, but the old "long barracks," the site of the final assault where a great many of the men had died, was in danger.

Miss Adina was convinced from her extensive research that the present building had merely an inappropriate wooden exterior structure which covered the original two-story stone building underneath it, the actual building where the last desperate moments of the battle occurred.

As early as 1892, before they had become a part of the DRT,

Miss De Zavala and her group had obtained a verbal promise of an option to buy the building from the Hugo-Schmeltzer Company should they decide to sell. When that day came, she approached them to discuss the possibilities of terms. The price quoted was $75,000. That was under the bids from others they claimed to have received, but it was still an impossible amount of money for this little group of patriotic women to produce.

Miss Adina was not one to be discouraged from attempting to achieve such a goal, though, when it involved a project she was as passionate about as she was this one. Her group, under her single-minded leadership, was ready to attack the challenge somehow when fate delayed their efforts with an unequaled hurricane in nearby Galveston, her actual birth-city, which interrupted their effort. Miss Adina went off to Galveston to help in the program to assist the flood victims. This delay, however, was merely an interruption for her in her goal to raise funds to save this building. It was followed soon afterward by another act of fate seemingly. This time it was a solution to the problem of raising that necessary money for her cause.

A very wealthy young woman by the name of Clara Driscoll, who was known to have expressed great concern over the unsightly surroundings of the Alamo Chapel, was brought to Miss De Zavala's attention as someone who might be interested in helping. It was not clear whether Miss Driscoll understood the significance of the Hugo-Schmeltzer Building or not, but Miss Adina apparently informed her of it very quickly and thoroughly. She joined the DRT soon after their meeting, which put her into a position to be able to exercise the option on behalf of the organization.

Miss Driscoll appeared to be as anxious to save the old building, as well as the entire site, as Miss De Zavala and her colleagues, and so Miss De Zavala took this new DRT member to meet the owners to discuss the possibilities of purchasing the property. As a result, after consulting with her financial advisors, Miss Driscoll agreed to put up $500 of her own money the very next day for a thirty-day option for the purchase of the convento/"long barracks" building. The arrangement called for another $4,500 at the expiration of the thirty-day period for an option of one year.

Under their new-found friendship and devotion to the cause of saving the building and what they agreed upon to be the site of the final assault on the Alamo, the two women began a campaign to raise the rest of the $4,500 for the purchase. They sent out letters statewide asking for donations from all patriotic citizens, from school children to philanthropists, and everyone in between. Their efforts were very disappointing, though, and the response was less than the proverbial 'drop in the bucket' to fulfill their need.

By the end of the thirty-day option period Miss Driscoll was committed, not only philosophically but financially. This time she put up the required $4,500 for an extended option of one year. The two women renewed their fund-raising efforts with revived hope and vigor, but, again, there was grossly inadequate response.

At the end of the year when the option was to expire, they had another meeting for negotiations with the Hugo-Schmeltzer Company. This time, Miss Driscoll agreed to put up the money for the required down-payment for purchase and sign five promissory notes to cover the entire $75,000, the sales price for the "long barracks". For this unprecedented generous gesture, she became known overnight as the "Savior of the Alamo," a title she still retains.

When the state legislature met a few months later, it passed a bill to appropriate money to reimburse Miss Driscoll for the total amount she had paid thus far and to assume her promissory notes. The bill also named the DRT the official custodian of the Alamo property.

(Author's Note: A brief synopsis of the event which became known as "The Second Battle for the Alamo" follows. Full detailed and documented evidence on the troubled affair is covered in Chapter Eight. Several colorful newspaper articles on the "barricade" episode are included as well. In order to fully understand and appreciate this period in the

life of Miss De Zavala, the reader may wish to refer to that
Chapter at this point.)

Miss De Zavala and her Chapter of the DRT began at once
to consider the matter of removing the unsightly exterior covering
of the Hugo-Schmeltzer Building and developing plans for the
restoration of the original building underneath it into the museum
they had envisioned. Before too long, though, it developed that
some DRT members, other that those in their own local chapter, had
very different ideas.

The opposing members made it clear they did not believe
that the old building covered anything and certainly nothing that
was historic, underneath it. They began to call for the dilapidated
"eyesore" to be torn down. They wanted to see a memorial garden
and park put in its place as a tribute to those heroes who may have
died on that site, but especially 'for all those who died in the
Chapel' where they mistakenly thought most of the defenders were
at the last moments of the battle.

Meanwhile, Clara Driscoll left for a career in New York as a
playwright and novelist, but, before she left town, she had expressed
a change of heart at some point regarding the old building. It seems
she no longer wanted to see the building restored for which she had
worked so diligently with Miss De Zavala. For some unexplained
reason she had joined the opposing members and now was insisting
it be demolished and a park and garden be built in its place.

The argument began to heat up and soon the DRT had split
into two hostile groups. Miss De Zavala was leading one group.
Those in the other group were identified as followers of Clara
Driscoll, who by now had become famous as the "Savior of the
Alamo" because of her financial support earlier, albeit not of the
Chapel itself which most identify as "The Alamo", but of the "long
barracks". The disagreement between the two factions finally
reached a critical impasse, and at the DRT annual convention in
1907, the meeting broke up with both sides claiming to be the offi-

cial DRT group. Soon thereafter the Driscoll followers obtained a temporary injunction against the De Zavala group to cease its claim of the DRT and hence custodians of the Alamo property.

Before the trial on the mcrit of the case (ie., to make the injunction permanent), a story appeared in the newspaper stating that an eastern syndicate planned to build a large hotel adjacent to the Alamo Chapel. They were reported to have reached an agreement with the DRT (the Driscoll group) on a plan to destroy the Hugo-Schmeltzer Building and put in its place the park which that group wanted.

This came as a great shock to Miss De Zavala, needless to say. She had spent years trying to save and restore the original building. To have it threatened like this by the opposing group after she had cause to believe it was secure, was simply too much. Most of all, she felt the Driscoll Group had no legal right or the authority even to take such a step until the court made a decision on which of the DRT groups was the officially recognized one. She also felt her group was on the "side of the right" in this issue and would naturally win the court battle and be named as the true Daughters of the Republic of Texas.

She immediately went to the owners of the Hugo-Schmeltzer Building, with whom she had been negotiating all those years. Because of their knowledge of her dedication toward the historic significance of the building and preservation of it, they gave her the keys and their permission to enter it and take possession. She took some men with her to guard the building and went inside to see that it was secure against intrusion by the other DRT group or anyone else. While she and the guards were inside securing the building, there was a loud knock at the main entrance and a voice demanded that the door be opened. Miss De Zavala, who was not always inclined to comply automatically, said nothing and did nothing. After more loud knocking, the voice outside announced if the door was not opened, they would break it down. When there was still no compliance, they did as threatened and breaking the door and lock open, they burst into the room. The intruders seemed very surprised to see Miss De Zavala there. Apparently, they had expected to see only the guards. They forced the guards out bodily and then stepped outside in some confusion for a conference. When they did, Miss De Zavala quickly shut, locked and barred the door again even more securely with some means of a "barricade." She refused to come out or listen to the court order on the temporary injunction they attempted to read to her. They continued to read through the entire court order but she refused to listen and visibly 'stopped up her ears,' according to a later report of the DRT.

Miss De Zavala refused to come out of the building and she remained there for three days and three nights. She would not come out she declared, until she had the complete assurance of the governor of the State of Texas that nothing would be done to the building before the court case had been fully and finally decided. When that assurance did come on the third day of her self chosen incarceration, she unlocked the door and walked out calmly as though nothing unforeseen had occurred.

This dramatic episode became known as the "barricade of the Alamo" by Miss De Zavala, and it made her name the famous one this time in connection with the hallowed shrine. A detailed account of this is covered in Chapter Eight with colorful newspaper stories describing it all,and a copy of her complete "Statement". She had absolutely refused to stand by and do nothing while her dream of a museum and library in the old "long barracks" building was destroyed by those who would not recognize and accept what she felt to be the 'true history' of the building's place in the Battle of the Alamo.

The long overdue case to determine which group was the official DRT representative was brought to trial after many long delays. The decision which was finally rendered came unusually quick in the final round, and the outcome was devastating for Miss

De Zavala and the few faithful colleagues who had stayed with her to the end. The court had declared the Driscoll followers the "official" DRT group, to the complete disbelief of Miss De Zavala.

Within a few weeks the victorious group made an unprecedented and never since repeated decision regarding the opposing faction. They declared the "De Zavalan" group "could no longer claim to be members of the DRT" and they removed the names of Adina De Zavala and her twelve supporting members from the membership list of the Daughters of the Republic of Texas. Not only had the De Zavala group lost their case and their cause, but they also lost their entitlement to membership in the organization for which they had worked so hard for so many years.

The "Second Battle for the Alamo," as the whole long affair came to be called, had lasted for almost five years. It had been a pivotal point in the life of Adina De Zavala, but by no means the end of it. Like the heroes of the Battle of the Alamo in 1836, she lost her battle, but, unlike them, she survived hers. Ultimately, she accepted her defeat with a certain kind of honorable resignation, but she came to look upon it as a "temporary loss," and she never quit trying to recover that loss to the end of her days. She never ceased trying to get everyone, from each subsequent governor to everyday citizens everywhere to recognize that what was left of the "long barracks" was the historic site she claimed it to be and that the skeleton of the remains of the building must be restored as a museum honoring the fallen heroes of the Alamo.

The De Zavala Chapter, Daughters of the Heroes and Pioneers of the Republic of Texas, placed a tablet on the corner of the old "long barracks" building of the Alamo complex. In the picture on the following page Miss De Zavala points to the spot where the marker was and which she claimed had been covered over by her opponents. Her comments on the back of the photo are shown in her own handwriting.

Being the indomitable spirit she was, she gathered her

ADINA DE ZAVALA AND MISSING PLAQUE
(Adina De Zavala Papers, CN10287, Center for American
History, University of Texas at Austin.)

strong will together and moved on to other battles to be fought on other fronts, even as she continued through the years to push the idea of a museum at the historic site. She formed other groups to work toward historic preservation, such as the Texas Historical and Landmarks Association. This organization included men as well as women, and the preservation projects of this group were many and varied and far reaching throughout the state. Her reputation as a state-wide preservationist became well established and respected and the picture on page 126 appeared in a 1929 edition of *Who's Who of the Womanhood of Texas.*

Locally in San Antonio she continued to work on the other four old Spanish missions which had been one of her earliest passions. She had studied the history of the early Spanish explorations of Texas and their establishment of missions throughout the state.

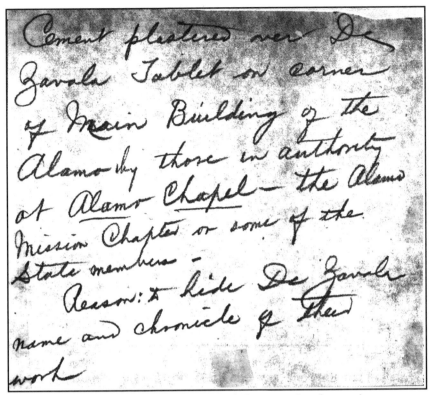

Cement plastered over De
Zavala Tablet on corner
of Main Building of the
Alamo by those in authority
at Alamo Chapel — the Alamo
Mission Chapter or some of the
State members —
        Reason: to hide De Zavala
name and chronicle of their
work

She had maps and plats of many of them and a fantastic memory regarding them it was said. She could "recite from memory," one admirer remarked, how two of the San Antonio missions, Espada and San Juan, "were constructed centuries ago." [35] The Alamo was obviously her favorite among the local missions though not only because of its role in Texas history which she had defended so fiercely, but because of its earlier significance as the first of the five missions in San Antonio.

She was devoted to the idea of the preservation and restoration of the San Antonio missions, but the missions established by the Spanish in the eastern part of Texas, which predated the local ones, had captured her attention, also. She was very interested in seeing that the sites of those earlier missions were identified with historic markers, even though the actual mission buildings themselves had all disappeared.

ADINA DE ZAVALA
"WHO'S WHO OF THE WOMANHOOD OF TEXAS"
(Adina De Zavala Papers, CN10284, Center for American History,
University of Texas at Austin.)

She made numerous exploratory expeditions to the East Texas area in search of the location of those early missions and other historic sites. Upon leaving for these expeditions, she was always concerned that the research material she was working on, which was notoriously unorganized, would be disturbed. On one of these trips she left the following handwritten note on the door to her study:

Please let no one whomsoever in my apartment. No matter what excuse, without my written orders!! Accept no excuse—no plea—I do not want anything touched or cleaned up—my historical notes are scattered every-where—and it would set me back to be worried about them—

Bebe likes plenty of water. We keep it in a pan under the sink and she could have some outside, too—convenient if she stays out sometime—.Love to our baby. Thanks for everything.

/S/Adina Z.[36]

Bebe was her pet dog. There is a picture of Miss Adina with her dog in front of the Governor's Palace on page 135.

One of her trips took her in search of the first Spanish mission in Texas, San Francisco de los Tejas, which was established in 1690, between the present day East Texas town of Crockett and a smaller community called Weches. She found that site, and today there is a bronze plaque on a pink granite boulder standing on the original "Camino Real," King's Highway, today's Texas Highway 21, marking the vicinity of the location of that early mission. The marker was placed there by Miss Adina's Texas Historical and Landmarks Association in 1934. A state park was built in the woods behind the marker commemorating the actual location that she determined to be where two earlier missions had stood.

This was just one of a total of 38 markers her group placed on significant Texas historical sites or buildings, not only of missions but of buildings and places of a great variety. In San Antonio alone, she placed 28 historical markers of all kinds, because of the city's unique historical heritage. Endless hours were spent on these projects and a considerable amount of her personal money was expended by her. The markers projects were spread over the years of the remainder of her lifetime, until travel and tramping through woods, where snakes and other hazards which abounded underfoot in the brambles and thorny underbrush, were beyond her physical capability and endurance.

Her good friend, Miss Frances Donecker, a San Antonio school teacher, accompanied Miss De Zavala on some of her exploratory trips to the "piney woods" of East Texas, and Miss Donecker always kept a neat, methodical journal of each trip. She too was a historical researcher, but unlike Miss Adina, she was a martinet about record keeping and filing of those records in an orderly system.

On one of those earlier exploratory trips, an anecdote that was typical of Miss Adina's practical and unruffled nature was recorded by Miss Donecker in her journal of a trip made in the summer of 1935. Miss Adina was 74 years old at the time. They made many stops in their route that began in San Antonio and went to La Grange, then wound through the East Texas mission sites, and on to historic Nacogdoches sites, and terminated in Western Louisiana. As they were tramping through the East Texas piney woods in search of a particular site, Miss Donecker became aware suddenly that "sand ticks" were plentiful there. She reports she looked down and noticed the front of the "light colored" dress she was wearing looked as if it were embroidered in red. "I was paralyzed, but Mr. Lambert [who had accompanied them to this site] grabbed a piece of brush and brushed them off in a jiffy." Miss Adina took no notice of the threat of such insects though and she plunged ahead with complete disregard for the "red-bugs" or any other critters, large or small. The "red-bugs" must have feasted on her, though, because Miss Donecker recorded, "poor Miss D. suffered the tortures of the damned for several days."[37]

Miss De Zavala's trips outside of San Antonio seem to have been confined primarily to the State of Texas in her search for those specific historic sites she knew of in the state. She never was privileged to travel to see the wonders and antiquities of the world around the globe it seems. She did, however, make at least one trip to Mexico City to research further the records there for some of her

projects. She said she was honored with a "private view" of the
Museo on a day it was closed to the public, and,

> . . . They even let down the white-satin-lined steps of
> Maximilian's coach and invited me to sit in it. They
> showed me so many fine courtesies all during my visit
> there.[38]

Other than her undying efforts toward forever trying to save
the "long barracks" as a shrine and museum, and the restoration of
the other local missions, the most significant contribution Miss De
Zavala made toward the preservation of an historic structure in her
home city of San Antonio, was probably the saving of a building
known as the "Spanish Governor's Palace."

This building is located in the center of downtown San
Antonio, where Spain established a military presidio in 1718.
Originally the building at the site was the residence of the presidio
Captain who was the ranking representative of the King of Spain.
When the presidio was deactivated, the substantial building there
was enlarged and enhanced and became the home of the ranking
civilian members of the community. At one time that person also
served as the governor of the area named by the royal ruler, and the
building became known as the "Governor's Palace".

Over the entrance of the doorway of this particular building
can be seen the original keystone on which is carved the coat of
arms of the Royal Hapsburg Family of Austria, who ruled Spain
and her possessions at the time. Below it is the inscription "Se
acabo 1749", which translated means "finished in 1749". It is said
to be the oldest Spanish residence in Texas, and possibly the U.S.,
which is still standing.

In 1915, when Miss De Zavala first became interested in
preserving and restoring it, it too had deteriorated into a true "eyesore" and had been misused for many purposes. Long gone were its
days as a "palatial" residence of an early Spanish governor of the

province. The noise that surrounded the building, the markets on the street, the "chili queens" and their open air food service, etc., had caused the last occupants, the Perez family, to move away. The historic home stood unused for a time and went into decline. The owners divided it into compartmented sections and rented each section to a variety of business establishments, such as a used clothing store, and antique (junk?) store, and even a bar and cafe at one time known as the "Hole in the Wall." The building had been well built initially with three foot thick walls of stuccoed rubble and stone masonry, and with this sturdy construction, the exterior had never deteriorated measurably nor collapsed, but much of it had been altered almost beyond recognition.

Fascinated by that keystone over the entrance door, Miss Adina sought out past owners to find what they might know of the history of the building. Their knowledge was limited to personal family history mostly of a later time, but her search continued with the study of old maps and documents. This led her to find, amidst other interesting facts, an account of a well known American explorer who had stopped there. Lt. Zebulon Pike, who later became famous for the discovery of Pike's Peak, on his journey to explore uncharted western areas of the North American continent, stopped in San Antonio as he was being escorted through Spanish territory. He recorded in his diary finding three provincial governors at the "Old Spanish Governor's Palace." One was the reigning governor of this province, Governor Cordero, and the others were two visiting governors, Salcedo and Herrera. He describes the color of their hair and eyes and tells how tall they were; describes the various people he met there and says that the grace, refinement, culture and elegance surprised him—that it was like a bit of court life transported from Europe and set down in the wilds of Texas; that Governor Cordero was very formal during business hours, but that "in the evening he was most democratic and danced with the populace in the Plaza."[39]

Miss De Zavala and two of her friends, Nellie Lytle (center) and Frances Donecker (right), in a 1926 photograph stand in front of the former Governor's Palace which serves here as a used clothing store.
(The Institute of Texas Culture, San Antonio Light, San Antonio, Texas)

Once Miss Adina found all of this history of such a place in San Antonio, and she saw that keystone which was still clearly visible, she knew beyond doubt this was the original "old Spanish Governor's Palace." It was a treasure of the past that she felt should be preserved and restored for future generations to see, and she embarked on a campaign to save it.

She first obtained and held an option from the current owner, and then turned her efforts toward raising the funds to purchase it. She appealed through the historical preservation groups she had formed. She appealed to the city, the state, and various other local civic groups. She and her supporters even resorted to "tag" sales, appealing to passersby on the street for "10¢, or whatever you wish to give."[40]

All these efforts led to very negligible results. However,

after months of "begging" for the building, the cause gained the
support of some of the women's civic groups, one of which was the
newly formed San Antonio Conservation Society, the primary historic preservation group of San Antonio today.

One of the women of that group, who later became presi-
dent of it, was the daughter of one of those ladies referred to in
Chapter Six who had taken food to Miss Adina during her "barri-
cade" at the Alamo. This was Mrs. Elizabeth Graham and she knew
Miss Adina well from her mother's association with her. Mrs.
Graham became the second curator of the Governor's Palace after
it was restored and opened to the public. She had this to say about
Miss Adina's part in saving the building:

> Two old San Antonio school teachers, "old maids" they
> might be called, specialists in San Antonio and Texas histo-
> ry, one a past-president of the Conservation Society, the
> other, . . . the organizer of the first San Antonio Chapter of
> the Daughters of the Republic of Texas Society, were my
> friends and history conservation counselors, Anna Ellis and
> Adena de Zavala [sic], respectively.
>
> They knew from their history studies that San Antonio,
> as no other city of Texas, could preserve, besides the world
> famed Alamo, six original buildings practically in the cen-
> ter of the city, buildings on their original settings, that
> would symbolize the history under the six national govern-
> ments whose flags had flown over Texas. . . .
>
> Their idea was to start with the restoration of the build-
> ing representing the first flag, the old Spanish flag. The
> choice of the still standing old building and long ago home
> of Spanish governors of Texas located on Plaza de las
> Armas (Military Plaza) in the actual center of our city was
> a foregone conclusion.
>
> Miss Adena de Zavala haunted the city council cham-
> bers with a constant plea that the old Spanish building be
> bought by the city and restored to a museum picture of early
> Spanish life. Miss Anna Ellis kept her plea before the ladies
> of the Conservation Society.
>
> Miss de Zavala was ignored by the city council until

those who manipulated city politics wanted a bond issue put before the citizens of San Antonio and were doubtful of its passage. Then one crafty old politician advised "Put into the bond issue something the ladies want and which they will work for, then we may expect to pass this bond issue."

I was told this, as a truth, by Ernest Altgelt, Sr., now deceased, who was present at that "behind the scenes" city officials meeting. The politicians considered it a great joke, but the bond issue did pass and the Spanish Governor's Palace was restored and rededicated with much ceremony.[41]

The building was reopened in 1931. It had been restored and re-furnished with great authenticity as a result of the careful research and skill of the restoration architect, and the many who had supported the project. There can be no doubt that Adina De Zavala was the initiator of the effort, though, and it was due to her perseverance that it ever came about, but this was not accomplished without another minor "battle" for her.

The Conservation Society had gotten on the band wagon in earnest once the bond issue was introduced for they had another project they wanted included in the bond vote. Their board had pushed to the forefront in the struggle, crowding Miss De Zavala to the side, if not out of the picture entirely. Shades of the "long barracks" all over again! She had promptly let them know in no uncertain terms "that that was her field . . . there was just room for nobody else," and she told them ". . . to clear out," according to Miss Emily Edwards, president of the Conservation Society at the time who reported this to the Society's board. Another board member, Mrs. Perry Lewis, stated she knew Miss Adina well and would take care of things. She did and reported back that she had called on Miss Adina and as Mrs. Lewis described it, "There were many tears but we will be permitted to exist."[42]

Not only did they "exist," but they did so to the exclusion of Miss De Zavala's role in the saving of this building, too. Mrs. Elizabeth Graham, however, in a statement made to Dr. Robert

Ables later, "without hesitation and unequivocally, gave Miss Adina credit for saving the palace: "The Conservation Society helped, but actually we didn't do so much compared to Miss De Zavala. She saved it [the palace], although we often get the credit."[43]

Miss De Zavala had pictured the building as originally having a second story, or at least a part of it as being two-storied. Others disagreed. At the time of the argument, a will written in 1804 was found in the court house records, which described the house as a one story dwelling,[44] and the building was restored with one floor.

The restoration architect, Harvey P. Smith, was convinced after extensive research the building had only one story, but looking at it from another point of view, it seems possible that there just might have been a second floor over at least a part of the building at one time, if for no other reason than to offer an explanation for the existence of a graceful semicircular, free-standing stairway that leads up to nothing more than a small room called a "pantry loft." It is unusual, to say the least, to have a pretty curving staircase, in a central passageway of the building, clearly visible from the front entrance-way, that leads merely to a food storage loft.

Miss De Zavala had believed so, in any case, for she was convinced there had been a second floor on at least a part of the building. She had hoped to restore this building to a replica of the grandeur of its early days, and possibly to use a part of the historic site as a museum of history, some of which would be used to honor the heroes of the Alamo and others, and some as a repository for a part of her collection of artifacts. She had hoped to use a part of the "long barracks" for this purpose, but she had lost her battle at the Alamo, and, alas, she lost this one, too, and her hopes for a museum site were thwarted once again and there is no second floor there. Of course, just how all of the rest of this was to have been financed, once she had persuaded the city to purchase the building in the first place, was one of those details that this lady of great dreams had not yet worked out, just as in the previous dream. But her hopes were always high.

ADINA DE ZAVALA AND HER DOG "BEBE."
(Adina De Zavala Papers, CN10286, Center for American
History, University of Texas at Austin.)

It had taken almost fourteen years of unrelenting effort for this goal of the restoration of the Governor's Palace begun by Miss De Zavala to be brought to a successful end. Once again her part in its success is little known or recognized. Perseverance was indeed one of her strongest characteristics, though, even if it required making a nuisance of herself, something she was not reluctant to do or freely admit she did and would do again, and even encourage her colleagues to do, if it was necessary to achieve the goal.

In addition to working for these various causes, she spent a

ADINA DE ZAVALA AT THE SPANISH GOVERNOR'S
PALACE, SAN ANTONIO.
(Adina De Zavala Papers, CN10286, Center for American
History, University of Texas at Austin.)

great deal of time writing, based on her voluminous research, but
the sum total of all her written material will probably never really
be known. She wrote many magazine articles, newspaper articles,
and pamphlets, as well as several books with her prolific pen.
Among the best known books that were published are three on her
favorite topic, the Alamo: *Story of the Siege and Fall of the Alamo,*
privately published in 1911; *History and Legends of the Alamo and
Other Missions in and Around San Antonio,* privately published in
1917; and *The Alamo, Where the Last Man Died,* published by the
Naylor Company in 1956, one year after her death.

The reprint of this last book, *The Alamo, Where the Last Man*

Died, was financed by final funds from the account of the Texas Historical and Landmarks Association which was disbanded soon after her death. In the foreword written by a member, Colonel Harry M. Henderson, he paid a tribute to Miss Adina's dedicated spirit.

> Miss De Zavala was a remarkable woman; her frail body had the strength of a giant. Once having a selected objective, she remained on the trail until it could be marked accomplished.[45]

Another of those three books, *History and Legends of the Alamo and Other Missions in and Around San Antonio,* which had been published originally by her in 1917, was reprinted in 1996, by Arte Público Press, University of Houston, Houston, Texas. It is edited by Richard Flores, with an introduction by him which reviews her life story briefly, but its greater purpose seems to be an overdone and confusing analysis of the psyche of Miss De Zavala. The introduction uses the name of Adina De Zavala for a fifty-two page discourse on what Mr. Flores feels is the injustice of discrimination against Mexicans of Texas, something that had very little to do with Miss De Zavala actually and even less to do with the legends and myths or other subjects she wrote about in her book about the Alamo. Flores' point is summed up in the final sentence of his over-long introduction quoted below, with which, incidentally, it is doubtful Miss De Zavala would agree. In fact, it would probably set her off again on another battle.

> . . . . With a fuller discussion of De Zavala's historical and folkloric work still needed, I want at this point, to allow her embedded critical discourse to remind us that keeping Mexicans in line has been a central plot of the Alamo all along.[46]

This claim by Mr. Flores that the Alamo has been a central plot as a reminder to "keeping Mexicans in line," came as a surprise to me, and actually, sounds somewhat ridiculous. After all, Mexico won that battle, and with a resounding Victory, with a capital "V". As for Miss De Zavala having this attitude, why would this highly intelligent and respected woman risk her public image and reputation, and even her personal safety, to save a building that was a reminder for such a purpose? And then, moreover, spend the rest of her life trying to get it restored? Clearly Richard Flores has misjudged her and her motives completely. Admittedly she was impulsive to a fault when something she valued was at risk, but she was passionately protective of the Alamo and all it symbolized - the supreme sacrifice made for liberty by the men who died there for it.

One more point about the book. The comments on the cover, which may or may not be his, describe this little book as focusing on Miss De Zavala's role as a "Texas Mexican" woman at a time when "Texas Mexican women had little influence".[47]

The fact is, as proud as she was of her Spanish-Mexican heritage with no reluctance to extol the achievements of her distinguished Mexican-born grandfather, she abhorred the term "Mexican-American", or "Texas Mexican", as the book cover refers to it today. Around the time the term "Mexican-American" first came into common usage, she wrote a letter in 1949, which Flores quotes in its entirety, wherein she deplores the use of such a term, which in fact had not been in common use during Miss De Zavala's earlier more active years. She stated in another letter on the subject at about the same time that she considered herself "an American of Mexican descent," but not a "Mexican-American." These two letters which are the only reference she made on this point, were the only such references found in the Adina De Zavala papers. Moreover, no indication was found in her extensive collection of papers wherein she alluded to her Mexican heritage as ever having been a deterrent in any way in her efforts to achieve the goals she set for herself.

Lewis Fisher, in a book entitled *Saving San Antonio* makes

this point in a footnote:

> As Holly Beachley Brear reports in *Inherit the Alamo, Myth and Ritual at an American Shrine*, (Austin: University of Texas Press, 1995), 93-94, some latter-day observers suggest that ethnic discrimination because of her Hispanic background caused Adina De Zavala the difficulties she faced in her struggles through the years. But there is no indication that such an idea ever occurred to anyone else at the time nor that it even occurred to Adina De Zavala, who openly spoke with pride of her distinguished Hispanic heritage, although three of her four grandparents were Anglo-Americans. She was accepted early on by founders of the Daughters of the Republic of Texas—some of the leading ladies in the state—and was elected to the DRT's state executive committee in 1902 and later to the executive council of the Texas State Historical Association and to membership in other leading statewide organizations.
>
> Miss De Zavala's difficulties appear to have been, instead, largely self-inflicted— "her forthrightness, her tendency toward stubbornness which bordered upon intractableness if she thought she was right, a quick tongue . . ."[48]

Dr. Ables sums it up simply by saying "Miss De Zavala was her own enemy."

Richard Flores may have been saying Adina De Zavala was not typical of the 'Texas Mexican woman' in the comments on the book cover and in his introduction of this reissue of Miss De Zavala's book.

She was held in very high regard by a great many people of all ethnic groups and the 'influence she held' was far reaching indeed. Certainly many state officials held her in the highest esteem if the Resolution they signed upon her death in 1955 is any indication. It is most unusual for this kind of a Resolution to be made for an individual. Miss De Zavala was made an honorary member of the Texas State Historical Commission ten years before her death, and she received other well deserved honors over the years. All this speaks very well for the influence this Texas American woman of Mexican descent had in her lifetime and afterward.

In one way, however, Mr. Flores does a service perhaps. This reprint did bring back into circulation some of the interesting myths and legends about the Alamo that Miss De Zavala unearthed, which had been out of print so long.

Another book relating to Miss De Zavala appeared in 1999. It is titled *Alamo Heights,* written by first time novelist, Scott Zesch. The author claimed to have been inspired by an exhibit he saw at the Witte Museum in San Antonio in 1986 (the same exhibit that got this writer started on all this), which included a very brief item describing Adina De Zavala's barricade of herself "in the Alamo".

The book was received well enough as an entertaining piece of fiction, but what it actually does is present a false picture of the culture and some of the history of old San Antonio. Even worse it further perpetuates the myth that the DRT saved the old long barracks. The story so distorts the historical truth it is almost laughable. Its continuation of the idea the DRT nobly held off commercial development of the building to save it is preposterous. The fact is the DRT under the leadership of the Driscoll faction would have had the old convento/long barracks destroyed to the ground if they could have, and a park built on the site.

In his fanciful story surrounding the "Second Battle of the Alamo" and its principal opponents, or proponents as he made them, the author uses characters by other names to represent Adina De Zavala and Clara Driscoll. Neither character bears any resemblance to the real-life people, either in personality or motives.

As a novel the book could be called entertaining reading for some, but as a reflection of historical facts it fails altogether.

Adina De Zavala had been collecting data for years on Texas history to use in writing the many things planned in her mind which never got into print as well as those that did. Her collection

140

of materials was monumental, but she never stopped long enough to organize the collection. Before her death, the large accumulation of papers, documents and relics saved over her lifetime were offered to the University of Texas in her letter to Dr. Carlos E. Castañeda, a professor in the Department of History at the University of Texas at Austin. His reply dated March 21, 1951, accepts her offer "with honor and pleasure".[49] These papers are now in the Archives of the Center for American History, University of Texas, and are available to the public for research.

As extensive as this collection is, not everything she collected found its way to the archives. In one of the boxes of her papers, there is a handwritten note expressing considerable annoyance over her sister Mary's disposal of some of her papers:

> Mary emptied out 57 boxes, by her own count, of my material! No idea it was so much. Though I know she denuded me shamelessly.[50]

Mary's attitude about Miss Adina's material was shared by some other people as well, and one in particular, but she was not free to do what Mary had done. Although the collection was appreciated as a source of some otherwise possibly unrecoverable information, it would not be a simple and uncomplicated acquisition. The archivist at the University of Texas at Austin at that time, Winnie Allen, received a letter from the secretary who had been sent to San Antonio by the University to help Miss Adina sort and catalog her material before transferring it to their archives. The secretary, Bess Fitzhugh, despaired over the condition of the task with which she was faced, and her letter describes the maze she was trying to wade through. In her own words, "you never saw so much 'junk—some good—some not so good'."[51] No doubt she must have wished she could 'empty out some boxes,' too.

Each summer, and at times during the academic year, from 1952 to the month of January 1955, two months before Miss De

Zavala died on March 1st, Miss Fitzhugh came to San Antonio and worked with Miss Adina in an attempt to master the situation. In spite of what must have been supreme efforts by Miss Fitzhugh, and even with some successful results, the papers found at the Center for American History were still an incredible maze for the writer of this book. One thing is clear though, even after the cataloging that Bess Fitzhugh was able to accomplish, and others since, the unmistakable stamp and spirit of the collector of it all is still evident. There are massive amounts of seemingly unrelated material, some in seemingly massive confusion, that would surely defy the best of archival catalogers.

All of these papers had been the result of years of memories of Adina De Zavala from the time of her birth near Galveston and her life and schooling in that city, followed by the years of collecting data and searching out the history of Texas during her later life in San Antonio and travels around the state. When advised to seek a dryer climate for his health, Augustine De Zavala had moved his family to San Antonio and established them on their ranch about twelve miles north of the center of town where they lived until his death. Following his death in 1893, Mrs. De Zavala, and her two children still at home, Adina and Mary, had moved in to their house in town at 141 Taylor Street.

The years that followed were among the most active years of Miss Adina's life, the years of her teaching career in the San Antonio schools, followed by all of those turbulent times connected with the Alamo event and all that had come after it.

In 1918, Miss Adina's mother died leaving Adina and her sister, Mary, to live on in the family home. After all those many very active years in her pursuit and preservation of Texas history, Miss Adina suffered a rather disabling fall in 1944 at age 83. She managed to recover to a limited degree and she held out for another ten years but she was slowed down considerably, her strength beginning to fail noticeably in the last few years of her life.

The death of her sister, Mary, in 1950, left Miss Adina as the last surviving member of her family, but she lived on in her home alone for most of the remainder of her days. She usually had the help of a servant who came in to take care of household tasks, and she had a very loyal and understanding secretary, Miss Pauline Williams, to help her continue to attempt to write. Miss Williams even moved in to live at the house with her for a period of time. Both of these helpers were of great assistance, but this tenacious woman was finally brought to being very limited in what she could

THE DE ZAVALA HOME AT 141 TAYLOR STREET IN SAN ANTONIO.
(Adina De Zavala Papers, CN10282, Center for American History,
University of Texas at Austin.)

do. Nevertheless, she still continued determinedly to live on alone, managing to care for herself except for faithful helpers who came in from time to time, until near the end of her life.

Much of this story of Adina De Zavala's life would have been impossible without the accounts written about her by Dr. L. Robert Ables from which so much of the foregoing has been taken with his kind permission. The closing remarks from his masters degree thesis, written in 1955 soon after her death, are quoted here as an unsurpassable description of the final years and days and the death of this remarkable woman.

ADINA DE ZAVALA AT HOME, 141 TAYLOR STREET.
(Institute of Texan Cultures, San Antonio Light Collection.)

LATER LIFE AND DEATH

Advancing age slowed the pace and mellowed the temper of the steel fibre within the patriarch of San Antonio historians during the last fifteen years of her life. Actually, Miss Adina's health began to fail about 1936 when a serious stomach disorder caused her to remain on a liquid diet. She was admitted to the hospital twice in 1944, once as the result of a fall that fractured her hip. Although such mishaps handicapped Miss Adina, merely being hospitalized did not stop her work. Miss Donecker visited Miss Adina during another confinement in the hospital and found the bed and a table strewn with Texana material and a small Texas flag mounted in the room.

During the 1940s Miss Adina's activities had slackened noticeably, and by the 1950s she had ceased much active participation in the continuing work of preserving and marking historic sites of the Texas Historical and Landmarks Association..

Plagued by cataracts on both eyes, she was partially blind during her last years. Miss Pauline Williams, her secretary for two years, said:

"Four years ago when I began with her she could see outlines of objects, but after about two years more she could only distinguish daylight from dark.

Sometimes when she signed something, she would ask, 'What color is this pen?' I would answer, 'Red.' (I had a red pen she often used when she signed papers or letters.) She sometimes replied, 'Well, I can't tell what color it is.'"

By the 1950's Miss Adina used either a wheelchair or she laboriously found her way about the house by utilizing furniture as support. Although usually someone was employed to help her, she often cooked with the gas stove without aid and handled her own money. She could recognize coins by touch and used only one and five dollar bills after devising a different method of folding each to distinguish them.

Her reticence to reveal her age remained until she lay on her deathbed. Miss Williams related that Dr. Wolf, her physician, once inquired if he could ask her age. Her face lighting up in humor, Miss Adina answered, "You may, but you won't get a reply."

Regardless of her physical inactivity, she remained intensely interested in the Texas Historical and Landmarks Association and followed other events in San Antonio and the state. She continued to write a little and encouraged others to do the same. The year before she died, the historical association had a proposal before it to change its constitution. Miss Adina wrote a letter to the group stating her views and opposing the change. In late 1953 a proposal was before the city council to make an underground parking space of Travis Park in downtown San Antonio. Miss Adina and the Texas Historical and Landmarks Association, the Conservation Society, and others took immediate steps to block what they considered a move to desecrate another historical landmark. Although the fierce flame of her youth had just about flickered out, Miss Adina demonstrated that sparks still could fly:

This beautiful park is the only one of its kind in San Antonio or any other city . . .

Perhaps the members of the city council do not know that this park is a unique monument to Travis.

She enthusiastically talked Texas history with her visitors and showed a deep personal satisfaction for various congratulatory messages received from time to time. But the end was near. Early in February, 1955, she re-injured her hip in another fall and was taken to the hospital. Three weeks later she lapsed into a coma and died at 6:18 P.M. on March 1, a few hours before the dawn of the anniversary of her beloved Texas' independence.

The funeral was held March 5 and . . . Her casket was draped with the Texas Flag . . . On its way to St. Mary's Cemetery, where Miss De Zavala was laid to rest in the family burial plot, the funeral procession passed by the historic Alamo in final tribute to Miss De Zavala who had so valiantly defended the Shrine of Texas Liberty, . . .[52]

The De Zavala family had never been what might be considered wealthy, although, as the last surviving member of her family, Miss Adina was "financially secure" with her remaining family funds and properties. For some time during those later years of her life, she had had a special interest in the nearby Incarnate Word College, today The University of the Incarnate Word. As a faithful and devout Catholic she was a great admirer of the sisters and their dedication to the teaching and nursing professions and their various charitable and educational projects. She made a rather sizable donation to the College during the latter part of her lifetime, and had specified in her will which was witnessed and signed on February 12, 1953, two years before her death, that all she owned was to go to the Sisters of Charity of the Incarnate Word upon her death.[53] In gratitude for her generosity, the sisters had taken a special protective and compassionate interest in her well being during her last years, knowing she lived alone and was in frail health. A group of nuns went regularly to check on her during that precarious period of her life.

Sister Margaret Patrice Slattery, formerly President, now Chancellor of the University of the Incarnate Word, was a very young nun at the time, but she recalls how the group was sent years ago to help care for Miss Adina, first in her home, and later how she was moved to the College campus and cared for there. From Sister Margaret we get another look at the final days of Miss Adina; how she spent the last weeks in the College Infirmary and had to be transferred to Santa Rosa Hospital after suffering another fall. At the hospital she slipped into the coma from which she never regained consciousness and soon afterwards died a peaceful death.[54]

Sister Margaret wrote a book on the history of Incarnate Word College entitled, *Promises to Keep*. In it we find in an endnote some of her memories of Miss Adina.

Many interesting stories about Miss Adina have been

147

preserved in the oral tradition of the College. When she became ill and was confined to bed in her later years, the sisters regularly went to care for her, taking the bus from the College to her home in the downtown area of San Antonio. The entire neighborhood, with the exception of Miss Adina's old homestead, was filled with parking lots and run-down business operations. The house itself was filled with empty boxes, paper bags, balls of string, etc. Miss Adina had evidently saved everything that she ever purchased, including the wrapping.

When her physical condition became critical, Mother Columkille convinced her to move to the student infirmary at the College. She insisted on bringing with her a very old cardboard carton [Sister Margaret corrected this in a personal interview later as actually "a trunk."][55] that was secured with heavy rope and covered with a blanket. No one ever saw the inside of the box [trunk] until Miss Adina died. When it was finally opened, the sisters found it full of cash, bills of all denominations, and even some confederate money that had been stored away for many years.[56]

This last recollection regarding "confederate money" is an amusing little side-light, but it should be remembered that Miss Adina was born just about the time the Civil War began, and she was only four years old when it ended. There is no explanation as to how she came to have some confederate money, but it is not likely she was one of those misguided folks who talked of the "South rising again." She was really too young to have developed such notions for one thing, and for another she had not grown up in a household with such a strong background in southern cultural tradition. The fact is, however, her father's boat had served as a blockade runner in Galveston Bay during the Civil War,[57] and perhaps the money was a treasured memento that had belonged to him. Who knows?

When her estate was settled upon her death, papers that had not been given to the University of Texas Archives in Austin earlier, were transferred to the Archives of Incarnate Word in San Antonio, along with some personal possessions, as she requested.

She was always described as a 'small woman of slight stature,' but her frail appearance in later years was a very misleading indicator of her inner strength. She seemed to have grown stronger with age. Through the years, the more demanding the challenge, the greater her strength. She was the oldest of her five siblings and yet she outlived them all, in spite of the dedicated, unending goals she set for herself, many of which required a great deal of physical effort as well as mental stress. Her light had burned bright and full for many years, but it had finally gone out on that final day, March 1, 1955.

Her accomplishments over a lifetime were numerous and impressive, but as some wise wit once advised, 'don't ever do anything you don't want to be the first line in your obituary.' Without intent Miss De Zavala seems to have done just that. Even though her accomplishments were numerous and impressive, that "barricade" will always be the thing for which she is most remembered. Sadly, despite its significance, there is also a greater irony to it. In the first place, very few could tell you just exactly what the legacy of that "barricade" was, even though it was a real contribution for which no one else should rightly claim the credit. The further irony is, by a twist of misinterpretations, Clara Driscoll has been given all the credit for years for "saving" the Alamo Chapel, not the long barracks. It is only recently that the misinformation is slowly being corrected. Further still, the "long barracks" actually was made famous by that "barricade" of Adina's, and it was the building Miss Driscoll would have demolished to the ground if she had had her way. (Possibly the only time she did not have her way in her entire lifetime, as some writer once observed.) The whole episode is filled with the kinds of misinformation that almost defy description.

And what ever happened to that old building called the "long barracks," after the "second battle" finally ended, and the restoration project had been abandoned?

There was talk occasionally, mostly as a result of prodding

by Miss De Zavala, about restoration, but nothing ever came of it. The remnants of the building that were left remained a roofless shell in a state of ruin and neglect, open to the elements for more than fifty years, but it was covered with those "graceful trailing vines." Nothing was ever done successfully toward the restoration of it until 1968, when an event called "HemisFair," an international type of world's fair, took place in San Antonio. As a feature for the fair the "long barracks" building was finally roofed, floored and finished off to make it into the single story museum building it is today. By then, Miss De Zavala had been dead twelve years. One half of her greatest dream, so to speak, was realized at last, but she didn't live to see it.

Until very recently there was no mention made anywhere around or in the building telling of her part in saving that part which is still there. The plaque put on the building by Miss De Zavala had been covered up and a bronze plaque was placed on one of the walls of the unfinished ruin on March 2, 1927, giving Clara Driscoll the credit for doing it all. It is still in place beside the entrance with no updating marker ever put up to include Miss De Zavala.

The DRT has made many commendable contributions toward the protection and preservation of Texas history, but their lack of acknowledgment of the error they made regarding the site of the battle remained a blemish on their record for many years. It was not until 1942, fifty years after their founding, that they made a public statement in writing correcting that error when they wrote a new version of their story on the history of the Alamo in their *Fifty Years of Achievement* publication. But their firm claim that Clara Driscoll alone had "saved the Alamo" was still made in the book and their position on that continued for many more years. A pamphlet they printed and published almost fifty years later in 1991 entitled "Clara Driscoll Rescued the Alamo," told the story again of how Miss Driscoll "was the savior of the Alamo" with still no mention of Adina De Zavala. The pamphlet did state that the "long barracks" was the major site of the final assault in the 1836 battle but it did not make any reference to Miss De Zavala's part in helping save that site.[58]

The DRT was not the only historically oriented Texas group which continually failed to recognize Miss De Zavala, however. In 1990, The Texas Historical Commission, an official state agency, printed in the March issue of their quarterly publication *The Medallion* an article entitled "Who really "saved" the Alamo?" After carefully reading the article, with the full expectation of seeing something at long last about Adina De Zavala, not a word could be found. The story was all about how a 'number of people' assisted in this patriotic effort, but that Miss Clara Driscoll was the one "who really saved the Alamo for all Texas and visitors from around the world." [59]

There may have been some protests, however, because in their 1991 March issue of *The Medallion* one year later, there was almost a full page story entitled "Adina De Zavala, Preservationist Extraordinaire," which described Miss De Zavala's part in the Alamo controversy and her tireless dedication in resisting the destruction of the "long barracks" building.[60] Reference is made in the article to her many other contributions toward the preservation of Texas historical landmarks, customs and heritage in general. It seems odd for this organization, the Texas Historical Commission (THC), to be so late in acknowledging all this about Miss De Zavala, though. She was a charter member of a much older statewide historical organization of similar general purpose called the Texas State Historical Association (TSHA), and had, in fact, been named an honorary fellow of that group in 1945, ten years before her death. Forty-six years after Miss De Zavala's death the THC recognized her as "a preservationist who understood the broad context of history."

The DRT position regarding Miss De Zavala finally seemed to change, too. In 1994, at long last, twenty-seven years after the "long barracks" was restored as it now stands, and eighty-six years after the "barricade" incident itself took place, an acknowledgment of Adina De Zavala's contribution was made by the DRT. Today, in the one-story museum building made of what is left of the very building where she barricaded herself, the old "long barracks," no doubt in one of the very rooms where many of the heroes died— there is a picture of Miss De Zavala and an account of her part in the "saving of the Alamo," including the story of her "barricade." The exhibit was put there by the Daughters in recognition at last of this dedicated, but overlooked and mistreated member, whom they put out of their organization. It should be a long overdue closure to the unfortunate past events.

One year later the DRT, as the only group authorized under the initial agreement by the State Legislature to make such additions as this and the placing of markers of any kind on the Alamo property, also put a small, unique porcelain marker in the courtyard near the entrance to the long barracks museum which reads:

Adina Emelia [sic]   Clara

De Zavala   Driscoll

1861-1955   1881-1945

Two loyal members of the

Daughters of the Republic of Texas,

each in her own way responsible

for preserving this historic site.

Another recognition of Miss De Zavala was made by the DRT when they placed a series of panels called "The Wall of History" in the courtyard near the Alamo Chapel and the Alamo Museum Gift Shop in 1997. It depicts the chronological history of the Alamo, beginning with the founding of the mission on this site during the Spanish mission period, the site during the battle of 1836, and the subsequent history of the area to the time of the installation of the "Wall of History". Adina De Zavala's picture and her part in the history of the Alamo are included on the wall at the appropriate place in the chronology.

Some may dismiss much of this account of the life of Adina De Zavala as just a story of a woman considered by some as a "zealot." Some will still insist that Clara Driscoll was the one who "really saved the Alamo." But it is sincerely hoped that they along with others will read this story of "Miss Adina," and perhaps begin to see both sides of that disagreement which never seems to die.

Until I investigated the whole story, I may have said the same thing as those who support Clara Driscoll. After all, that's what I had always been led to believe, and in fact, what I was taught as a school child in the state of Texas—that Clara Driscoll "saved the Alamo," and paid for it with her own money. I was never taught that she was reimbursed and that it was the "long barracks" that was in danger.

When you see both sides, there is abundant evidence to show that both women indeed did save the Alamo, "each in her own way." However, there is also enough evidence, some of it in her own words, to make me question whether Clara Driscoll actually would have "saved" anything at the time except a plot of land for a park next to the Alamo Chapel, had she been left to her own wishes. Certainly not the "long barracks" building itself, for she repeatedly tried to have it completely destroyed. Later she was to make more than one generous monetary contribution, without reimbursement, to the DRT for other projects. But the fact remains, the money she advanced toward the so called "saving of the Alamo" was actually for the "long barracks," and the money was reimbursed to her, minus a relatively small contribution toward the purchase from her own private funds.

Adina De Zavala was not just a determined woman with a mind of her own whose only legacy to the state of Texas was that one dramatic act of highly publicized courage, as significant as that act was. In fact, her many contributions over an entire lifetime are a reflection of much of the preservation of the history of the state and the city she called home, San Antonio.

An article I once read related an experience the writer of the article had which caused her to come to the conclusion that she now understands who heroes really are. She says: " . . . [they are] people who face adversity and commit themselves completely to overcoming the most staggering of odds. . . . Heroes may not always triumph, but true heroism is in their spirit and will to succeed."

Adina De Zavala, a passionate patriot, was also a true "Savior of the Alamo" in my mind, and a hero in the truest sense of the word, 'whose spirit and will to succeed overcame all kinds of staggering odds' even though she did not triumph in her battle at the time. Without question, Clara Driscoll's money was very necessary at a critical time in preserving the Alamo "long barracks" and the site where it stood, but had Adina De Zavala not barricaded herself inside that building later at the critical time she did, and had she not continued to fight for it for so long, there would be none of it left today. Was it worth all it had cost her? Her sister, Mary, once told her, "No relic in the world was worth the trouble this has caused." But Miss Adina did not agree.

This loyal and brave Texas woman was the final defender of the Alamo and the most enduring of them all.

Because of that, a part of the evidence of her dedication and the silent triumph of her famous act of courage is still there in Alamo Plaza, for "all Texans and visitors from around the world" to see. And echoes of her voice, along with those of the "heroes of the Alamo," can still be heard in the "long barracks" by those who listen.

~ ~ ~ ~ ~ ~ ~ ~ ~ ~

ADINA DE ZAVALA IN THE CHAPEL ROOM AT THE GOVERNOR'S PALACE.
(Adina De Zavala Papers, CN10285 Center for American History,
University of Texas at Austin.)

CLARA DRISCOLL
(Adina De Zavala Papers, CN10283, Center for American History,
University of Texas at Austin.)

Chapter Seven
Clara Driscoll

"I don't think the Alamo should
be disgraced by a whiskey house."

Clara Driscoll, known as the "Savior of the Alamo," made the above statement on December 28, 1911, in an open meeting in San Antonio,[1] the city where the honored symbol of Texas liberty is located. The meeting had been called by O. B. Colquitt, the current governor of the state, for the purpose of attempting to obtain the facts regarding the Hugo-Schmeltzer Building, a grocery and whiskey warehouse adjacent to the Alamo Chapel, and the storm that was now raging over what should be done with that building and the area surrounding it.

Clara Driscoll had joined the Daughters of the Republic of Texas (DRT) in 1903, eight years prior to this 1911 meeting. She had been active off and on during that time in the program they had sponsored to protect this site, which was a part of the original Alamo mission complex and the "Battle of the Alamo." At the beginning of the effort to save the building itself and the surrounding site, she felt so strongly about the matter that when the need arose to either purchase the property or lose it to further commercial development, she had purchased it with her own money on behalf of the DRT who did not have sufficient funds for such a purchase. She was reimbursed by the State of Texas which bought it from her as a state historic property in 1905 and was left afterward with the problem of how to settle the continuing disagreement over the way the site should be developed.

For some reason, Miss Driscoll had reversed her original position to save the Hugo-Schmeltzer Building itself and repair and restore it to become a museum. Instead, she was now the leading member of the group who took the position that the dilapidated "eyesore" was merely an ugly wooden building that had been erected years after the battle of the Alamo in 1836 had occurred, and that it had no historic significance whatsoever. Moreover, it obstructed the view of the hallowed Alamo Chapel which her group contended was where most of the men had died. They felt the unsightly structure should be completely demolished and replaced with a memorial park, honoring the heroes who died in the battle.

An opposing group, also in attendance at the meeting called by the governor, were former members of the DRT who had been removed from the rolls of the organization for their active part in trying to protect the building from total destruction. Led by Miss Adina De Zavala, they continued their efforts to protect the site, even though they were no longer members of the DRT. They believed the wooden exterior, now visible there, was merely a false exterior that had been built at a later time to cover the original two-story stone building which had begun to deteriorate. They further believed the original stone structure underneath still stood and that it was where the final assault occurred, not the Chapel. This group wanted to see the wooden superstructure removed in order to reveal the original stone building, which they proposed should be properly restored and made into a museum to honor the heroes of the entire Alamo compound and a proper park created around it.

The governor was attempting to learn what if any documented evidence there was to support either side of the argument. Since the building was now state property, his opinion would be a major factor in the final decision on the matter. A concise summary of this meeting was written by the editor of the *Dallas Morning News,* Tom Finty, Jr., for the general public to read at the time of the meeting. Later Governor Colquitt covered it thoroughly in his "Message to the Thirty-third Legislature Relating to the Alamo Property," parts of which are included at the end of Chapter Eight.

Miss Driscoll had become famous nationwide earlier for

putting up the money to save the Hugo-Schmeltzer Building. Now, however, she was saying it was "disgracing The Alamo," and she was identifying it as a "whiskey house" and campaigning to have it torn down. What had caused her about face?

Who was Clara Driscoll to make a public statement such as this? And how had a young, twenty-two-year-old woman come by such an amount of money of her own to do what she had done in the first place? Where had she come from, and what led her to do what has made her famous ever since as the "Savior of the Alamo"? Most of all, though, why had she reversed her position? This last question will in all probability never be answered, but there are answers on record for some other questions.

Clara Driscoll was born on April 2, 1881, to Robert and Julia Driscoll in a small South Texas port town called St. Mary's. The little community sat on a bluff overlooking Copano Bay on the Gulf of Mexico about 175 miles north of the Rio Grande River and just a few miles north of the large port city of Corpus Christi. St. Mary's was an active small port for several years but a series of disasters caused it to dwindle in size and importance over the years and eventually the town went out of existence officially and is no longer shown on the map.

The biography of Clara Driscoll by Martha Anne Turner relates that Miss Driscoll's paternal grandfather had arrived from Ireland around 1834 in a group recruited to colonize the Texas area during the time it was still a part of the Republic of Mexico. Daniel O'Driscoll was the name he was listed under originally, but the descendants dropped the O' as the prefix to the Irish surname, and they went by the name simply as Driscoll.[2]

Clara's paternal grandmother, Catherine Duggan, was also an immigrant from Ireland. Her first husband had come with the original group but died in a cholera epidemic soon after their arrival in New Orleans where they had first landed. Catherine Duggan had moved on to Texas with the group and later married Daniel

O'Driscoll. They had two sons, Jeremiah and Robert, and the latter became the father of Clara. Daniel O'Driscoll was killed in an accident in 1849 and his wife, Catherine, died three years later. The young boys, Jeremiah and Robert, were raised by their half-sister, the daughter of Catherine Duggan's first marriage, Lizzie Doughty (sometimes spelled Doty), and her husband.[3]

When Jeremiah and Robert reached maturity, they divided a tract of headright land inherited from their parents, and each took his share and embarked on his separate path in life. Those paths were quite different and Robert's took him on to a vast fortune in due time. He was an able businessman as well as a successful rancher, and he managed to parlay his original share into one of the large ranching and trail driven cattle operations, and later into oil holdings, in South Texas. He also went on to establish the largest banking institution in the area at the time, the Corpus Christi National Bank. His starting point had been relatively humble, but before it was all over he had accumulated a multi-million dollar empire.[4] Upon his death, this fortune would be passed on to his only surviving heirs, his two children, Robert, Jr. and Clara.

Clara Driscoll's mother, Julia Fox, was the daughter of James Fox, who was said also to have been in an early emigrant group, and he came from either Ireland or England. James Fox was trying to establish a new life in this new land, too. He had a small ranch in South Texas in Refugio County but he moved his family in to the little county seat called Refugio, where he opened a boardinghouse in an effort to establish a more secure life for them. Julia was described as "a pretty little blond girl" who "was considered something of a scholar." Her family was not able to provide a special schooling opportunity for her, but she was fortunate enough to have an affluent godmother, a Mrs. Norton, resident of their little town, who financed her education at a private Catholic convent, the Ursuline Academy in nearby San Antonio.[5]

Robert Driscoll and Julia Fox were married on December 7,

1870, while Robert was still a struggling young cattleman. Their first child was born one year later and they named him Robert, Jr. Their only other child, a girl they named Clara, was born ten years later on April 2, 1881. The brother and sister grew up as very compatible siblings and they were said to have been especially devoted to one another all their lives.

Because of his industriousness and good business sense, Robert Driscoll, Sr., had risen from those simple beginnings as a common ranch hand with moderate land holdings to become a highly successful rancher and businessman of enormous wealth in the truest of American traditions. Even though he was a self-made and self-educated man in the same pioneer American spirit, unlike some other occasional such successful pioneers, Driscoll had a firm respect and appreciation for the value and importance of a good formal education. It was probably more of what was described as his wife's "scholarly disposition" though that resulted in his children receiving their education primarily in select private schools,[6] especially in the case of their little daughter.

Robert, Jr. did attend the public schools in areas near his hometown, but upon graduation from high school he was sent to college at the Jesuit school of Georgetown University in Washington, D.C. He then attended Princeton University in New Jersey where he graduated with a law degree in 1893. Following his graduation he maintained a law office in New York City until 1903.[7]

While Robert was in college, Mrs. Driscoll took young Clara off to school in the east, also. She enrolled her in the "select private school, Miss Thompson and Peebles," in New York City, and in 1892, when Clara was only eleven years old, Mrs. Driscoll took her to Europe to complete her education. There she attended a private Catholic convent, Chateau Dieudonne, near Paris, where she "studied French and German along with her other studies."[8] The study of language, especially French, was considered one of the marks of a distinctive social education for a "refined" young lady of that day.

Presumably Mrs. Driscoll had remained with Clara, both in New York and in France, and upon her graduation from Chateau Dieudonne, Clara and her mother toured Europe and Asia. For a time they even lived on a houseboat on the Godavari River in Bombay, India. This adventure led to an acquaintance with an Indian woman who, Clara was to tell friends later, had a "great influence on her philosophy of life."[9]

When Clara and her mother were ready to return to Texas they were scheduled to leave Europe from England on their ocean voyage home. Soon after arriving at London from the continent, Mrs. Driscoll became ill and she died there quite unexpectedly on May 23, 1899.[10] Young Clara returned home alone, leaving her mother's body in London under apparently temporary interment arrangements since her remains were brought back to the U.S. for final burial later.

Both the Fox and Driscoll families were of long-standing Catholic heritage and the descendants had been raised 'in the faith' and all were said to be earnest Catholics.

Robert Driscoll, Sr. was also a Mason and soon after his wife's death he had ordered a mausoleum built at the Masonic Cemetery in San Antonio with four vaults in it, one for each of the four family members, father, mother, son and daughter. As life turned out, each of them was buried in their specified vault just as Mr. Driscoll had planned it. Thus, ultimately the family was reunited in death in this way.

Six months after her untimely demise and the completion of the mausoleum and other burial arrangements, Mrs. Driscoll's body was returned to the United States for final interment. As the first member of the family to die she was laid to rest in her vault in the mausoleum in San Antonio on December 2, 1899.

Under the heading of the MORTUARY section in a local San Antonio newspaper, the following account appeared the day after her body arrived:

The remains of the late Mrs. Julia Driscoll, wife of Mr. Robert Driscoll, arrived from London, England, yesterday evening over the Southern Pacific at 5:20 o'clock and were immediately conveyed to the Alamo Masonic Cemetery and there deposited in a vault recently prepared for their reception. The family of the deceased and a few friends were in attendance. There was no special ceremony, as religious services had previously been held in London.[11]

Clara Driscoll was eighteen years old when her mother died. The unexpected death of Mrs. Driscoll must have been a shock to all the family, but especially for Clara since they had been so close all her young life. She had in fact seldom ever been out of her mother's sight. Her trip home was most surely a sad one for her. Before reaching her destination at the family ranch, the "Palo Alto" near Corpus Christi, she had stopped briefly in San Antonio as was to become her custom after travelling abroad.

The travels with her mother had included visits to many of the historic treasures of Europe and the Orient, and those places had given young Clara a deepened appreciation of sites where events of great moment had occurred. They also reminded her of the fact that there were historic treasures in her own native state, not the least of which was the Alamo, a place she learned that was becoming internationally famous. She was appalled now when she returned home and saw the shabby condition of the historic shrine and the lack of respect shown for this Texas symbol of freedom and liberty.

Her concern about the status of the Alamo was so great that she wrote a letter to the *San Antonio Express* newspaper hoping to arouse the same concern in others. Her letter was published on January 14, 1901, but she was to be disappointed in the lack of response to her plea for 'every Texan to give his little mite' to see improvements made to the area. She described in noble terms her shock and disbelief about the condition of the building and the way it was treated. She wrote:

To live for any length of time in the Old World spoils one for things and places which savor of newness. They love to cling to the old traditions and romances. Their monuments, that speak to them of the valor of their forefathers, are held as things sacred, and each stone is guarded with the utmost vigilance. Every respect and deference is shown to any edifice that boasts of historic interest, by the way they preserve and care for it. Tourists are not allowed to lay a finger on one of the cherished stones, so carefully are these places guarded. We uncover our heads and speak in hushed voices in their pantheon's, where are buried their famous heroes. We tread with timid feet the battlefield of Waterloo, and yet, there is standing today, right in our very home, an old ruin, a silent monument of the dark and stormy days of Texas, when her sons were sacrificing their lives and shedding their blood for her Independence . . . It is our ALAMO . . . and how do we treat it?

How can we expect others to attach the importance to it that it so well deserves, when we Texans, who live within its shadow, are so careless of its existence? There does not stand in the world today a building or monument which can recall such a deed of heroism and bravery, such sacrifice and courage, as that of the brave men who fought and fell inside those historic old walls. Today the Alamo should stand out, free and clear. All the unsightly obstructions should be torn away. I am sure that if the matter were taken up by some patriotic Texan a sufficient amount could be raised that would enable something of the kind to be done. Yes, every Texan would give his little mite to see the Alamo placed amid surroundings where it would stand out for what it is . . . the Grandest Monument in the History of the World![12]

The trip with her mother was not the last of Clara Driscoll's travels abroad. She was described as "an inveterate traveler" in Martha Anne Turner's biography of this famous Texas woman. Turner states Miss Driscoll circled the globe three times, once by

164

the time she was eighteen on that first trip with her mother, and then she made at least fourteen more crossings to Europe in her life- time.[13] (And this was in an age before fast jet air travel.) That first trip obviously had awakened in her a desire to see more and more of this world.

She made another trip abroad in the early 1900's and this time she was accompanied by her close friend and contemporary from San Antonio, Miss Florence Eager.[14] The extensive trip of these two young women was perhaps the most colorful and excit- ing trip Clara ever experienced, for she still was of an age when her mind was filled with fabled tales of far-away places of fantasy and romance. These are mere "reliquary" reminders of a bygone era to those in the fast-paced, continuous travels of today's society, many of whom have literally been everywhere, and seen everything, more than once.

Clara's return to Texas after her first trip had awakened her to the plight of the Alamo, but the return after her trip with her friend, Florence Eager, made her even more acutely aware of the precarious and shameful condition of the hallowed shrine. The two had visited some of the sites Clara had explored on her earlier trip, and others she had not yet seen, including some of the treasures of many other famous historical and literary places which she had studied and read about that held such fascination for her.

After returning from abroad on this trip, she stopped in San Antonio as usual and stayed at the Menger Hotel which stood just at the south side of the Alamo. It is possible she could even look from her hotel window and see the historic Alamo Chapel sur- rounded as it was by commercial buildings, especially the run- down one known as the Hugo-Schmeltzer Building, which was lit- erally attached to it by a common connecting wall. The whole scene undoubtedly aroused her concern about the place all over again.

This time she did more than just write a letter to the news- paper. She apparently called on one of the owners of the building,

Mr. Gustav Schmeltzer, inquiring about the availability of the property for purchase. She wrote a letter later to the other owner, Mr. Charles Hugo in which she referred to her visit with Mr. Schmeltzer.

> Robert Driscoll
> Palo Alto Ranch
> Banquete, Texas
> Feb. 5th, 1903

Mr. Hugo:
Dear Sir:
    While in San Antonio a few days ago I saw Mr. Schmeltzer in regard to the property adjoining the Alamo. He said it was for sale. The Daughters of the Republic are anxious to procure it in order to make a park about the old ruins.
    They are about to present a bill to the Legislature asking for an appropriation to assist them in their plans. Would you kindly let me know the price of the property? Also if you would give the Daughters of the Republic the option on it, and if in payment of a certain sum by them, you would hold the property until they could pay full amount?
    I am sure you, as well as every Texan, would like to see the property used for this purpose in which the Daughters of the Republic wish to utilize it, and I feel convinced that you will work to the interest of the Daughters in this matter.
    It is important that I should hear from you at your earliest convenience.

> Sincerely yours,

Clara Driscoll
Chairman of Committee on Alamo
And Mission Improvements[15]

    Miss De Zavala, the leader of the group who opposed the destruction of the Hugo-Schmeltzer Building, always said that she had taken Miss Driscoll to meet Mr. Schmeltzer, and Schmeltzer himself stated that was how he met Miss Driscoll in his detailed

"Notarized Statement" included in Chapter Eight. Also, according to the thesis of Margaret E. Goodson, "Clara Driscoll, Philanthropist-Politician," Miss Driscoll was "accompanied by Miss Adina De Zavala" when she called on Mr. Schmeltzer concerning terms for the property.[16]

Regardless of how the young heiress and the property owner became acquainted, they did meet for the purpose of discussing financial arrangements for the purchase of that particular part of the Alamo battle site known as the Hugo-Schmeltzer property. Mr. Schmeltzer told Miss Driscoll, as he stated in his testimonial, that ten years earlier in 1889 his Company had given Miss De Zavala a first option on the property on behalf of her group called the De Zavala Daughters.[17] The option was transferred to them under their new name, De Zavala Chapter when they joined the DRT, once that organization was formed.[18]

Mr. Schmeltzer's "Notarized Statement" reports they had quoted the De Zavala Chapter a price of $75,000 and further said they were in no hurry to sell yet. This would give the women, as the new DRT Chapter, time to re-group now and work toward coming up with a plan to raise funds for the project. So far, they had been unable to devise a successful plan or collect much money toward the purchase of the property, and the interest now of the wealthy Miss Driscoll joining the effort was most welcome indeed.

Miss Driscoll was not yet a member of the DRT when she first talked to Mr. Schmeltzer, and after their meeting she lost no time in joining the organization. She had written her letter to Mr. Hugo on February 5, 1903, which refers to seeing "Mr. Schmeltzer in regard to the property adjoining the Alamo," and she is recorded as having become a member of the De Zavala Chapter of the DRT four days later on February 9, 1903.[19]

The timing of Miss Driscoll's visits with the Hugo-Schmeltzer Company owners is a little unclear, but in any case, they were able to come to terms. The company agreed on the price still as $75,000, with an option of one year upon payment of $5,000. At the expiration of that year a payment of $20,000 would be due, and the remaining $50,000 would be paid in five annual installments of $10,000 each, plus six percent interest.[20]

The DRT had no treasury to supply an amount such as the immediately required $5,000 option payment, let alone the rest of the amount later. Miss Driscoll consulted with her personal financial advisors, including her father, and shortly thereafter, on March 16, 1903, she called on the Hugo-Schmeltzer Company again, accompanied this time by two of her advisors, as well as Miss De Zavala. The outcome of this meeting was that the company agreed to accept a $500 payment for a thirty-day option and the remaining $4,500 at the end of the thirty-day period. Apparently there was not even $500 in the DRT treasury, because the very next day, to the surprise no doubt of the entire DRT, Miss Driscoll gave Hugo-Schmeltzer a check for $500, dated March 17, 1903, for that thirty-day option.[21]

An immediate meeting of the De Zavala Chapter was called and a plan devised to write letters to all Texans everywhere with a plea to donate fifty cents and the names of three friends they might contact to do the same.[22] A finance committee was formed and Miss Driscoll was named chairman.

It was also voted to appeal to the State Legislature for an appropriation of state funds for the cause of purchasing this historic Alamo property. The decision was to make this appeal in person since the Legislature was now in session. Two members of the Chapter, Clara Driscoll and Mrs. R. A. Coleman, were chosen to go to the State Capitol and make the appeal, with Miss Driscoll acting as spokesperson.[23]

In the meantime, the DRT continued the fund raising efforts they had begun. When the immediate thirty-day option period had expired, they had collected only $1,021.75, which was woefully short of the $4,500 needed. Miss Driscoll again came to the rescue, and she wrote another personal check on the deadline date of April 18, 1903. This time, her check was for $3,478.25, which was the difference between the $4,500 needed and the DRT check of $1,021.75, the amount collected thus far.[24] The Hugo-Schmeltzer property was now safe for one more year, thanks to the generosity of Clara Driscoll, plus the contributions thus far of other DRT members.

The amount the DRT had been able to collect was far below what they had hoped for but the dedicated women were not discouraged. Inspired by Miss Driscoll's act of unselfishness, and with more time now, they set about the monumental task of raising the larger amount of $20,000 due at the end of the one year, plus additional money hopefully with which to repay Miss Driscoll, although there is no record that she had asked for it.

The appeal to the Legislature earlier was passed by both houses and it was voted to appropriate $5,000 for the purpose requested, but the governor had vetoed it on the basis there was no fund the money could be taken from in that year's budget. The measure would have to be introduced again for consideration next year.

Meanwhile, time was moving forward toward the one-year expiration date, and the DRT women proceeded to work vigorously to raise funds by means of bazaars, "chain letters" requesting contributions, benefits of all kind and solicitations for donations from any source possible. They even made a patriotic appeal to school children for their "mite."

When they were so far below their goal it began to appear the effort to save the Alamo property would have to be abandoned after all. If they defaulted now, though, the property next to the Alamo Chapel would probably be lost forever to commercial development. But Clara Driscoll like her colleague Adina De Zavala was not one to accept defeat so easily when she was in pursuit of something she wanted. She had put not only her effort into this project, but she had put a substantial amount of her own money into it, too, which she was set to lose along with the object of her pursuit. And so she now had in mind a very bold plan.

As she customarily did on decisions of the magnitude she was considering now, she consulted her father. Her plan was to obligate herself for the entire remainder of the $75,000 price for the property. Her father is said to have asked her about the chance of reimbursement if she put that much money in the project. There is no indication Miss Driscoll ever did what she did regarding the purchase of the Hugo-Schmeltzer property with the expectation of reimbursement, but it was a very logical question for her father to ask, being the businessman he was. After some deliberation with her, he is quoted as assuring his daughter she would have enough in her bank account to cover the purchase price.[25] Clara Driscoll was always known to have a strong will, however, to put it one way, with which her father was surely familiar. Once her mind was made up, it is doubtful he could have dissuaded her anyway.

When the one-year option period was drawing to a close, the DRT had collected only $5,666.23 toward the needed $20,000.[26] It was clear they could never meet the deadline. Just prior to the expiration date in early February, Clara Driscoll made her decision to do just what she had told her father she would do, and she arranged for another meeting with the Hugo-Schmeltzer officials. This time she stunned everybody connected with the matter by giving the owners of the property her personal check for $14,333.77, which was the difference between the amount collected thus far by the DRT of $5,666.23 and the $20,000 for that first payment on the purchase of the property. She then signed five promissory notes of $10,000 each, bearing six percent interest, to be paid yearly over the next five years. This transaction took place on February 10, 1904, and it secured at last the Hugo-Schmeltzer property for the Daughters of the Republic of Texas.[27]

In fact, Miss Driscoll made it very clear in the transaction that although parts of the payments for the property were in her name, she was purchasing it for the "use and benefit" of the DRT. In the deed is the statement that the property "is to be used by them for the purpose of making a park about the Alamo, and for no other purpose whatsoever."[28]

This is an interesting point because Adina De Zavala's announced purpose from the outset was two fold: first, to make a museum out of the old "long barracks" building which she had maintained was still underneath the wooden covering of the Hugo-Schmeltzer Building; and, second, to create a park around the museum building. According to all evidence available, such as letters between the two women, and Miss Driscoll's letters of appeal to the public cited earlier in Chapter Six, the two had been working apparently in harmony for the same purpose for almost two years. It should be noted here, however, that in Miss Driscoll's letter to Mr. Hugo, quoted earlier, she had said the DRT wanted "to make a park about the old ruins," but she had not spoken outright of destruction of the building. What actually was her intention from the start? Whatever she may have had in mind originally, she appeared outwardly to have accepted what Miss De Zavala said earlier concerning the building. Once she had learned the facts about the part the building had played in the battle, she seemed very willing to follow Miss De Zavala's plan, but later she seems to have changed her mind for some reason. Regardless of the reasons behind it, her position had changed.

News of Miss Driscoll's magnanimous act of making the payment on the property and signing the promissory notes now spread all over the state at once and then over the nation. Overnight she became famous as the "Savior of the Alamo" and she was the darling of the press and the public everywhere.

Other than some people in the immediate proximity of the site and those who were aware of the true historical facts, almost everyone seems to have mistaken the building she saved to be the Alamo Chapel rather than the old Hugo-Schmeltzer Building. So accustomed had people become to the belief that the famous Chapel was where the battle had taken place, they assumed that was the building under discussion.

After all, for as long as almost anyone alive at that time could remember, the Chapel was all that could be seen standing there which could be identified with the Battle of the Alamo. When visitors came to see the hallowed site where the heroes had 'never surrendered, never retreated, and the defenders had all died,' that was what they were shown, because the only other building left had been enshrouded in the dilapidated structure known as the Hugo-Schmeltzer Building for years.

Miss Driscoll, without any doubt, knew what she had purchased, however, and it wasn't the Chapel, the building which had become the famous symbol of it all. That restored building had been bought in 1883 by the State of Texas and had never been in any danger since it had been rebuilt by the U.S. Army in 1849. It was later placed under the care and management of the DRT. Oddly enough, there is no record of Clara Driscoll ever protesting about any misunderstanding on this point, though. After all, the Chapel certainly appeared to be a more historic and visually focused site to picture the noble sacrifice of the heroes of the Alamo battle than the run-down Hugo-Schmeltzer Building. By now, the Chapel was where the memorable scenes that had come to surround the story were pictured to have happened in everyone's mind. And, most important perhaps, it was the building that her friends and supporters in the DRT insisted was where the heroes had all died.

(Author's Note: A condensed version of the episode which came to be called "The Second Battle of the Alamo," as it happened in the life of Clara Driscoll follows. In order to fully appreciate the complete story, full details and documented information on the entire event can be found in Chapter Eight. The reader may wish to refer to that Chapter at this point.)

172

Earlier, as stated, Miss Driscoll had appeared to be in support of the plan of Miss De Zavala to restore the stone building that the latter believed to be under the wooden covering of the Hugo-Schmeltzcr Building. Since the public had dramatized the battle as taking place in the Chapel, as did her friends, Miss Driscoll apparently had changed her mind and now joined the other Daughters in considering it the real battle site, too. Could it be these were the things that had influenced her to change her opinion and now say the Hugo-Schmeltzer Building was nothing more than a "whiskey house" that should be torn down? Or had she really felt it should be destroyed all along and had intended doing so when she could obtain control of it?

One more common misconception by the general public was that Miss Driscoll had bought "The Alamo" outright by paying the entire purchase price of $75,000 at once out of her own personal funds. This was far from the fact. She had simply paid only a part of the initial payment for the one-year option and a part of the first payment of the $20,000 needed later and signed promissory notes for the remainder. This was a very sizeable amount relatively speaking, of course, but she did not put down the entire amount for the property all at once. The other seldom publicized fact is that the Legislature of the State of Texas voted to reimburse Miss Driscoll less than one year later, and within that year had appropriated funds for that purpose, notwithstanding that had not been a requirement of the transaction. The purchase and transfer of ownership had been settled on February 10, 1904, when Clara Driscoll signed the contract with Hugo-Schmeltzer, and the Bill providing for transfer of ownership to the State of Texas and her reimbursement was signed by the governor on January 26, 1905. The money was appropriated by the legislature and paid to her in full in August of 1905.[29]

In September of that year Miss Driscoll departed for New York City, and she did not return to her home state to live until nine years later. She made periodic return trips to Texas, but she was not present during a great deal of the turbulent time of the struggle later between the two factions over control of the Hugo-Schmeltzer property. During this time except for those occasional trips she handled much of her association with the DRT by long distance or left things in the hands of other Daughters on the scene.

As for her change of heart about the Hugo-Schmeltzer Building, no matter what she had intended at the outset, her reason for that is still unexplained and within two years after her initial venture into the matter with Miss De Zavala, she had taken the firm position that the building should be torn down and a park created on the site as did her friends.

After the departure of Clara Driscoll from the scene, almost three years of disagreements in a quasi-polite atmosphere took place. Finally, the split in the two groups erupted into a complete breakdown in their relationship, with both groups claiming to be the official Daughters of the Republic of Texas. The end result was a court case to decide the matter.

In 1908, before the case came to trial, Miss De Zavala had actually "barricaded" herself inside the Hugo-Schmeltzer Building for three days and nights to prevent the opposing group which originally had been led by Miss Driscoll, from taking possession of it. After assurances from the governor of the state this would not be allowed to happen until the decision of the court had been rendered, Miss De Zavala came out of the building. Delays that had lasted almost three years were soon brought to an end following this highly publicized event, and the case came to trial not long afterwards.

The court's decision was in favor of the group who had followed Miss Driscoll and they were now officially acclaimed the Daughters of the Republic of Texas. Miss De Zavala and her by now very small group of twelve supporters were removed from the membership roles of the DRT because of what was described as "continual annoyance of the De Zavala faction," and their active role in operating as the authorized official group. Of course, the

174

other group had operated as the official group, also, although neither group yet had the sanction of the court. It was a very awkward and almost impossible period of time in the history of the DRT, no matter which side one might have been on, and the entire episode came to be called "The Second Battle of the Alamo." Miss Driscoll, as noted, was seldom on the scene however, for much of this "battle" at critical moments. The fight had been a long and bitter one that left scars that sadly are still unhealed and are sensitive to this day.

Clara Driscoll's image was unsullied through it all though. She was established forever as the "Savior of the Alamo," no matter what she had actually saved or whether she was reimbursed or not. Her generous act had been a critical factor in a time of need, of that there can be no denying, and so for that she has been given complete credit for having "saved the Alamo." Never mind the fact that it wasn't the Alamo Chapel she saved, as most people thought, and that she would have completely destroyed the building she did save, and the original long barracks underneath along with it, had she been allowed.

It was not until 1995 that any public acknowledgement was made by the DRT on the Alamo grounds concerning the other principal person in the "second battle," Adina De Zavala. Eighty-seven years after the episode, a small marker was placed in the court yard of the "long-barracks" naming Miss De Zavala along with Miss Driscoll, as one of two who "each in her own way" had saved the site. There is a brief account of Miss De Zavala's special "fifteen minutes of fame" of the "barricade" episode in the "long barracks" one-story museum which has now been established at the site, as well as on a panel called "The Wall of History" in the courtyard.

As a matter of fact, though, everything had not always gone Miss Driscoll's way on some minor things during the "second battle." Once, at the DRT annual meeting held in the historic town of Goliad in 1906, the year before the conflict had come to a climax, she wanted the DRT to purchase a portrait of one of the heroes of the Alamo, David "Davy" Crockett, with funds from the DRT treasury. She was outvoted on this, however, not only by the De Zavala Chapter, but by the majority of the membership as well. They felt that at that time any available funds should go toward making that hoped for museum of the "long barracks." This was followed by another vote in favor of giving the De Zavala Chapter (later to be referred to as the De Zavala "faction") custody of the Alamo rather than Clara Driscoll. Rejection of her on these two issues, one after the other, but especially the matter of custody, had caused her such displeasure she had risen and "tendered her resignation of both the custody of the Alamo and of her membership in the society."[30]

The Clara Driscoll supporters at the meeting were appalled at the very thought of such a thing and felt the action of the majority of the convention was discourteous to Miss Driscoll. One month later a member reported in her local Corpus Christi paper:

> As a bright little lady in the heated discussion pertinently remarked: "It was not sentiment that bought the Alamo, but hard old cash that did the work."[31] [Referring, of course, to Clara Driscoll's mistaken payment for it all.]

No matter what other factors may have contributed to the process of "saving the Alamo," whatever that may have meant in the minds of some of the members, it was 'money, and money alone that had saved it' as far as they were concerned. A reprint later of the article quoted from above appeared in the same newspaper in a "50 Years Ago" feature, and there was a very insightful handwritten comment on the file copy found, which said, this was "so like our Daughters of today."[32] Some beliefs never seem to change, though. Once all the facts are known, it becomes apparent that it took more than just money to save what is left of the long barracks, the building where so many of the heroes actually died.

Miss Driscoll's resignation was not accepted by her faithful followers, needless to say, but she was quite unhappy about the things that had happened in the meeting in Goliad, and she stayed away from close involvement with the organization for quite a long time. She busied herself with her new life now in New York City. She did resume her association with the organization in time, however, and she made other generous contributions to the DRT at later times for which she did not receive any reimbursement. They were her gifts in support of projects for improving other areas of the Alamo property.

Clara Driscoll did have a life full of a variety of experiences other than her association with the DRT and the Alamo, and she was off to pursue one of an entirely different nature after her financial rescue of the Alamo property.

She had always had a colorful imagination and a flair for the written word. This was evidenced in her letters to the newspapers regarding the plight of the Alamo. And now she had moved to a completely different environment to embark on a career as a novelist and playwright, where she could put to use her talent for writing. The subjects of her novels and plays were based on scenes and imaginary characters from her own background and place of origin in South Texas. There were even stories revolving directly around the Alamo and the other old Spanish missions of San Antonio.

Her first novel, published in 1905, was entitled *The Girl of La Gloria,* and the setting of the story is a ranch in South Texas, Clara Driscoll's own home area. The name of the ranch belonging to the heroine of the story is "La Gloria," which is the name of one of the real life Driscoll family ranches. The life of the heroine of the story closely parallels that of Miss Driscoll in many ways, and thus she brings to life scenes from her own past and relives and fantasizes some of her own personal memories. In fact, the heroine's name of "Ilaria" is said by some to be a Spanish style variation of Miss Driscoll's name of Clara.[33]

The second novel, issued in 1906 by the same publisher, is titled *In The Shadow of The Alamo,* and its title story revolves around that early Spanish mission in San Antonio under its later name at the time of the battle, "The Alamo," which had brought it such worldwide fame and her such sudden fame as well. Unfortunately there are a few uses of "writer's license" of liberal fictionalizing that create a wrong interpretation of the true facts about the site and the battle. Either that or Miss Driscoll herself was under the wrong impression. In one instance the heroine is leading a young man through the old mission/battle site and she says of the doomed Texas heroes:

> The Texans desperately contested every inch of ground until by the overwhelming force of numbers they were forced back into the chapel, where the last stand was made.[34]

This is misleading because the old convento/"long barracks" across the courtyard has been established by historians as described in Chapter Eight in this book to be the site of the major "last stand" where most of the last of the defenders died. Miss Driscoll and her followers had all insisted the Chapel was the site of the "last stand," however, as does her heroine in this story.

She further relates a story of how one of the best known defenders, James Bowie, was killed in "the Baptistery" room of the Chapel.[35] Again, this is misleading. It is pretty well accepted that Bowie died at another location. According to one of the women named Susanna Dickinson, who was in one of the Chapel rooms at the time of the battle, Bowie died in a room on the second floor of the old "long barracks" building. Susanna Dickinson was one of the real women who survived the battle and lived to tell what she had seen and of the horrifying experience of it all as told in Chapter One of this book.

The young heroine in Miss Driscoll's story about "The Alamo" leads her visitor to the front door of the Chapel and directs his attention to a building across the courtyard. She says:

178

That old building outside is soon to be cleared away and
a fitting surrounding given this Chapel.[36]

She is, of course, referring to the building across to the side
of the Alamo, the Hugo-Schmeltzer Building, which she had put up
the money to purchase for the DRT then campaigned so vigorously
to have torn down and the area cleared so a proper park could be
built in its place. She was still working toward that end at the time
her book was published.

At the end of *In The Shadow of The Alamo,* there is a fic-
tionalized story about the "most remote" of the old "missions that
cluster around San Antonio" that "stands on the bank of the San
Antonio River . . . ." Mission San Francisco de la Espada is the last
in a chain of five missions built along the winding San Antonio
River, starting with Mission San Antonio de Valero, known as "The
Alamo." The story is a charming and romantic one set in the last
mission in the chain, Mission Espada, as it is referred to, with a
very nice drawing done by her friend, Florence Eager, presumably
illustrating the mission named in the story. The only thing wrong,
though, the drawing is of Mission San Juan Capistrano, the other
smaller mission.

She also wrote the text for a comic opera entitled *Mexicana,*
which was produced in New York City at the Lyric Theatre. It is
reported to have been backed financially by her brother, Robert, for
the cost of the production. A contract was arranged with the pro-
ducers, also, specifying other details such as a percentage of prof-
its, royalties for Clara as the author, etc.[37] The show had only a very
short run, but it gained her a great deal of publicity and recognition,
primarily, it must be said, as being the "Savior of the Alamo" rather
than as an especially talented writer.

From the moment of her arrival in New York her initial
focus had been on her exciting new literary career in the big city.
The critics' focus, however, seemed to have been on the young

author herself. Clara Driscoll had become famous by then as the Texas heiress who was known as the "Savior of the Alamo". The following review of her first production was found in Miss De Zavala's Collection in a handwritten letter from one of Miss De Zavala's friends. It tells her this is a copy of a review of the operetta "Mexicana" found in a "swell New York monthly":

> The most striking feature of "Mexicana" the new musical play that came last week to "The Lyric", is the patriotism of its author. There are excellent opportunities for stage pictures, but what stands foremost in impressiveness about the play is the fact that its author, Miss Clara Driscoll, purchased the historic church of the Alamo at San Antonio, Texas, and presented it as a highly prized memento to the State. This was the church that Jim Bowie and Davy Crockett and this handful of brave frontiersmen held against Santa Anna's army until they fell before overpowering numbers; but after which Houston's little army with its battle cry of "Remember the Alamo" routed the Mexicans and saved the territory which became the Republic of Texas, and in 1845 was annexed to the United States. The defense of the Alamo was not only one of the most thrilling deeds of courage in all history, but as one writer says, "it was the most stupendous, the most sagacious, and the most 'nervy' real estate transaction ever consummated by man in the brief period of eleven days."

~ ~ ~ ~ ~ ~ ~ ~ ~ ~ ~

Miss Clara Driscoll
The author of "Mexicana" who <u>bought</u>
the historic Alamo and <u>gave it</u> to Texas.
[Letter writer's underlines.]

~ ~ ~ ~ ~ ~ ~ ~ ~ ~ ~

The article came from:
Town and Country Magazine
289 4th Avenue
New York
February 10, 1906 [38]

Without intention possibly, the review of Clara Driscoll's operetta "Mexicana" sounds more like a lampoon of the production than a serious critique. From its opening lines about Miss Driscoll's "purchase of the historic church" and presenting it to the state as a "memento", to the final line about the "eleven days" (which in reality were thirteen), it is obvious the critic had not done his homework very carefully.

However, this kind of inaccuracy seemed to be a common fault with articles in the press at that time on the subject of 'saving the Alamo'. In fact, it is a fault that never seems to have been corrected altogether unfortunately.

There was one perceptive reporter on the home front back at the Alamo who analyzed the situation of the growing "second battle" though, with this report:

> She [Miss Driscoll] was feted and made much of in all quarters of the United States. . . She quite eclipsed Miss Dezavala [sic] and other members of the Daughters . . . and in her sudden rise their long efforts seemed almost forgotten. They had worked when obstacles were many and when recognition of their plans was slow. They felt that they had made Miss Driscoll's somewhat meteoric success possible.
>
> Unquestionably there was some resentment of Miss Driscoll's success and a little jealousy, but the Daughters put it behind them for the glory of the cause. Then came the resolution of the executive committee to make Miss Driscoll custodian of the building for one year, and on top of that, the statement is made, Miss Driscoll, instead of sacrificing her New York work and pleasures for the honor, attempted to turn it over to her friend, Miss Eagers [sic]. This was too much--the last straw . . . [39]

Clara Driscoll's career as a playwright and author was a brief one of less than two years, but her stay in New York did not end when her writing career ended. Nor, however, did her life there completely disassociate her from matters concerning the Alamo. She occasionally came back to Texas on family business and the Alamo situation as well. The latter was the case when she attended the open meeting in San Antonio regarding the disposition of the Hugo-Schmeltzer property in December of 1911, the account of which opened this chapter on the story of the life of Clara Driscoll.

Soon after this meeting in 1911, Miss Driscoll wrote a notice addressed "To All Texans" appealing to them to help promote the DRT plans for a park to be built on the site next to the Alamo.

To All Texans:

As legal custodians of the Alamo, the Daughters of the Republic of Texas request your signature in endorsement of their plan for the beautifying of the Alamo Mission grounds adjoining the Chapel of the Alamo, more generally known as the Hugo-Schmeltzer property.

It is their desire to convert this property into a beautiful park filled with swaying palms and tropical verdure, enclosed by a low wall, with arched gateways of Spanish architecture. They also wish to restore the roof of the Chapel of the Alamo, and have a replica of the original doors placed at the entrance to the Church.

The Daughters of the Republic of Texas ask for your support in their honest endeavor to be worthy the obligation imposed upon them by the Twenty-ninth Legislature of the State of Texas.

CLARA DRISCOLL SEVIER,
CHAIRMAN ALAMO AUXILIARY
COMMITTEE,

Menger Hotel, San Antonio, Texas,
or
37 Madison Avenue, New York, City,[40]

This notice was followed by a more detailed one under the

same heading, but apparently directed to the members of the DRT. It was a report on the meeting where the original notice had been issued, and in this letter instructions were given to the various DRT Chapters to form committees for the work, and the responsibilities of those committees were outlined. They were told:

> . . . They do not approve of the erection of a modern building which would have no historic or sentimental value, but on the contrary be incongruous and overshadow that sacred edifice so dear to the hearts of all Texans--the Chapel of the Alamo. These patriotic women would have that hallowed shrine standout clear and unobstructed, the most glorious monument in the world today to the immortal glory of the men who gave up their lives that Texas might gain its freedom and independence. They would restore the roof of the Chapel . . . as . . . a replica of the original . . . keep its walls in repair . . . and make it a fitting mausoleum for the heroes who so willingly gave their lives for Texas liberty.[41]

Miss Driscoll errs regarding the roof of the Chapel being restored as "a replica of the original." In actual fact there had never been a completed roof to the building. The one that was begun collapsed and work on it was never resumed. Further details on this are given in Chapter Eight.

These plans of Miss Driscoll and the DRT nearly came to pass, but the plan did not succeed in the final arrangement.

After the open meeting called by the governor in December of 1911, he received documents from Miss De Zavala which he had requested regarding the history of the Hugo-Schmeltzer Building and the part the original building underneath had played in the Battle of the Alamo. These, plus the inspection trip conducted on the site following the meeting, convinced him that the original building was still there under cover of the wooden exterior, and these facts were the basis of his decision on the property. He ordered that the wooden exterior be carefully stripped away and any remains of the original stone building be restored and the building completed.

The project had begun, and when the wooden exterior was removed, most of the two-story skeleton of the long building Miss De Zavala claimed would be there was revealed. It was partially restored according to plan when the state appropriated funds for the project ran out, leaving only a roofless structure with gaping window openings and incomplete arches standing there. Later in 1912, when the governor was out of the state, the lieutenant governor as the authority pro tem had the second story removed, possibly in acquiescence to pressure from, or even in sympathy with, Miss Driscoll's group, because, as he said, it "obstructed the view of the Alamo."

After the removal of the second-story walls of the original old building, work was halted altogether, leaving only a roofless one-story shell. At that point, Clara Driscoll's active participation ended, also, in that so-called "second battle of the Alamo." Nothing further was done on the remaining ruin left standing there for the next fifty-four years except for those "trailing vines" that the Daughters requested be planted to cover it. It was not until 1967-68 that work was resumed and the remaining first floor was finished into a one-story interpretive and artifacts museum. Neither of the two principals in that "second battle" lived to see those final results. This restoration and interpretation effort took place twenty-two years after Miss Driscoll's death and twelve years after Miss De Zavala's.

Returning to the chronological story of the life of Clara Driscoll, which was underway before the above digression into the "second battle" and its conclusion, when Miss Driscoll had appeared before the State Legislature as DRT spokesperson in 1903 with their appeal for money for the purchase of the Hugo-Schmeltzer property, a young representative by the name of Henry Hulme Sevier had been very impressed with her presentation. So

CLARA DRISCOLL CHAPTER SEVEN

impressed that he introduced the bill later which called for her reimbursement of what she paid for the property with her own funds. The two met at that time through mutual friends and for a brief time they were considered a "twosome"⁴² around and about Austin but their relationship had apparently remained one of simply "good friends."

Clara Driscoll had left for New York City in September of 1905, once the purchase of the Hugo-Schmeltzer property and the reimbursement matter was settled, to pursue her short-lived writing career. Hal Sevier, as he was known, moved to that city in January of 1906. He was employed as the financial editor of the *New York Sun,* a post he held until 1912.⁴³ Sevier had been in the newspaper business in the small West Texas town of Sabinal prior to his election to the Legislature as a representative from there.

The friendship between Miss Driscoll and Hal Sevier was resumed on a more serious basis this time with the result they were married just a few months after his arrival in New York City. It was not exactly what might be called a "whirlwind affair," because after all they had met three years earlier. However, there had been very little personal contact since, and, in fact, the wedding was said to have come as quite a surprise to some of the bride's friends. The gossip columnists back in San Antonio obviously were keeping up with Clara's personal life in spite of the distance and lack of frequent visits home, though, as this social page account from a San Antonio paper in August of 1906 records.

> While it has been a dainty morsel of gossip for several months that the most favored suitor in Miss Driscoll's eyes was Mr. Sevier, the marriage announcement brought surprise to even many of the young lady's most intimate friends.⁴⁴

The two were married in New York City at high noon on July 31, 1906, at St. Patrick's Cathedral on Fifth Avenue. The wedding was a small affair with only a few family members and friends in attendance, but it was no doubt a fashionable one, even if subdued. A New York newspaper in its report of the social event identified her as the author of "Mexicana," her comic opera, which had appeared at the Lyric Theater there the past season, and some presses described the marriage in such sentimental terms as "the romance of the Alamo" and the bride as the "Alamo Queen."[45]

The wedding had not come as an immediate surprise to Clara's father and brother though, but just how much advance notice they had is unrecorded. They were present for the marriage ceremony, of course, and the celebration luncheon afterward at Delmonico's fashionable restaurant. Her brother, Robert, was asked later what he thought about the marriage and he, a lifelong bachelor, said something like, "Well, I never thought she'd make it, but I'm glad she did. Thank goodness, now I won't have to lug her packages all over town."[46]

One month after the wedding the couple left for Europe on an extended honeymoon trip. They visited England, France and Italy, and they reported that they especially enjoyed the theaters of London, the gaieties of the night life of Paris, and the beauty of Italy. Clara kept a memory book of post cards, theater programs, ticket stubs, and all sorts of memorabilia. She entered diary-like notes on special events and days on the pages of her "scrap-book," plus some other more personal comments about various things.

One of those more personal comments, as described in Martha Anne Turner's biography, was a cryptic one of: "Six glasses a day!" Apparently Clara was becoming concerned about her husband's consumption of liquor, according to Turner. The hotel receipts showed frequent orders for whiskey and other alcoholic beverages, along with ginger ale.[47] This may have been an early indication of a matter that was to become a major problem for them in the future.

186

Upon returning to New York where they were to live for the next eight years, the Seviers built a beautiful home of Spanish style architecture with romantic Mediterranean detailing reminiscent of their recent honeymoon trip to that area of the world. The residence was quite large, surrounded by spacious lawns and gardens, and was located in the exclusive Oyster Bay area on Long Island next to the home of the Theodore Roosevelt family.[48]

Clara Driscoll, now Mrs. Hal Sevier, entered into her career of married life with great enthusiasm. She became a bona-fide "housewife" and hostess, with all that accompanied her new role. She became interested in cooking and collected recipes as all young housewives do, and she entertained lavishly and with great flourish. Her personal files and newspaper accounts reflected this side of her home life during those early years of her marriage while living in New York. She also is said to have developed an avid interest in gardening, and she is recorded as even having found time to write several stories and articles which were submitted for publication.

These new home activities, an exciting social life with an elite group, both as a popular hostess and a guest, along with her hobby of writing, kept Clara Driscoll Sevier and her husband Hal quite busy. Those were very happy years for the newlyweds.

After six years on the *New York Sun,* Hal Sevier resigned from his post, but he continued his newspaper career as a correspondent with some Washington, D.C. papers. For several years he was also a cotton merchant in New York City.[49]

Following a trip to California in 1914, the Seviers went to San Antonio to see Clara's father who had been ill there for some time, and to their shock he died during their visit. Clara had always been closely attached to her father and had been dependent on him for advice, and she felt this loss very keenly. Robert Driscoll, Sr. was laid to rest in the family mausoleum in San Antonio beside his wife, Julia Fox Driscoll. The death of her father brought to an end those happy years of early married life in New York City for the

Seviers. In order to be closer to her brother and share in the respon-sibilities of the Driscoll family business, Clara decided the time had come to move back to Texas.

The Seviers chose the capital city of the state, Austin, as the location of their new "dream home." She and Hal Sevier had fallen in love with the Lake Como area in Italy where they had spent a part of their honeymoon trip, and the style and atmosphere of the homes they saw there were the inspiration for their new Mediterranean style home in Austin.

The architect they engaged was Mr. Harvey L. Page of San Antonio. It is possible she may have become acquainted with him around 1911 when she was struggling so to convince the governor that a Spanish style memorial garden should be built next to the Alamo to replace the Hugo-Schmeltzer "whiskey house." Shortly before that Mr. Page had designed an elaborate amusement palace to stand at the northeast corner of the Alamo Chapel and his plan had been well advertised. In front of the building he designed, he planned a garden to stand where the Hugo-Schmeltzer building stood which was the same type of garden Mrs. Sevier proposed for her home later. The building and garden for the Alamo property are described in Chapter Eight and copies of some of the drawings for it are included, also.

Mr. Page, at the request of the Seviers, included in their dream home both Spanish and Italian elements suggestive of each of those two countries which they had traveled through. He also included a very unusual detail. It is a copy of a window in the old Spanish Mission San José in San Antonio, which is called the "Rose Window" or, more accurately, "Rosa's Window." The win-dow is in the shape of an elongated quatrefoil, with clusters of pomegranates carved around the opening. There is a romantic leg-end about how it came to be called "Rosa's Window" which tells of the unrequited love of the sculptor for a beautiful young maiden named Rosa. One version of the story tells that Rosa died before the window was finished and that the sculptor dedicated it to the memory of his lost love. This was just the kind of story that a young Clara Driscoll had fantasized about in the dreams of her youth and which she had included in her novels. The window is a beautiful one and quite a unique piece of sculpture, but there is no real proof of the romantic tale of the inspiration for it. Incorporating a copy of "The Rose Window" into her house in Austin was an expression of Clara Driscoll's genuine love for the old missions of San Antonio though and her South Texas heritage in general.

Another bit of evidence that reflected her affection for her native state was the fact that the site chosen for her home which overlooked Lake Austin was land once owned by Stephen F. Austin, for whom the city is named, and who is called "The Father of Texas." Stephen F. Austin, following his deceased father's plan, was the organizer of one of the first colonizing groups brought to Texas while it was still a part of Mexico. He had bought the land in 1832 for a prospective home but he never built there.[50] All of this was learned by the Seviers when they purchased the site in 1914 for the sum of $4,750, an amount hard to believe by today's market prices.

They called their new home, which was located at a lagoon on Lake Austin, "Laguna Gloria." They chose this name because it was part of the name of one of the Driscoll ranches in South Texas, "La Gloria,"[51] and also, possibly because that part of the name is in the title of Clara's earlier novel, *The Girl of La Gloria,*[52] which had been named for the same family ranch of real life.

Once they were settled in their new Texas location, Hal Sevier continued his newspaper career as founder, owner and editor of the *Austin American,* an occupation he pursued until 1917.[53]

Life for Clara and Hal Sevier in Austin was a very happy time for them, and even more satisfying and fulfilling for Clara probably because she was "home again." Their social life was a busy and pleasant one and "Laguna Gloria" was a showplace in Austin during those years and a mecca for local dignitaries and international visitors as well.

Both of the Seviers were interested in politics and state and national political groups were frequently entertained at their home. It was during this time that Clara Driscoll Sevier herself became personally involved in the Democratic Party, and later in 1928 she was elected by the Party as Democratic National Committee Woman from Texas.

The Seviers had a varied social and civic life in Austin at "Laguna Gloria" from 1916, the year of the completion of the home, until 1929 when life brought about an abrupt change again for them. Clara's brother, Robert, Jr., died quite unexpectedly on July 7, 1929, from complications following an illness which had required the amputation of one of his legs.

Robert Driscoll was ten years older than Clara, but they had always been very close to one another. Not only were they a devoted brother and sister but they were described as being very "good friends" as well. They had been co-managers of the family business interests since their father's death, but Robert, in fact, had been the responsible partner on the scene. That he had been the principal manager of the Driscoll businesses of ranching and banking was a well-known fact, but he also had been extremely active in many facets of the industrial, commercial and civic enterprises of the port city of Corpus Christi.

The Driscolls had been a small, close-knit family of four, and now with the loss of her brother Robert, Clara was the only one left. She felt the loss of this last member of the family very deeply, not only because of her attachment to him, but along with it there was the realization that the management of the family fortune, which had grown to multimillion dollar size, was hers alone now. It was quite a challenge, but as she always seemed to have done in time of crisis, she rose to meet it.

Clara arranged for Robert to be interred in his place in the family mausoleum in San Antonio. Once again family tragedy changed the life of the Seviers. They decided they would have to close their much loved home of "Laguna Gloria" in Austin and they moved to the Driscoll ranch headquarters at "Palo Alto," which was located twenty-five miles from Corpus Christi. The City of Corpus Christi was where the major part of the family business interests was centered.

They still spent occasional week-ends and other special times at "Laguna Gloria", but in later years Clara stayed there only briefly from time to time. In 1943, just two years prior to her death, Clara Driscoll donated "Laguna Gloria" to the Texas Fine Arts Association to be used as a museum. In 1995 it was incorporated into the combined properties of the Austin Museum of Art, as an individual museum open to the public as Clara Driscoll had hoped it would be.[54]

Initially, after their move to the ranch, the Seviers commuted from "Palo Alto" to her office in downtown Corpus at the family owned bank. Mrs. Sevier had suddenly been thrust into a situation with a highly varied and demanding assortment of administrative responsibilities. Some people, it was said, wondered if a woman so accustomed to such a busy social and politically involved life could handle it all. She apparently took over those new responsibilities with considerable business acumen and skill, however, and in time she became recognized as 'one of the most astute businesswomen in the nation' according to one local newspaper account which stated:

> As her brother had succeeded her father, Mrs. Clara Driscoll [she had dropped her married name Sevier at this time] followed the footsteps of her brother and was recognized as outstanding among the nation's businesswomen . .[55]

Clara Driscoll Sevier managed her varied business interests with the support of her husband for a time, and with the help of her associates in her enterprises who were her trusted advisors over the remainder of her lifetime. With it all, though, she mixed other major interests, primary among which were those of politics and as club woman extraordinaire. Both of these activities required a great deal of personal involvement, but they also took a great deal of her money as well.

In support of her interest in politics, she made a $25,000 donation quadrennially to the Democratic Party, and her personal involvement became a significant factor in her life when she was elected as Democratic National Party Committee Woman from Texas

MRS. CLARA DRISCOLL SEVIER, TEXAS MOST NOTABLE WOMAN
FROM TEXAS CENTENNIAL MAGAZINE, SEPTEMBER 1935.
(Vertical Files, Daughters of the Republic of Texas Library.)

in 1928. She held this post for sixteen years consecutively until 1944. That was longer than anyone else had ever served in that position.

It is believed by many it was this active participation in the Democratic Party that led to her husband, Hal Sevier, being appointed by Democrat President Franklin D. Roosevelt as Ambassador to Chile in 1933. It was rumored, that Mrs. Sevier was first offered the ambassadorship, but declined in favor of her husband's appointment.[56]

The couple were sent off on this assignment with a round of parties and good wishes from Texans throughout the state, but especially by those in Austin and Corpus Christi where they were best known personally on a social basis as well as politically.

Their departure from the Driscoll enterprises did present a problem for them, of course, since she and her husband were key members in the management of her business affairs. Fortunately, however, the advisors and colleagues she had depended on since her assumption of the management of it all were there to take over and she confidently left everything in their hands.

Unfortunately, Mr. Sevier's performance in his job as Ambassador was rumored to be less than up to standard from the outset and criticisms accelerated to a pretty high point as reflected in an article that appeared in *Fortune Magazine* six months after their arrival:

Hal Sevier, Ambassador to Chile, isn't really an Ambassador at all. His wife is. Sevier is an active Texas Democrat (Tennessee-born), a protege of Garner, and an Austin newspaper publisher. He's pretty impressed with the importance and the dignity of being Ambassador but doesn't quite know what to do about it. Mrs. Sevier ("The Woman Who Saved the Alamo") does her best to tell him, does, in fact, just about whatever is done. His Spanish is feeble; hers is fluent. Washington gossip is that when Hull wandered about South America recently, he discovered that in conference Sevier will say "yes" affably enough to anything but doesn't know half the time what he's saying "yes" to. From a business point of view, Sevier's main job is to smooth the way for exports of Chilean wines.[57]

Because of continuing criticism of him, Hal Sevier resigned his post in Chile in 1935, two years after his arrival and two years before the expiration of his term, and the Seviers returned to Texas. For the next two years their marriage, which was said to have been in a precarious state for some time, began to decline visibly.

From the time they returned they had withdrawn from par-

MR. AND MRS. HAL SEVIER, CHILEAN AMBASSADOR
(Institute of Texan Cultures, San Antonio Light Collection.)

ticipation in public functions and it soon became apparent that in effect they were "separated." They maintained separate suites in downtown hotels in Corpus Christi, but they displayed no open hostility. They simply stayed apart from the public in general for reasons they kept to themselves. According to the Turner biography:

> Upon their return to Texas in 1935 the Seviers were separated. Regardless of what had happened in Chile to precipitate the break, both remained silent. Speculations as to the reasons for the domestic discord were advanced. Some people felt that Sevier's occasional flights of infidelity might have contributed. Others were of the opinion that Sevier's immoderation was a factor. Some wondered if Sevier had not tried to wrest full control of the Driscoll empire from his wife's hands. Still others theorized that for Clara Driscoll, Hal Sevier, her husband, had lost integrity - a trait upon which she placed exceedingly high value. Since neither of the estranged couple was inclined to confide intimacies to others, none of these probabilities were ever confirmed as fact.[58]

Then in May of 1937, while they were in San Antonio staying at the Menger Hotel where Hal Sevier was attending a banking convention, the newspapers carried a story stating that Mrs. Clara Driscoll Sevier had filed a suit for divorce.[59] The news was apparently a complete surprise to her husband judging from his reaction when reporters approached him in the lobby of the hotel and asked him if he had any comment to make. His response was:

> "I am distressed by this information and I want to remonstrate with Mrs. Sevier before I make a statement."[60]

He then went to their rooms and after talking with her he returned to the reporters and said:

> "She is ill and nervous and I think we had better not disturb her anymore. You can say for me that regardless of any action my wife wishes to take, my affection and esteem

remain as they always have been for her. But nothing, either legal or moral grounds, would prompt me to contest the suit."[61]

There was some talk soon afterward that Mrs. Sevier was considering dropping the divorce proceedings and a reconciliation was possible. This did not happen, however, and on July 9, 1937, the divorce was granted on grounds of incompatibility and mental cruelty. There was no community property and no children.[62] Thus the thirty-one year marriage ended. Mrs. Sevier kept her husband's name until immediately after his death when she took legal action to resume her maiden name, but she retained the married title of Mrs., and from that time on she was identified as Mrs. Clara Driscoll.[63]

According to some accounts Clara Driscoll offered Hal Sevier a settlement of several thousand dollars which he was said first to have refused, then later to have accepted $250,000.[64] Reportedly from still other sources he also later reversed himself and instigated litigation to have the divorce set aside and have it granted in his name, and further, to have the property valued at $5 million upwards divided, which he contended was jointly earned.[65]

Attorneys for both sides appeared in court and the judge upheld Mrs. Sevier's divorce as granted, and the suits were dropped. It was said that she then made some kind of settlement, the amount of which was not disclosed. Whatever it may have been, when he died two years later, Hal Sevier died a relatively poor man. He had moved back to Tennessee near the area of his birthplace. He died in Chattanooga on March 11, 1940.[66] The actual cause of his death was not stated. Rumors concerning her husband's "immoderation," as Turner termed it, had always surrounded the life of Clara and Hal Sevier and it is possible that may have been a contributing factor.

Life for Clara Driscoll after her marriage ended proceeded as it had after every other crisis for her - with some difficulty and adjustment, but as always she coped.

Prior to their departure for Chile in 1933, she had become actively involved in the DRT again. When a substantial amount of money was needed in 1932 to purchase the area immediately south and to the rear of the Chapel for converting it into gardens, she donated the necessary $65,000 to make up the deficit needed to match the purchase price of the property. There was no reimbursement this time, though, nor talk of any.

This purchase resulted in obtaining the area on the right side as you face the Chapel, the south side, extending to Crockett Street, and in the rear back to Bonham Street, the eastern perimeter of the property. Within this area today are the Alamo Hall meeting building and the DRT Library, with a large garden area behind the buildings, which has been planted with native trees, shrubs and flowers. On the left side of the Chapel as you face it, the north side, is a courtyard with the remaining one story of the "long barracks" building and a gift shop building behind it. A high rock wall encloses the entire compound. There are gates to several entrances in the wall that are closed and locked at night, securing the area. This entire compound is now state property under the care of the DRT. Thus, the Alamo Chapel is protected from close-in encroachment on all sides at last, with only a threat to the so-called "viewshed".

Only the front of the Chapel which faces onto the Plaza is fully visible twenty-four-hours a day. It, too, is locked and secured at night, of course, but it is brightly lighted. And the Texas symbol of liberty, The Alamo, with the "Lone Star" state flag flying over it continuously, can be seen "unobscured" night and day, as Miss Driscoll felt it should be.

Other than efforts toward continued protection and restoration of the Alamo property such as these from time to time, Clara Driscoll never really participated in the actual cause of historic preservation. She was a philanthropist for many causes, but historic preservation per se was not one of them. She was both a clubwoman and a political supporter, but politics seemed to be her real passion as time passed.

Her interest in a variety of women's clubs filled a great deal of her time and her social life. She was active in a number of them throughout her lifetime. She was made President for Life of the DRT by the Daughters for her unequaled generosity to that organization, and she also was extended the same honorable title by the Texas Federation of Women's Clubs. Competing with her contributions to the DRT, was her financial support to this latter organization. Her gift to them may have surpassed that made to the DRT in fact; if not, it came close.

The Texas Federation of Women's Clubs had built a very large and impressive clubhouse in Austin in 1929-30, and hundreds of clubs and thousands of members of them statewide contributed to the financing of it. The two-story, red brick building of colonial design was completed and enjoyed by clubs from all parts of Texas for eight years, but unfortunately, because of poor financing arrangements, a near disaster was encountered in 1938. The mortgage payment was overdue and there was a $92,000 indebtedness and no solution in sight.

A club member and friend of Mrs. Driscoll contacted her about a loan, and Clara Driscoll, as a banker, consented to refinance their current loan. She presented to them a very favorable refinancing program which was described by one member as "a plan handed to them on a silver platter." Mrs. Driscoll's plan was a great help but that was not all she did for them. A year later, Clara Driscoll unexpectedly once more performed a "fairy godmother" act - she converted the $92,000 loan into an outright gift, and the clubhouse was theirs, debt free.[67]

There was a day-long schedule of festivities in her honor a few months later, on October 4, 1939, in gratitude for the generous gift to the clubwomen of Texas and to the city of Austin. It was celebrated by the governor and many other celebrities, as well as clubwomen from throughout the state. An elaborate banquet held at the Clubhouse climaxed the festivities at the end of the day, and speeches in praise of Mrs. Driscoll were made by various dignitaries and clubwomen. One member, Mrs. R. C. Cochran, caused considerable amusement with her comment: "When Clara Driscoll gave $92,000 to lift the Club debt, she also lifted the faces of 60,000 women."[68]

The city of Corpus Christi, where Miss Driscoll made her home for the final years of her life, was also a recipient of her sense of community service. Just as her brother before her had done, she made many contributions toward official activities and the civic progress of the city. She was a strong supporter of the program directed toward attracting tourists to the area of the port city, including the as yet undeveloped potential of the coastal island just off shore known as Padre Island.

One of the things she did toward this goal was to build a luxurious hotel on an esplanade along a bluff above the downtown district of Corpus Christi to accommodate some of the visitors being urged to visit the area. She conceived the idea of building a hotel in 1937, but construction did not begin until 1939.

Actually, there was a large hotel already there in the same area, which her brother had built in the 1920's, possibly with the same purpose in mind, and it had been a part of her inheritance when her brother died. When she was away in Chile, an outside party had gained control of the hotel which was named the White Plaza Hotel, and upon her return she brought suit to regain it. The federal court where the case was tried decided in favor of the other party, however.[69]

The story that grew up around this unpleasant situation has become legendary in the tales told about this legendary lady. In one version she was said to have sworn "a mighty oath that she would build a hotel next to the hotel her brother built, the White Plaza, so tall that she could stand at a window and vent her displeasure on it in the most suitable way that occurred to her. And she did." [70]

The story has another variation wherein she supposedly came into town on one of her unannounced trips and went to the White Plaza Hotel where she asked for a room and was told there were none available.

Thinking the clerk did not know who she was she told him that she was Mrs. Clara Driscoll Sevier. Still he insisted there were no vacant rooms. Angry, Mrs. Sevier demanded to see the manager. When he arrived, Mrs. Sevier repeated her request for a room and was again told there were no vacancies. Then she is supposed to have said:

> "Alright, if you won't give me a room in your hotel, I'll build one next to yours and I'll build it high enough and close enough that I can stand on top of my hotel and spit on yours."
>
> The fact that she built her hotel on the same street with only a narrow alley between the hotels seemed to make the story true and has served to keep it going. Like most stories the older it gets the more it is changed until the present version told in Corpus Christi, is not fit to repeat. [71]

Neither version has any verification but the story still circulates to this day. The hotel she built was done in memory of her brother and it carries his name, The Robert Driscoll Hotel. Several factors entered into her reason for building the hotel and one of them was to provide a suitable place for her to live when she decided to move into town permanently from her Palo Alto ranch home after her divorce. She built a palatial penthouse on top of the twenty-story edifice and she did build it two stories higher than the other hotel for whatever her reasons may have been. It was designed to meet her special tastes and needs, and featured the latest of everything. A penthouse on top of your very own building is quite a dream to realize in any age, but in Clara Driscoll's day it was a real rarity and it received a lot of publicity for that reason alone.

The support of Clara Driscoll for causes that appealed to her was always an intensive thing with her. She gave generously of her wealth for them, but she put a lot of personal effort into them, too, and none of those causes was as intense and long lasting as her passion for politics. She had been abruptly introduced to the political arena when she began her campaign to save the property next to the Alamo Chapel to be developed as she thought it should be. And although that effort never turned out exactly as she planned, she became famous for it, nevertheless, and this may have whetted her appetite for the challenges of the uncertainties of political contests. Not only did she like to win, she expected to. Politics became the vital interest of her life and remained so almost to the end of it.

Mrs. Driscoll was elected National Democratic Committee woman from Texas at the Texas State Democratic Convention in 1928, and she held that position for sixteen consecutive years. Over the years, in addition to her quadrennial donation of $25,000 to the Democratic Party, she sponsored dinners, birthday balls, and various other political and entertainment events. She also made other substantial donations from time to time for special occasions.

One of the more spectacular events she participated in for the National Democratic Party was one on the occasion of the inauguration of President Roosevelt for his third term in office. For the parade on the great day she imported a thirty-six piece Cowboy Band from Hardin-Simmons University in Abilene, Texas, with six beautiful white horses and six pretty young college girls to ride them, thus giving the parade a showy Texas flavor. The climax of the day was a tremendous reception for the distinguished Texans who attended the festivities, and the Cowboy Band played for dancing throughout the evening.

When a split in the Democratic Party occurred later, inevitably Clara Driscoll's position in the organization was caught up in the situation. She undoubtedly suffered considerable distress over this, plus apparently she had begun to feel the strain of the

continuous competitive environment of politics. Besides disturbances within the party, though, there was a greater reason for with-
drawal from her active participation in politics. She was ill. Earlier
in her life she had suffered an injury in an automobile accident that
gave her trouble for the rest of her life. Because of it, or some other
undisclosed reason, she had developed a limp and ultimately she
was seen as usually being transported in a wheelchair during the
last period of her life.

She finally resigned from her post in the Democratic Party
in 1944, one year prior to her death, bringing to a close her involvement with it in sponsorship of those many events and public
appearances. She sent the following message to the State
Democratic Convention that year:

> I have long been a member of the Democratic Party and
> for sixteen years I have served as National
> Committeewoman from this state. I love politics and the
> Democratic Party. This is the first time since I was first
> called on to serve my party, that I have failed it. It is with
> regret that I must refuse now, but I am ill and do not feel that
> I would be able to serve my party as it should be served and
> therefore I must refuse.[72]

She had held strong sway and influence over the party for
all those years of ups and downs. Her presence would not soon be
forgotten among friends or enemies. As one commentary expressed
it: "Politicians liked her or seemed to fear her . . .,"[73] and *Time* magazine described her thus:

> . . . a fiery-eyed, saber-tongued heiress . . . Politicians soon
> learned to respect her; she could drink, cuss and connive
> with the best of them, out-spend practically all of them.[74]

Some have suggested that Clara Driscoll may have had a
drinking habit that bordered on being a problem toward the end of
her days, as it was said her husband may have had. There is no

recorded evidence of this, even though the *Time* article refers to her drinking with politicians in competitive situations. Her close friends always insisted such was not the case, and her personal physician and long-time friend, Dr. McIver Furman, described her, when asked later, as a "controlled drinker."[75]

Clara Driscoll had built the Robert Driscoll Hotel to memorialize her brother, and she spent her last days there in her penthouse as a virtual recluse much of the time apparently without the company of friends around her. It would seem she became one of those "poor little rich girls" at the end of her life, whose illusions had suffered over the years, and now she had become a very lonely woman and no one with whom she felt she could share her final days. She is reported to have locked herself in her apartment periodically, refusing to see or talk to anyone for days at a time during the last of her life.[76]

After one of these self-chosen confinements she made a remark to a Corpus Christi friend that seems to conflict with her public image but might be surprisingly revealing of some of Clara Driscoll's inner psyche. She told Mrs. J. C. Wilde that "she preferred her white-faced Hereford cows to people as the cows didn't ask her for money."[77]

Clara Driscoll died of a cerebral hemorrhage on July 17, 1945. She was alone in her penthouse except for her nurse and her physician. She was sixty-four years of age.

The entire state and the Democratic Party throughout the nation mourned her death. There were many tributes from near and far from those who had benefited from her generosity.

The Daughters of the Republic of Texas requested that she be given a burial site in the State Cemetery in Austin, but it was declined by her estate trustees, because of her previously stated preference that she be buried in the family mausoleum in the Masonic Cemetery in San Antonio.

Her body lay in state in the Alamo Chapel from 10:00 a.m.

to 1:00 p.m., one of the few people ever accorded this honor. Simple funeral rites were held at St. Mark's Episcopal Church in San Antonio and she was laid to rest with her father, mother and brother in their mausoleum as requested.

Clara Driscoll had been very generous with her money in many instances with seemingly no limit to her generosity in an almost impulsive spirit it appears in many cases. In other instances, though, as her Last Will and Testament reflects, there are some almost penurious gestures with regard to some of her more humble personal servitors. Yet, all of those loyal people were remembered on a long term basis, even if not a grandiose one.

She did make a grandiose and extremely generous gesture, however, toward leaving a legacy for a very worthy cause that had been her long-term dream. The major recipient of the bulk of her fortune was the Driscoll Foundation Children's Hospital in Corpus Christi. The Foundation conducted nationwide studies which gathered information that resulted in a hospital with some of the most remarkable pediatric services and facilities for children in Texas and all of the Southwest. The Foundation provided for a free clinic and hospital "for crippled, maimed or diseased children born in Texas whose parents cannot pay for assistance." No Texas child who cannot afford treatment has ever been turned away. "It is an institution that is a living memorial that testifies to the magnanimity of the childless woman who dreamed of its creation,"[78] and it is another glimpse into the inner part of the complex mind and personality of this "poor little rich girl," Clara Driscoll.

There are many varied images of this legendary Texas woman that come to mind in reflecting on what she was really like, and each one seems to fit a special event or time in her life. But one image that is attributed to her that doesn't seem to fit, is that of a "ridin', ropin', rancher," which she is reported to have called herself. At the same time, though, she also was quoted as saying on one occasion that "while she liked ranching, she did not think it was an occupation for a woman to be engaged in." [79]

Martha Anne Turner's biography of her describes her ranch image in these words:

> Quite literally Clara Driscoll attained young girlhood with the bawl of a yearling in her ears and the hot burning acrid smell of hot burning cowhide in her nostrils. By her own admission she was equally skilled behind a revolver or a rifle, was born and bred to the saddle, proficient with a lariat. In fact she was capable of doing almost anything her father's ranch hands could do except bulldog a steer. [80]

The puzzlement about that picture is the fact that young Clara left home sometime before she was ten years old to attend the private school in New York City and then went on to France to finish her schooling there. She did not return for quite some time after that to the ranch home in Texas and by then she was eighteen years old. Her life following that soon took her away from the ranch again until after her brother's death in 1929 when she was forty-eight years old.

And so, when did Clara Driscoll acquire all those skills of the open range she is said to have had? There were no pictures found of her demonstrating twirling a rope nor even riding a horse. Very few ten year old girls and younger, as a matter of fact, have achieved great proficiency in most of those things other than riding, at least rarely at that tenderfoot age. Somehow, that image doesn't seem to fit this lady, anymore than the one suggested by the *Time* magazine article.

An entirely different picture of Clara Driscoll does come to mind, however. The image that does fit, beyond any doubt, is the one associated with the Alamo. That famous act of Miss Driscoll's in 1905 of advancing her own money made her an instant and indelible icon in Alamo lore. In an era that idolized and immortalized its heroes and heroines, no one could touch her reputation as the sole "Savior of the Alamo," the edifice that became the symbol of Texas liberty and freedom, and no one has been able to touch it since. She is a figure of unequaled admiration and respectful devotion in the minds of the Daughters of the Republic of Texas, and they have repeated the story of her generosity as a mantra through the years. Consciously or otherwise, they in turn have helped perpetuate that story, whether it is entirely factual or not, just or unjust.

Clara Driscoll's name is synonymous with the Daughters of the Republic of Texas and with the Alamo. No matter what else may ever be said about her, there is no disputing the fact that her generosity at that moment of crisis most assuredly made it possible for her to do her part, "in her own way," to help "save the Alamo."

~ ~ ~ ~ ~ ~ ~ ~ ~ ~

Echoes Are Still Heard

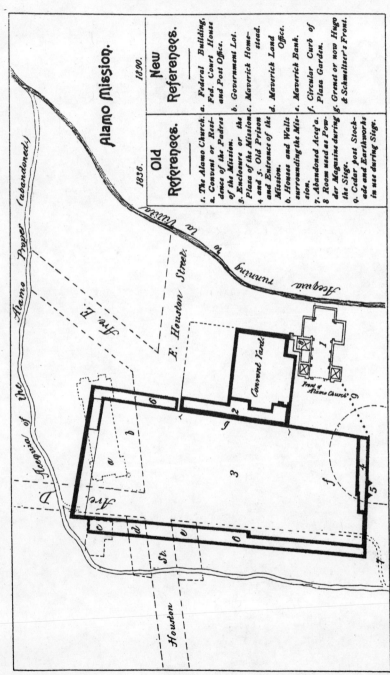

FROM WILLIAM CORNER'S *SAN ANTONIO DE BEXAR*, SAN ANTONIO, TEXAS, BAINBRIDGE & CORNER, CHRISTMAS, 1890.

This map from *San Antonio de Bexar* by William Corner depicts his conception of the plan of the old Mission San Antonio de Valero compound at the time of the Battle of the Alamo in 1836. The dotted lines show the changes that had been made by 1890. This map may have been used as a reference by Miss De Zavala along with other more in-depth research material.

Chapter Eight

Echoes Are Still Heard

— ". . . if the men had blown it up, the women
wouldn't have been blowing it up ever since."[1]
— Nettie Houston Bringhurst

*T*hat remark was made in 1909 by the daughter of Sam
Houston, Antoinette "Nettie" Houston Bringhurst. She was the fifth
of the eight children of Margaret Lea and Sam Houston. Born in
1852, she died in 1932 at age 80, as the result of an automobile
accident and is buried in the "Alamo City" of San Antonio, where
she lived the last several years of her life.

She lived a long life filled with colorful stories of her
famous father and Texas history facts and folklore of all kind, and
she was herself an acclaimed storyteller. She was a noted poet and
a historian, college educated and married to a college professor.
"Nettie" Houston Bringhurst was a forthright champion of what she
stood for, but a fair and controlled one. She served as State
Historian of the DRT for several years, including that turbulent
time of the "Second Battle for the Alamo."[2] She also was said to
have been opposed to the destruction of the Hugo-Schmeltzer
Building, the cause of that "Second Battle," because of what she
believed to be the historic role it had played in the original Battle
of the Alamo.

Sam Houston's daughter always contended that historic battle would never have happened if her father's order had been followed. His order to 'blow up' the Alamo was the result of a significant event that took place just prior to the time of the battle in
February of 1836.

In September of 1835, a contingent of Mexican troops
arrived in San Antonio on a mission to restrain local citizens from

active resistance to the centralist tendencies being established by the President of Mexico, General Antonio Lopez de Santa Anna. The troops under the command of Santa Anna's brother-in-law, General Martín Perfecto de Cós, had come to San Antonio and they were quartered in the old Mission San Antonio de Valero compound which had been converted into a military fort earlier by Spain. Three months after the Mexican troops had moved into the Alamo Fort, as it had begun to be called, they were overwhelmed by a group of the resisting Texians in a skirmish in an outlying area of town. General Cós was forced to sign a treaty agreeing to take his troops and return to Mexico and never come back.

Sam Houston, the commander of the army of Texian revolutionists, learned just six weeks later that the Mexican Army was returning in great numbers, this time under the command of an outraged President, General Santa Anna himself. Houston ordered that everything in the path of the approaching army which could be of any use to them be destroyed, or 'blown up'. This included the Alamo Fort, of course. The order obviously was not carried out and the result was the well-known defeat and tragic loss of lives of all the defenders. Some have said that the claim of his order to 'blow up the Alamo' was concocted by Houston afterward to win favor with the public.

In any case, Nettie Houston Bringhurst had grown up with the story of her father's order to 'blow up the Alamo,' and other stories of the Texas Revolution, and from her own study of history her knowledge of the part of the Hugo-Schmeltzer property in the battle was well grounded. Her somewhat sarcastic sounding but nonetheless rather sad conclusion made in 1909 regarding the Alamo, whether based on a true claim by Sam Houston or not, still seems to be appropriate at times. As with all sensitive subjects, the pros and cons of this Alamo battle never seem to become final. And so, echoes from women of the "second battle of the Alamo" as well as those from the first, have continued and are still heard from time to time, even today.

Yes, the story of that Alamo controversy which took place in the early 1900's, which became known as the "Second Battle for the Alamo," is still a sensitive subject and it has many conflicting accounts. Over the years the DRT has had many members who have carried on those accounts of how Clara Driscoll was the "Savior of the Alamo," but the contributions toward that cause by another "savior" of the famous site, Miss Adina De Zavala, seem to have died with her, except for a few voices in the wilderness which are heard from time to time. And, Clara Driscoll continues to be given all the credit for "saving" it by most people.

In trying to determine the best way to handle this complicated matter of stories within a story, it became evident that no matter how it was told, a certain amount of duplication was unavoidable. The arrangement finally chosen was to give the fuller account in this chapter and a briefer summary in the chapter on each of the two principal women involved as it occurred in the life of each.

The more detailed account in this chapter, which is really necessary for a more complete understanding of both sides, evolved into an account told primarily from the viewpoint of Adina De Zavala as it turned out. The reason for this is more than just an effort to bring better balance to the fact that versions of the story have been told and re-told in the past by numerous writers, all based on the well publicized accounts relating Clara Driscoll's part in this famous Alamo event, with Miss De Zavala's contributions rarely being mentioned. The other and more important reasons for this are based on two even more simple facts: (1) Miss De Zavala was on the scene and in the thick of the battle at all times, and (2) she wrote her own personal accounts of what happened and she kept her own records. Many of these records, unfortunately, are not readily available at a variety of sources, but they are available in the De Zavala Collection at the Center for American History at the University of Texas in Austin, as well as some at the Library of the

University of the Incarnate Word in San Antonio. They are all accessible to anyone for research or review.

In the case of Miss Driscoll, on the other hand, she was not always present, and even when she was, the accounts of what happened were told by others. Also, oftentimes, in addition to being written at a later time, they were written by people who were not present for the happenings. An exception to this is one account of the famous "barricade" of the Hugo-Schmeltzer Building by Miss De Zavala. Two of the members of the Driscoll group obtained entry to the building in the middle of that three-day incident at the request of the leader of their group. One of them made a report on the situation as she viewed it. Her report can be found in the DRT *Fifty Years of Achievement*, a history of the first fifty years of their organization which can be found at the DRT Library at the Alamo. This and other accounts, which were written later, have been printed in several publications and are available at the Alamo and other libraries and research centers elsewhere. They all reflect, almost exclusively, versions of the events according to Miss Driscoll and her followers.

There are published reports of all the DRT Annual Meetings relating to this controversial incident, but these reports which are on file at the DRT Library at the Alamo are now only accessible there to the Daughters of the Republic of Texas.

In the final analysis, however, everyone must make up her/his own mind as to who really "saved the Alamo", but that decision should be based on accounts from both sides, not just one that tells only the Clara Driscoll side of the story.

The "Second Battle for the Alamo" did not begin nor end with that dramatic incident on February 10, 1908, when Adina De Zavala barricaded herself in the old "long-barracks" building, as is often thought to be the case. The "second battle" had begun quite some time before that. Miss De Zavala, in fact, had been concerned about the use of the Hugo-Schmeltzer Building and its future since the moment she learned years ago, both from Texas history talk in her own home and her research that told her of the historic event that had occurred there. In 1889, when the city of San Antonio condemned the building,[3] she promptly took positive steps toward doing something about trying to save it. By then, which was before the DRT was formed, she had organized the group called the De Zavala Daughters for the purpose of the preservation of sites such as this and others that had been identified as historic. By 1908 she had been working one way or another, first with her own group and later as a member of the DRT, for a total of close to twenty years toward the objective of the preservation and ultimate restoration of this special place, which she felt should be a hallowed shrine.

From her research of the history of the old mission and the 1836 "Battle of the Alamo", she was convinced that underneath the wooden exterior structure of the commercial building, which now stood on the site, was the original two-story stone convento/barracks where some of the last few desperate moments of the Alamo Battle took place and where many of the Alamo heroes had died. Surprisingly, the general public in 1908 was under the misconception (as some still are to this day!) that the battle had occurred in the old church building itself and that most, if not all, of the 180-plus men had died within the church walls.

Adina De Zavala knew that the old "long barracks" and the church were both a part of the battle site, and a large area surrounding them as well, all of which had been a part of the original Mission San Antonio de Valero, founded at that location in 1724. She also knew the defenders who were not killed in the open compound, as the enemy scaled the walls, had retreated into the "long barracks", where the final assault was said to have occurred and the last of the defenders to have died. This building had originally been built as the convento to house the priests at the old Mission San Antonio de Valero.

The question arises with visitors today, as it must have then, if the complex was founded as a mission, how did that particular building come to be called the "long barracks", and how did the old mission get the name "The Alamo"? Weren't missions traditionally named for saints of the church?

During the period when Spain was establishing its claim in the New World, it built a great many missions in the area. The purpose was not only to spread the faith, but also to teach the native peoples a new life style, new skills and make of them loyal Spanish citizens. Therefore, the mission was not just a church and a house for the priests. The missions in this area were a community built around a rectangular walled-in plaza primarily for protection against hostile Indian attacks and possible French intrusion into the area. There was a convento to house the priests assigned to the mission, but there were apartment rooms along the outer enclosing walls to house the resident mission Indian families, also. There was a granary for food storage, shops in the center area of the compound for carpentry, blacksmithing, weaving and other skills, as well as various other buildings supporting the needs of the mission. The Alamo mission compound once had all of these in the area surrounding the church building and convento.

The mission as founded by Spain was named originally "Mission San Antonio de Valero" in honor of its patron saint, St. Anthony de Padua, and the Marquis de Valero, the viceroy of New Spain at the time of the founding. The so-called "long barracks" building was built originally as the convento to house the priests at the mission. The church originally was designed to have twin bell towers, with an elaborately decorated facade and a dome. It had been near completion with these features, when "it fell to the ground because of the poor skill of the architect" according to one inspection report,[4] and "through the ignorance of the builder", according to another.[5] It was never completed during the mission years nor for some time afterwards, and the building itself was never used as a church or a "chapel." An adjacent room on the north side of it was used for religious services during that time, however.

When the mission period ended in 1793, the properties were divided among the resident Indian families of each mission. Any buildings that remained standing at the site usually were left unoccupied and began to deteriorate. These of course always attracted squatters and looters, as was the case with Mission San Antonio de Valero.

Early in the 1800's, about ten years after the mission closed, a company of Spanish cavalry soldiers was sent up to the town of San Antonio de Bexar from a village in northern Mexico called El Alamo de las Parras. Their duty was to subdue possible uprisings in the area related to Mexico's struggle for independence from Spain. They were to reclaim and occupy the buildings of the old religious mission.

The church ruins were of no use to them but the remainder of the compound that was salvageable was repaired and adapted for their use. The convento was converted into quarters to house the troops and it became known as the "long barracks", not only because of its new use, but because of its unusually long, narrow shape. The men who were quartered there were called "los soldados del Alamo", referring to the village from which they had come. Thus the two names, "long barracks" and "The Alamo", were a natural evolution. They became so commonly used in fact that the original names were almost completely forgotten, even to this day.

Many people do not know that the old church building ever had any other name than "The Alamo". It has been said some of the men who died there in fact never knew the complex had ever been anything but a military fort known by that name.

At the time of the battle the church was nothing but a roofless shell with collapsing walls barely enclosing the intended church area. The "long barrack", however, and some other parts of the rest of the compound walls were still standing. A few months before the 1836 battle, during the latter part of 1835, the Mexican army had reinforced the walls making it into a fortified compound to control the Texas revolutionary uprisings, just as the Spanish had done earlier to control Mexico. In the "Siege of Bexar" in San Antonio in December of 1835, the commander of the Mexican troops, General Cós, was captured by the Texans and a treaty requiring the Mexican army to return to Mexico was signed. When the Mexican troops vacated the Alamo compound, the Texans quickly moved in and set up their own defense operation there. Six weeks later the Mexican army returned under General Santa Anna and the "Battle of the Alamo" began. The thirteen day assault ended with the fall of the Alamo on March 6, 1836, with no combat survivors left among the defeated Texans, and the compound in almost complete ruins. Some accounts state that Santa Anna had ordered most of the complex destroyed after the battle ended.

After the battle, the remains of the old mission/fort laid in silent abandonment and continued to deteriorate for the next ten years or so. In 1845 Texas voted to join the United States and the flag of the Republic of Texas was finally lowered for the last time in February of 1846. In 1847 the U.S. Army leased the property from the Catholic Church to establish a supply warehouse operation for the forts along the southwestern U.S. frontier. All that was left of the complex by then were the walls of the church ruins and the deteriorating convento/"long barracks" building. The rest had fallen down completely and most of the loose stones had been carried off by looters.

The U.S. Army covered the roofless church with a peaked roof and finished off the jagged front wall ruin with the now famous "stair-step-and-loop" parapet and used the building as a storage warehouse. The fancy facade not only finished off the front of the building nicely, but it hid the peaked roof from view as well.

THE ALAMO AND "LONG BARRACKS" CA. 1868.
(The UT Institute of Texan Cultures, from the *San Antonio Light* Collection)

Shown above are the two rebuilt structures, the "long barracks" on the left and the church with a horse-drawn wagon being driven through the front door of the hallowed shrine of today.

The "long barracks" building was converted into offices for the army supply depot and it was given a peaked roof, also. The two buildings were occupied by army personnel, either federal or confederate, for over 25 years. In 1876, with the opening of the new United States army post, Ft. Sam Houston, on "Government Hill" at the edge of town, the military supply depot operation moved out of the Alamo site and left it unoccupied once more.

The buildings did not remain vacant for long this time, though. The next year a new merchant in town, Honoré Grenet, purchased the "long barracks" site from the Catholic Church for $19,000.[6] Mr. Grenet converted the building into a fancifully designed warehouse and general merchandise store with an incredible variety of goods. When he opened his doors for business, a local newspaper described the event:

"Mr. Grenet signalized the commencement of the New Year by moving into the Alamo building . . . which he has thoroughly renovated and painted and dedicated to the peaceful arts of commerce, although it is still suggestive of warlike purposes, with its imposing facade on the north, south, and west sides, and its towers bristling with cannon pointing in every direction. A handsome gallery extends along the whole building, and this corridor in connection with the aisles running through the store will allow a promenade of nearly a mile in length, which feat of pedestrianism must be accomplished if a person makes an inspection of the entire array of goods displayed on counters and tables provided for the purpose. Upstairs and downstairs there is an ocean of goods of every imaginable description which it would be next to impossible to give a tithe of, besides extensive warerooms filled to overflowing with tier upon tier of domestic and imported liquors, flour from the most celebrated St. Louis mills, while piles on piles of sacked coffee and barrels of refined, and hogsheads of Louisiana sugars, tierces, kegs and cases of lard, butter, etc. etc. . . . The second story is conveniently reached by four stair-ways of easy ascent where dry goods, clothing, notions, boots, shoes, plated ware, china and fancy goods and attractive novelties abound in bewildering profusion."[7]

The wooden exterior structure was painted, the peaked roof the army had put on was either partially removed or hidden from view by the top of the entire structure which was finished off with a crenelated border, suggestive of a medieval military fortification, with corner look-out towers and some large wooden cannons on the roof. It was Mr. Grenet's interpretation of what the fortress might have looked like from which the Alamo defenders fought, as he imagined it.

HONORÉ GRENET EMPORIUM, 1882
(From a handbill, 1882, advertising sale of the Alamo property, as reproduced in
The Texas Pioneer, Vol. X, No. 2, p. 5. Daughters of the Republic of Texas Library, CN94. 47.)

Of course, it bore only a faint resemblance to the original structure, but it certainly proved one thing—that he apparently must have known that was the building where much of the fighting had occurred. Miss De Zavala had undoubtedly informed him of it. In any case, it was Grenet's tribute to the heroes, whom he greatly admired, at a time when their sacrifice had not yet captured the interest of the world of commercial "progress". He even made an area in the building into something of a museum to honor them and showed it off with reverent pride. According to Miss De Zavala he had announced his plans to leave the building as a gift to the people of San Antonio and Texas in memory of the heroes.[8]

Mr. Grenet's untimely death in 1882, only two years after opening his enormous emporium, prevented that plan from being executed, however, and it brought about another change in the "long barracks", and the status of the "Chapel" as well. His estate sold the "long barracks" building to another merchandise company, Hugo-Schmeltzer, for $28,000 and the Catholic Church sold the "Chapel" to the State of Texas in 1883 for $20,000.[9] The State turned the management of the "Chapel" over to the City of San

219

Antonio to be operated as a museum on the Battle of the Alamo and Texas history in general.

HUGO SCHMELTZER STORE CA. 1880'S
(Institute of Texan Cultures.)

The Hugo-Schmeltzer Company removed some of Grenet's bizarre fortification features from the "long barracks" structure and created an "eyesore" of their own in the opinion of some. For a time they operated a business similar to Mr. Grenet's with a variety of goods including a retail/wholesale liquor business according to deed records.[10]

Before long, however, they closed their business at this location and built a new store on East Houston Street,[11] but they continued to use the "long barracks" as a storage facility. After they moved out, it went into serious decline and the city condemned the misfit building, declaring it unsafe.[12]   During this same time period a business called the "Alamo Beer Garden Saloon and Restaurant" opened on the other side of the Alamo Church.

Soon afterward the Hugo-Schmeltzer Company decided to make their property available for sale and Miss De Zavala was contacted about the option to buy. A letter from the Honorable W. O. Murray, a member of the state senate at the time described the situation that led to Mr. Schmeltzer's contacting Miss De Zavala. The letter was included in Governor O. B. Colquitt's *Message to the Thirty-third Legislature Relating to the Alamo Property (See p. 323)*. The Senator's letter with Governor Colquitt's introduction to it are quoted here:

TRUSTWORTHY INFORMATION.

The following letter from Hon. W. O. Murray, now and for a long time a member of the State Senate, and before his membership in the Senate, a member of the House of Representatives, is of importance, because it shows how the negotiations for the sale of the part of the Alamo owned by Mr. Schmeltzer and his associates began:

AUSTIN, TEXAS, February 19, 1913.

Governor O. B. Colquitt, Austin, Texas.

DEAR GOVERNOR: Knowing that you have devoted a great deal of time gathering data, both modern and ancient, with reference to the history of the Alamo and its purchase by the State of Texas, it occurs to me that I might be able to give you a little inside information with reference to the sale of the property from Hugo & Schmeltzer to the State.

In the early spring of 1899 or 1900 - I am not positive as to the date - I was in the office of Hugo & Schmeltzer, engaged in a business transaction between the firm and myself. It was about 1 o'clock p. m. I was in Mr. Schmetlzer's private room when one of the office men opened the door and told Mr. Schmeltzer that Mr. . . . . had been in the office in the morning and had requested him to tell Mr. Schmeltzer "that he would give him $85,000 for that property." The old man arose from his seat and motioned his hand to the young man, saying, "Tell him it is not on the market, not on the market, and that I do not care to see him."

He turned to me and asked me if I could spare the time to talk with him a while. I replied that I could. He began to talk to me about the early history of Texas, but we were interrupted every few minutes by someone opening the door and addressing him with reference to some business matter. He finally remarked, "We can not talk here; come with me to some quiet place where we can talk." We went across the plaza and into a back room of Kalteyer's drug store, or that vicinity, I think.

The old man rehearsed his early life, telling me of his boyhood days and of how he earned his first dollar, giving biographical sketches of many of the old Texans and of the early history of the State.

He also fought again the battles of the Confederacy and seemed to be an unreconstructed rebel. I suppose we began this conversation about 2 o'clock p. m., and about sundown he asked me what could he do with the Alamo property; if there was not some way by which the State of Texas could be induced to take it and guarantee the proper care and preservation of the Alamo?

I concluded from all he had said that he contemplated, or rather was anxious to make the State a present of the property. I told him that I could only speak "extempo," as it was a matter I had not given much thought to, but that in my judgment, people as a rule did not think much of anything unless they paid for it; that the Alamo was a shrine at which all Texans would be glad to bow; that it ought not to be preserved to posterity by charity on the donation of a private individual, hence my advice would be to arouse public sentiment first, educating the people to the point that they would be willing to purchase and preserve the Alamo.

He replied: "I am very old; I can not live but a short time, and what I do I must do quickly; if I leave the matter open until such time as the people may become interested in same, I will have passed to my reward beyond, and besides," he remarked, "I have never been in the public eye of the people of Texas and do not believe they would pay any attention to my suggestions."

I told him he would not be expected to do the work necessary to call the matter to the attention of the people of Texas; that he could find someone else who would gladly do it. He asked me who. I told him of Mrs. Looscan of Houston, who is known to be a very patriotic woman and a sister of my most intimate and personal friend, and that I was sure she would be willing to undertake the work in Houston, and that I felt constrained to think that Miss Adina De Zavala would be glad to take up the work in San Antonio.

We discussed this plan at length, he arguing that an effort of that kind was too uncertain; that he was too old to expect to live to see a consummation of this plan. I then told him not to wait; that it was not necessary to wait; that if the ladies would undertake the work that he could give them a contract of sale which would provide for consummating the sale even though he should die in the meanwhile.

After mature reflection this seemed to please him, and he told me he was going to act upon my advice. He then asked me what he ought to ask for the property. I told him that he ought to place as near the real value upon same as possible. I asked him what he thought it was worth by comparison to other property adjacent. After thinking a while he said he thought about $75,000. He said: "You heard the offer I had this evening of $85,000, and I am almost certain that I could sell the property in twenty-four hours for $100,000."

I then suggested that he place his price at $100,000 and head the subscription to the purchase with $25,000. This seemed to please the old man very much, and he thanked me kindly for so patiently listening to him and for the advice I offered, and remarked: "I think this is all right; I think I shall do it right away."

It was but a short time after this conversation when I saw in the newspapers that he had contracted with Miss De Zavala to sell her the property.

Very truly yours,
W. O. Murray.[13]

Mr. Gustav Schmeltzer tells of his part in his relationship with Miss De Zavala in a notarized statement issued later. The testimony of Mr. Schmeltzer on events as they occurred to the best of his recollection follows, corroborating what Miss De Zavala had always claimed.

"Testimony of Mr. Gustav Schmeltzer"

In order to assist in keeping a complete and correct record of the several transactions relative to the purchase of that part of the old Alamo, (the main building of the Alamo) occupied by the firm of Hugo, Schmeltzer & Co., I wish to state that Miss Adina de Zavala called to see me about the year 1892, with reference to securing the Alamo property owned by us; explaining the objects of the society of which she was President, and asked me to obtain for her the promise of all the owners, not to sell or offer the property to anyone else without notifying her, and giving the Chapter the opportunity to acquire it, to save it to the people of Texas, to be utilized as a Hall of Fame and Museum of History, Art, Literature and Relics.

This object meeting with my full approval, I spoke to the other parties in interest, and on her second visit, informed her that we would do as she had asked, giving her the refusal of the property. Miss de Zavala called again at various times, to inquire if we remembered our promise, and we answered that we did, and were in no hurry to sell. In 1900, she called again and stated that the Chapter was about to start an active campaign for the purchase money, and asked us to get the price. On consultation with Mr. Hugo, and the other owner, we agreed to contribute $10,000.00 and make the purchase price [to her Chapter] $75,000.00.

Miss de [sic] Zavala immediately went to Galveston and Houston in behalf of the cause, and shortly thereafter, the frightful disaster of the Galveston storm occurred; Miss de Zavala just missing by a few days being caught in Galveston. On account of the necessity of aiding the storm sufferers, the De Zavala Chapter again postponed its call for money for the purchase of the Alamo, and it was not until 1903 that the Chapter felt justified in bringing the matter before the public again. Miss De Zavala then brought and introduced to me the Chairman [Clara Driscoll] selected by herself, and ratified by the vote of the Chapter to take charge of the collections for the purchase, and to prosecute the work outlined by the Chapter. A written option was paid for and signed, and on February 10, 1904, the payment of the $25,000 was completed, and the several notes arranging for the balance of the amount due, were duly made out and signed.

(Signed.) G. SCHMELTZER.
San Antonio, Texas, September 24, 1908.

Affidavits as to signature of Mr. G. Schmeltzer were sworn to by Mr. Aug. Briam, Jr., who worked for the different companies of the Hugo, Schmeltzer people for 25 years, and who was secretary of the corporation at the time of the agreement and sale of the Alamo property; by Mr. Charles Heuermann, son of one of the members of the firm, who was also employed in the business.

By Mr. A. Sartor, a life-long friend of Mr. G. Schmeltzer.

By W. A. Wursbach, who was also employed by the firm and was acquainted with Mr. G. Schmeltzer for 30 years.

And by Mr. J. N. Brown, President of the Alamo National Bank, of San Antonio, Texas.

All subscribed and sworn to this 10th day of February, 1914. I, Wade H. Bliss, a Notary Public in and for Bexar County, Texas, do hereby certify that the foregoing is a true and correct copy of a statement dated September 24, 1908, signed "G. Schmeltzer," and of the affidavits attached thereto.

Witness my hand and seal of office the 10th day of February, 1914.
(Seal.)
Wade H. Bliss,
Notary Public, Bexar County, Texas[14]

According to a notarized statement for Mr. Charles Heuermann, the son of a founder member and himself an employee of the company, Miss De Zavala began what he described as: ". . . her frequent visits . . . during her negotiations and campaign for purchase of the old Alamo Fort".[15]

She made these "frequent visits" over an extended period of time, first as the representative of the De Zavala Daughters, a group of historic preservationists she had organized earlier, and then continued on behalf of the De Zavala Chapter of the DRT which they became when that organization was formed and her group joined it in 1893. She made many repeated visits during the years from the

226

time the property had been offered for sale in the 1890's up to the time of the crisis that was to arise in 1903.

Neither of the organizations she represented had funds of the magnitude for a purchase such as this, but Miss De Zavala was never one to be daunted by a challenge, not even a seemingly impossible one. She began a campaign appealing "to all Texans everywhere to assist in saving the Alamo Fort by contributing funds for its purchase", according to Mr. Heuermann. He further says:

> Miss De Zavala's patriotic work for the historic research, the marking and preservation of historic land-marks . . . , her zealous and untiring endeavor to save and preserve the Alamo appealed to me as a noble work and I gladly offered her such assistance as I could give.[16]

From her lifetime of research, Miss De Zavala knew the complete history of the entire landmark site, but the story of the significance of both of the only two remaining buildings of the Battle of the Alamo was to fall on deaf ears for the most part. To make her case more difficult it should be remembered that the "long barracks" had undergone many changes in the variety of uses it had endured following its famous use in the battle for Texas independence. First, the U.S. Army had made such drastic changes that the battle scarred building had all but lost its identity. Next, Mr. Grenet had created tremendous changes when he covered the two-story stone building with his "inartistic" wooden exterior. And then, the Hugo-Schmeltzer Company had made even further changes, making the building's identity still more obscure. But, according to Miss De Zavala's firm belief, none of these interim occupants, not the U.S. Army, nor Honoré Grenet, nor Hugo-Schmeltzer had destroyed the original two-story stone walls of the convento/"long barracks". Each had merely covered up what remained after the battle was over and they came into possession of it.

Miss De Zavala was convinced beyond all doubt that underneath the false wooden facade stood the hallowed stone walls of the original "long barracks", blood stained by martyrs, that should be preserved at any cost. In other words, by her adopted motto, 'she knew she was right and she went ahead'!

With characteristic determination she continued under her arrangement with the Hugo-Schmeltzer Company on the option to buy, but how to get the money to consummate the option was the real problem, and the solution seemed nowhere in sight. It was at this point that Clara Driscoll came upon the scene, and before long she would become known as the "Savior of the Alamo". For a time she was just exactly that for the De Zavala Chapter. The introduction to Miss Driscoll almost seems providential.

Mr. Heuermann's notarized statement continues with:

> When the firm received several other offers and was ready to sell, Miss De Zavala was notified, and she brought to the store and introduced a member of the society, Miss Clara Driscoll, stating that the society was now ready and willing to venture on the final purchase, and that Miss Driscoll, as Chairman and Treasurer of the De Zavala Chapter, Alamo Committee would conduct the business for the Chapter.[17]

Mr. Schmeltzer also had stated that Miss Driscoll was brought to him as shown in his testimonial quoted earlier.

Another story tells of how Miss De Zavala and Miss Driscoll first met and how a whole new perspective to the bleak future for the preservation of the "long barracks" building came about when Miss Driscoll was brought to Mr. Schmeltzer.

Pompeo Coppini, the eminent Italian born sculptor, who had emigrated to America and first settled in New York before moving to San Antonio, tells the story in his autobiography, *From Dawn to Sunset,* of how he helped bring the two together almost by chance. Miss De Zavala was one of the first people Coppini met soon after moving to San Antonio. When he told two of his new acquaintances

228

that one of his goals was to learn all he could about the history of the state of Texas which he had chosen as his new home, he was immediately referred to the person they considered to be the best one in town to help him. In his own words he described his meeting with Miss De Zavala:

> As I expressed myself to both Charlie Tobin and Frank Bushick, it was my desire to get a thorough knowledge of Texas history, in order to become a real Texan, and they both agreed that I should meet a noble woman who was carrying on a patriotic crusade to preserve all the historical landmarks, especially the Alamo and all other missions, and who was the granddaughter of the first Vice President of the Republic of Texas, a school teacher, and the president of the local chapter of The Daughters of the Republic of Texas, and a member of many other patriotic organizations. This was Miss Adina De Zavala, who was then living in the same house where she lives today, [1949] on the corner of Fourth and Taylor Streets.

> Mr. Tobin did not lose any time, and from Mr. Bushick's office at the old *San Antonio Express* Building, on the corner of Crockett and Navarro, by the river, we walked to Miss Adina's home. She received us immediately. I will never forget that eventful moment. She was an exceptionally beautiful woman, with gorgeous black [blue-black?] eyes, black hair and very fair complexion. She carried herself with dignity but also with a gentleness of manner, and there was friendliness in her speech, and indeed all that was necessary for the inspiration I had looked for, from one who was to be my first teacher of Texas history. She seemed delighted to meet me, and to look forward to furnishing me with all that I told her was required, in order to learn to love Texas, and especially San Antonio, as if it were my birthplace, and to dedicate not only my art, but my whole life in order to contribute my very best to its glorification! . . . Miss Adina De Zavala opened the gate of

a new road, . . . I felt that I was re-born a Texan.[18]

Coppini's wife, Elizabeth, and Adina soon became fast friends, too, over their common interest in historic preservation. Mr. Coppini told how "Lizzie" and "Miss Adina" made daily rounds in the Coppini horse and buggy, pleading with merchants for contributions of brick, stones, lumber, cedar posts, wire and any such items they could get to repair the fences, walls, etc. of the four old Spanish missions located on the outskirts of town.

Coppini's talent as an artist and a sculptor of skill soon became recognized and he began to receive commissions both locally and throughout the state.

The Hugo-Schmeltzer property had been on the market for quite some time when one day Coppini was in consultation about a commission with one of San Antonio's leading architects of the day, Mr. Harvey L. Page. Mr. Page made Coppini an offer that at first sounded like "a joke" to him. Page said:

> "I have something big for you, Pompeo, something real big—a ten foot statue to be made of Italian marble of David Crockett." I smiled as though it were a joke, but he showed me the plans he was making for a big hotel that was to join the so called Alamo, the San Antonio de Valero Chapel.

> "Oh no!" I said, "They could not do that, for it is sacred ground. It would be a sacrilege to commercialize that spot!"

> "Come, come," Harvey said: "these people had many chances to save that property, but there is not a soul in the city who would subscribe a five-cent piece to make it a shrine of patriotism, while if this Yankee syndicate built a hotel there, and put up a big statue of David Crockett in the foyer, they would do more to call the visitor's attention to the history of the Alamo than what

these Texans, or San Antonians, are able to do for themselves."

He was surprised at my lack of appreciation for getting a good job, and at my morbid sentimentality for thinking so much of the commercialization of that spot. "What in the name of common sense do you call that ugly building there?" he asked. From his office window we could see the Hugo & Schmeltzer Building, a grotesque half stone, half gingerbread lumber misfit construction of a country wholesale merchandise store and warehouse, certainly not fit to be in the most prominent location of the town. "They want to sell, even though they realize themselves that if a hotel gets there, it is the end of any chance for that sacred ground to be reclaimed by the people or by the State! Well," Harvey said, "the Daughters of the Republic of Texas have had option on that property for some time, but it will soon expire. They have not been able to do a thing about it. The people are not interested, and a beautiful hotel in that spot will mean more to them that the saving of sacred soil. The Menger Hotel is too antiquated, and they are making no improvements; there is not a decent hotel in town to attract tourists, and the Eastern syndicate will mean business, and will get the property as soon as the Daughters of the Republic of Texas option expires, which will be very shortly."

I walked out of his office as if he had had me standing on burning coals, and I made a beeline for Miss Adina De Zavala's home on Fourth and Taylor.[19]

Knowing of her long time efforts to purchase the property, Coppini had run practically all the way from Page's office near Alamo Plaza to Miss De Zavala's house, which was only a few blocks away, to warn her of the unbelievable threat to the sacred site. Breathless and excited he related the devastating news:

"You know Miss Adina [as she was customarily

called] they are going to build a hotel alongside of the Alamo Chapel if you do not find a way to purchase the Hugo-Schmeltzer Building before your option expires. Mr. Page is drawing the plans for an Eastern syndicate. They know that you cannot raise the money; but we must find a way."[20]

He described her reaction as that of one who is abnormally calm momentarily "as when stunned by an unexpected blow". She finally said:

"Well, what can I do about it? You know, more than anyone else, what struggles I have to go through, even to keep up the missions so they will not fall to pieces, or go beyond repair. What is in your mind?"[21]

He was appalled that commercial greed was behind such a scheme rather than the patriotic respect for the site he felt should be there. The idea occurred to him that perhaps a counter plan by the Menger Hotel which was already right next door to the Alamo Chapel might be the answer to the unthinkable idea of such desecration. He suggested that the two of them go immediately and appeal to the operators of the Menger to fight the competition of another hotel so close by.

The two hurried off to the Menger Hotel to present their case, only to find the owners, the Kampmans, away on a trip to Europe. Mrs. George Eichlitz, sister of Mrs. Kampman, received them but said regretfully neither she nor anyone else associated with the hotel had the authority to commit to anything of that nature. According to Mr. Coppini's account, Mrs. Eichlitz then remembered a rich and prominent young woman who was staying at the hotel and suggested she might be someone interested in helping them. Her name was Miss Clara Driscoll.

The twenty-two-year-old young heiress from Corpus

Christi was a member of an early Texas pioneer family that had risen from very modest means to become one of the wealthiest families in the state. They had extensive land and ranch holdings, and had become a family of influence. She was indeed an appropriate person to appeal to for help.

Miss De Zavala and Coppini presented the problem to Miss Driscoll in full detail describing in patriotic and passionate terms the outrageous sacrilege and insult of such an unthinkable thing happening to the sacred shrine, and so on. When the meeting was over, the two of them left the hotel with, as Coppini described it, "good reason to believe they had prevented the Hugo and Schmeltzer building from falling into the hands of an Eastern syndicate and that the sacred spot would be saved from commercialization".[22]

Miss Driscoll's followers did not tell this story however. Their accounts never explain just how and when Clara Driscoll learned of the facts surrounding the possible destruction of the "long barracks," but the claim is made that Miss Driscoll initiated the first contact with the Hugo-Schmeltzer Company that led to meetings with Adina De Zavala and others for the negotiations on the purchase of the property, and that she was responsible, almost exclusively, for the movement to obtain control of the building for the ultimate purchase.

Since there are differing claims still as to who initiated the move to purchase the Alamo "long barracks", Miss Driscoll or Miss De Zavala, it seemed appropriate to present the above testimonials here.

In the absence of other documented evidence of how Miss Driscoll became acquainted with the fact of the possible destruction of the "long barracks", it seems reasonable to accept Mr. Coppini's story and most certainly the letter of Senator Murray and the sworn testimony of Mr. Schmeltzer and that of Mr. Heuermann. From these accounts it appears Miss De Zavala had led Miss Driscoll to the point of putting her in the position to become the so called "Savior of the Alamo."

Regardless of who initiated what, it was known that Miss Driscoll was already upset over how little attention was paid to the preservation of this important site of the battle for Texas liberty, and surely must have felt also that it would be a sacrilege to desecrate it further with such a crassly commercial project. She had stated her dismay over the way the Alamo was treated in a letter earlier to the *San Antonio Express* newspaper upon returning from a trip abroad. She was to say this in eloquent terms later many times. And now to the good fortune of all who were concerned about the fate of the historic site, the rich young heiress was able to come to the rescue.

Along with her patriotic respect for the heroes of the Alamo, there can be no doubt that Clara Driscoll also had an instinctive sense of high drama, and a flair for expressing it as well. She was to display this talent quite noticeably in her theatrical ventures in New York soon thereafter, as well as in other ways in her lifetime subsequently. In all probability this trait helped her make the bold and prompt decision she was to make about saving the Alamo property. Plus one other very helpful attribute—money. As one writer observed, "It is doubtful if she ever wanted anything she could not get"[23], because money will usually buy most things one wants.

Clara Driscoll did not offer to purchase the property outright, however, as was mistakenly thought to be the case by most people at the time, and surprisingly is still thought to be so by some today. But when negotiations began and there was no other alternative, she did provide personal funds for the immediate emergency by making the initial down payment and pledged her continued financial help as the fund raising efforts went forward.

Hugo-Schmeltzer had given Miss De Zavala and her organization first refusal on the property as indicated in the testimony of Mr. Schmeltzer.[24] When the matter of the hotel possibility arose, Hugo-Schmeltzer notified her as promised that they were ready to sell, and she was ready with a plan, thanks to Mr. Coppini's warning and Miss Driscoll's offer to help. As described, she brought Clara Driscoll to the Hugo-Schmeltzer office and introduced her as the chairman of the committee of the De Zavala Chapter in charge of the transaction of business regarding the purchase of this property and a written option was signed and the initial payment paid by Miss Driscoll,[25] as stated in Schmeltzer's sworn testimony.

Under the agreement the purchase price was set at $75,000 and Miss Driscoll gave them her personal check for $500 for a thirty day option on the "long barracks" building.[26] At the end of the thirty days, the DRT De Zavala Chapter was to pay $4,500 more, whereupon the option would be extended for one year. This would allow time to continue to raise funds, enabling them to be in a position to come to an agreement for payment of the full amount.

A vigorous campaign was launched by Miss De Zavala and Miss Driscoll to raise the money, first of all to repay Miss Driscoll her initial $500 advance, and then continue toward the $4,500 needed for the one-year extension. From the beginning, the campaign fell far short of their goal just as Harvey Page had speculated it would. When the thirty-day period ended, they had collected a moderate amount, but were nowhere near $4,500 necessary to extend their option for the next year. Since Miss Driscoll in effect had obligated the DRT for funds not yet raised, it would appear that the better part of such valor would be to pay the needed amount herself. And this she did with her personal check for $3,478.25. This, plus the amount of funds raised thus far, was paid to Hugo-Schmeltzer to meet the $4,500, thereby securing the option one more year until February 10, 1904.[27]

The campaign toward that next goal continued then with letters throughout the state requesting donations, plus various fund raising activities by all the DRT chapters statewide. At the end of the year, they were still far short of their goal, and once again Clara Driscoll generously came to the rescue. This time she made the big decision that was to make her famous as the "Savior of the Alamo". If she had not done this, not only would she have sacrificed the entire amount she had advanced thus far, but more important, the DRT would have lost the historic property to commercial development, in all probability.

Again Miss Driscoll met the requirement, this time with her personal check for $17,812.02. This was the balance between what had been collected in contributions thus far, amounting to $7,187.98, and the total $25,000 down payment required on this date. The terms of the agreement called for the new owner, Miss Driscoll, then to sign five promissory notes of $10,000 each , plus interest at 6 percent per annum, to cover the balance of the total purchase price of $75,000.[28]

Clara Driscoll was now the owner of what she had once described as a "hideous barracks-like looking building,"[29] but which to Adina De Zavala was a sacred and historic site under disguise. However, not only had Clara Driscoll shown fine patriotic spirit in these generous acts, but all of her contributions to save the building had been made with no real assurance of reimbursement. Why would she do this?

There is no question that what Miss Driscoll did was magnanimous and extraordinary, but the fact is, whether reimbursement was a factor in her decision or not, she was reimbursed less than a year later. This is something that was not known by a great many people then, and strangely enough is still unknown by most today.

Six months later, in August of 1904, after she made these initial payments and obligated herself for the balance, the Democrat Party of Texas voted at their convention to include a plank in their platform proposing that the state legislature purchase the property and reimburse Miss Driscoll. On January 26, 1905, when the Texas Legislature met for the 29th Session, they voted to approve the reimbursement of Clara Driscoll for the amount she had advanced to date, and assume the notes she had signed to complete the purchase of the Hugo-Schmeltzer property. This became a matter of official record when it was signed into law under the Legislative Act dated August 31, 1905, Twenty Ninth Legislature of Texas, House Bill No. 1. This Bill also gave custody to the DRT of "the property thus acquired, together with the Alamo church property already owned by the state."[30]

Since Miss Driscoll was reimbursed, it seems safe to say her actual contribution to the project of "saving the Alamo", when all was said and done, was not what the public has been caused to believe, either then or now.

In the De Zavala Papers there is a sheet of "DRT General Society" stationery which is reproduced on the following page. This hand written listing of the expenses and receipts in connection with the Hugo-Schmeltzer (Alamo) property shows a very clear financial picture.

This informal looking paper may have been merely a hand-written draft, but it contains figures that do not seem to match the accounting usually publicized. The figures show the total expenses as $82,334.62, and the total receipts as $79,767.74. This would leave a deficit of $2,566.28. The paper then states, "The expenditure of the sum of $2,566.28 was paid by me. (signed) Clara Driscoll." This would seem to suggest this was Miss Driscoll's only outright donation, if this accounting was final.

The "Statement" also shows under "Receipts, Received from the State—$65,000.00."This and other records clearly show that Miss Driscoll had been reimbursed for her other "donation," which was actually only an advancement of money, as it turned out. This was a fact neither she nor others seemed to speak of much at the time. In later years though it is stated more often, and frequently appears in print now.

This is a photostatic copy of that sheet:

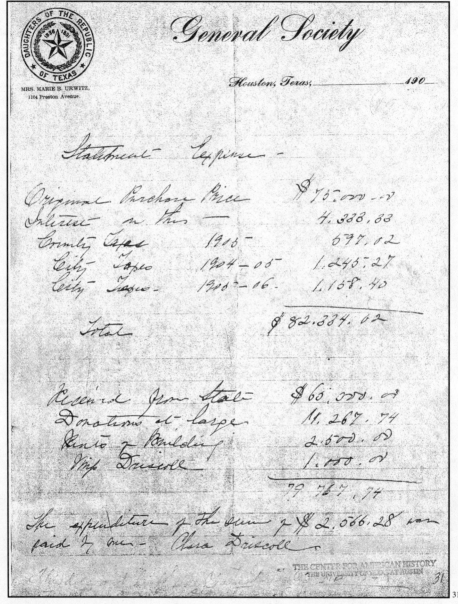

31

[Authors Note: The item second from last under the receipts listing is for "Rents of Building.." The building had been rented back to the Hugo-Schmeltzer Company as a storage facility after the DRT purchased it from them.]

Regardless, Clara Driscoll's unquestionably generous act of underwriting the funds needed in time of emergency, however it may have been offered, caused her to become known overnight and famous forever after as the "Savior of the Alamo".

This "glorious sounding" title, was due somewhat to the dramatic stories of the press throughout the country at the time. The stories presented merely the glamorous picture of a rich and beautiful young Texas heiress putting up the money to save a historic shrine from destruction. All the endless preliminary efforts to raise money and the tiresome and tedious financial arrangements that were involved were never included in those stories, nor was the specific building identified in most of them. The result was a mistaken belief, which for some people persists, that Clara Driscoll put up, without any repayment at any time, $75,000 needed to save "The Alamo", the Chapel, which was in danger of destruction. Of course, to the public in general "The Alamo" had come to mean simply the Alamo Chapel building. Nothing could be further from the truth all around.

To begin with, she did not put up all the money as has been shown, but only the "down-payment" needed at the moment to secure the property, with promise of the balance in the future. It should not be forgotten, however, that some money, even though it was far from the needed amount, had been collected already in the fund raising campaign from sincere and patriotic adult citizens who had answered the call for help, plus even some small contributions from earnest young school children. And, of course, the various DRT Chapters throughout the state had raised a moderate amount. All of this, small though it may have been, went in to the "saving" fund. Moreover, Miss Driscoll did not save the building that most people identified as "The Alamo", which was not in any danger. Instead she saved the "long barracks" building which was in danger of destruction.

Throughout the lifetime of Miss De Zavala and Miss

Driscoll, the so-called "Alamo" had looked the same to them as it looks today. They had never been concerned about its being destroyed because it was never in any danger.

The Alamo "Chapel," which had stood in ruins before and during the Battle of 1836, plus at least eleven years afterward, had been "saved" years ago when the U. S. Army leased it from the Catholic Church in 1848 and rebuilt the main body and gave it its famous facade. It had never been in danger of being destroyed from that day forward. Interestingly enough, although the interior was renovated more than once before the restoration as it appears today, no major changes have ever been made to the facade since the Army engineers finished their now famous design, circa 1850. Many people, even now, are under the misguided notion that at the time of the battle it looked as it does now. It did not—it was just a jagged ruin of four walls piled with rubble, except for two or three small roofed rooms built into the church originally, where a few women and children had huddled in terror during the battle.

In summary, the facts are: Miss Driscoll had not put up any money to save the "Alamo" Chapel itself. She had put up enough money to complete the down payment to save the "long barracks", plus obligate herself for the remainder. Further, she was reimbursed soon afterward for most of what she did contribute.

All the stress and uncertainty that had surrounded the attempts of Adina De Zavala to purchase the site or have the state do so, since as far back as the middle of 1890, had finally come to an end in the middle of 1904. The disappointment that she and Miss Driscoll had suffered during their unsuccessful efforts to raise the money needed—all this was over now, thanks to Clara Driscoll's generosity followed by the prompt action of the legislature.

The legislature's vote to reimburse Miss Driscoll and assume the responsibility of the site was a real triumph for all of the Daughters of the Republic, but it was especially so for the two who had spearheaded the campaign, Clara Driscoll and Adina De Zavala.

More so for Miss De Zavala undoubtedly than for Miss Driscoll—not financially, of course, but psychologically. Getting the Legislature to assume the responsibility of this site had been a major effort for Adina De Zavala for many years. At last it had done so.

Miss Driscoll's advancement of down payments and guarantee for the balance had indeed saved the "long barracks", and the world was well informed by the press of her act of generosity at that time, but the fact that she was reimbursed was never well publicized, not then nor now.

Miss De Zavala's role, not only during this dramatic period but prior to it, should never be underestimated. To give Clara Driscoll sole credit for "saving the Alamo" as has been done for so long is a grave discredit to Miss De Zavala. It is doubtful that money alone, not Miss Driscoll's nor anyone's, could have saved the historic place. Adina De Zavala had worked in many ways toward saving this site during much of the adult period of her forty-four years of life. This meant she was already hard at work on the problem when young Clara Driscoll was only a toddler.

In addition to all those years of work, credit should go to Miss De Zavala, also, along with Mr. Coppini, for bringing the matter to the attention of Miss Driscoll in the first place, if in fact the sequence of events was as he recalled it to have been. Unquestionably, Clara Driscoll was aware of the significance of the hallowed site of the Alamo, as were all Texans, but there is no recorded instance of any active involvement on her part to reclaim the site until around the time Miss De Zavala and Mr. Coppini are said to have appealed to her for help. There is evidence of her concern about the condition of the site which was expressed in writing in her letter published in the *San Antonio Express* newspaper at an earlier date. In that letter she deplored "the rundown appearance of the Alamo, huddled amid surroundings that were both distasteful and unworthy . . . and disgraceful".[32] She speaks in dramatic terms of how the "sinister old face frowns . . . as if it were still fighting".

. . . of how you might "Search the histories of the world and you will not find a deed to equal that of the men who died within the Alamo that Texas might be free . . ."[33]

Clara Driscoll's appreciation for this historic site of her Texas heritage was an apparently recent attitude. She had been taken by her mother as a young child to attend a select school in New York City and then at age eleven to Paris for further schooling. After she was graduated from the school in Paris, she and her mother traveled throughout Europe and the Orient where she had seen "the ancient wonders of the world", the glories of Greece and the ruins of Rome and more.[34] She had come home at age eighteen and seemed to have been suddenly awakened to some of the historic landmarks of her native land and what was literally in her own backyard—most notably the Alamo.

Miss De Zavala at that time, from evidence available, had not seen the splendors of the ancient world that might have made her aware of the history around her. She was born in the midst of the history around her and she lived her entire life surrounded by it. It had sustained her as her life's blood, and now she sustained it with her dedication to the preservation of it as her life's work.

When Clara Driscoll came back at age eighteen from an extended stay abroad, she had been struck by the lack of concern about the deteriorating condition of the Alamo and its surroundings and had written her letter to a San Antonio newspaper about the treatment of the hallowed site. Upon returning from her travels again two years later when she stopped in San Antonio, she was appalled to see that still nothing had been done, and she expressed her feelings about the place in writing again. It was at this fortuitous moment in time that Adina De Zavala and Pompeo Coppini had approached her for help and she had readily agreed. Inasmuch as the DRT, which Miss De Zavala represented, had an option on this property that distressed Miss Driscoll so much, obviously the best thing to do was join ranks with them, as no doubt Miss De

Zavala urged her to do. As the daughter of a family who were residents during the days of the Republic of Texas she was unquestionably eligible for membership and she took immediate steps to join the organization. She is recorded as joining the DRT on February 9, 1903, which was just days before the meeting arranged by Adina De Zavala with the Hugo-Schmeltzer Company to discuss the purchase of the Alamo property.

Adina De Zavala on the other hand joined the DRT soon after it was organized. Prior to that she had had countless talks with the Hugo-Schmeltzer Company for several years and had persuaded them to give her earlier group, the De Zavala Daughters, first option on the property.[35] When they joined the DRT as a new chapter, she arranged to have the option transferred. All this was before Miss Driscoll had come on to the scene and joined the DRT. Miss De Zavala had tried for years also to interest the state to support her plan for the restoration of the historic "long barracks" and the creation of a Texas history museum out of it.

In light of later developments, it is ironic that as a finale to all her years of preliminary work, Miss De Zavala, who is credited with drafting the bill the legislature passed which secured the purchase of the building, removed the coveted and expected control of it from her grasp simply by the way she worded the bill. This oversight did not become apparent to her at first, but its impact hit her with devastating results later. In addition, the bill as added on to by the legislature and passed, not only approved the appropriations for purchase of the property, but it also included the reimbursement of Miss Driscoll. Pearl Howard's article in *Holland's,* a popular magazine of the day, states from a personal interview with De Zavala:

> It was Miss De Zavala's persistence over a period of many years which resulted in the purchase of the Alamo. The Bill asking for appropriations of State funds to supplement the amount previously subscribed by private citizens earnestly solicited by Miss De Zavala and

her co-workers—was one which she herself drafted. It was adopted by the legislature and signed by the Governor as written by her, with practically no change in text:[36]

Thankfully, all of those years of uncertainty and the struggle for money to save the hallowed ground were over now—or so Miss De Zavala thought. The "long barracks" was now safe and secure, and the museum she had dreamed of establishing for so many years was to become a reality—or was it? Little did she realize that an even graver crisis would arise in the not too distant future that would cause her to do something that would put *her* name on the lips of thousands this time. It was a crisis that would be the highlight of her preservation efforts and it would overshadow anything she ever did before, or would ever do afterward, in the eyes of the public, and it would remain the one major thing that would be identified with her name forever.

For the moment though, the problem at hand was the matter of the design of the museum and the restoration process.

When the monumental business of saving the "long barracks" was finally accomplished, the complex question of the way the restoration would be handled and who would be in charge needed to be clarified. This was where the trouble would begin which apparently Miss De Zavala had not anticipated.

Adina De Zavala had written an actual draft of a bill which she submitted to the State Legislature requesting funds to purchase the Hugo-Schmeltzer Building. Further, she asked that custody of the two buildings, the Chapel and the "long barracks", be given to the DRT, but she failed to specify that the De Zavala Chapter be in charge of the restoration plan. As requested, the state gave custody to the DRT, with no mention of any one group within it who would be in control of the two buildings.

At the outset in 1903 when the two women began their project to save the building, this did not seem to be a problem because Miss Driscoll's preservation plan seemed to be quite in agreement with Miss De Zavala's; but it was to change dramatically later. By all accounts, Clara Driscoll was working toward saving the Hugo-Schmeltzer Building and removing the false exterior to save the remains of the historic building underneath in order to establish a museum in it, just as Miss De Zavala was, and to make a park of the area around it. Or so it appeared. Later in a complete reversal, Miss Driscoll was to declare the building was nothing more than a "whiskey house"[37] that should be torn down and the entire area made into a park. Just why she did such an about-face has never been explained clearly.

During the years of 1903 to 1905, right up to the date of the purchase of the "long barracks" and for a brief time thereafter, no difference of opinion in the two women nor split of any kind in the DRT organization was evident. Adina De Zavala and Clara Driscoll became fast friends in fact, or so it would seem, and appeared to be working harmoniously toward their common cause. Their love for their native state and its history was shared along with a few other commonalities of natural bonds that came from each one's birthrights. By some odd coincidence, both had Irish Catholic mothers who had been born in Ireland and emigrated to Texas; each mother was named Julia; and both mothers had been educated at Ursuline Convents. Julia Fox, Clara's mother, attended and was graduated from the Ursuline Academy in San Antonio, where it is said by some accounts Clara began her schooling, and from which Adina was graduated. Adina's mother, Julia Tyrell, had attended the Ursuline Academy in Galveston, where Adina began her schooling. The most important common bond between Clara and Adina, though, was still that almost religious fervor and respect each one had for the Alamo as a symbol of an heroic episode in the history of Texas.

Some original handwritten letters and a photograph from

Miss Driscoll to Miss De Zavala found in the De Zavala Papers reveal the concerns and plans of two good friends dedicated to saving the "long barracks". The letters open with "Dear Miss De Zavala" and close with "Much love, Always", followed by the personal signature of Clara Driscoll,[38] and the photograph on the following page found in the De Zavala Papers is signed "with love Clara."

A handwritten letter in draft from Miss De Zavala to Miss Driscoll opens with "My dear Miss Driscoll" and contains little personal things about mutual friends such as one concerning the mother of Mrs. Adele Looscan, one of the founders of the DRT. She describes Mrs. Looscan's mother as "being quite old and needs constant attention as she is confined to her chair—having had a hip dislocated by slipping on a banana peel in alighting from her carriage several years ago." Miss De Zavala's letter continues, saying she [Adina] told Mrs. Looscan: ". . . that I believed you [Clara] had the genuine patriotic spirit and could work single-minded and single hearted! There [indecipherable—is given to you(?)] to do [that] which is given to few women! . . ."[39]

These letters exchanged between the two women seem to show a genuine friendly feeling and admiration for one another, in sharp contrast to the bitter feeling that would develop between them later. In addition to this bond of affection there was an expressed dedication to their common cause. That cause is clearly stated by Miss Driscoll, not only in the personal handwritten letters to Miss De Zavala, but also in the printed letters of appeal for donations bearing her signature that were sent out statewide during the same time period. These letters state that the purpose is to "raise a sum sufficient to purchase the property adjoining the Alamo . . ." and make a "worthy and artistic monument to the memory of those valiant martyrs who fell inside its walls."[40]

Miss De Zavala's expressed dream had always been to restore the building called the "long barracks" and convert it into a museum to depict the history of Texas in general and in particular

MISS CLARA DRISCOLL, CHAIRMAN AND TREASURER OF ALAMO MISSION FUND, DE ZAVALA CHAPTER, DAUGHTERS OF THE REPUBLIC OF TEXAS, WHOSE PATRIOTISM PROMPTED HER TO GIVE OF HER WEALTH TO SAVE THE MISSION OF THE ALAMO.

(Adina De Zavala Papers, CN01490, Center for American History, University of Texas at Austin.) [Note: The inscription above was written by Miss De Zavala on the back of the photograph which was found in her papers. It appears Miss De Zavala may have trimmed the picture to fit in a frame possibly since part of the signature on the picture is missing.]

the Battle of the Alamo. It was to reflect the sacrifices made by the heroes of the Alamo who had fallen at this very site in this very building, the "long barracks", as well as in the Alamo Chapel and all those who had fallen in the rest of the compound which had disappeared over time.

The post card, which Miss De Zavala had printed and mailed out soliciting donations to save the building, carried an illustration drawn by Rolla Taylor, a well known artist of San Antonio at that time.[41] It appears to have been based on Miss De Zavala's concept of the style of a convento as one might have appeared during the mission period. It pictured a long, two-story building with an arcaded gallery containing numerous arches on both first and second floors and an imposing tower at each end. It was a Spanish colonial style building similar to the arched arcades of the two-story convento at Mission San José, the most beautiful of all the area missions which Miss De Zavala and her co-workers also had worked hard to try and save. She had published a similar drawing in the newspaper earlier.

Her interpretation of the building may have been inspired by something she found in the *Documentos Para la Historia de la Provencia de Texas* (MS) folios 164-167. (Translation:*With the Makers of Texas: A Source Reader in Texas History,* by Bolton & Barker, pp. 61-66). It contained a description of the entire area and then described the mission itself thus:

> The settlement contains a convent fifty yards square
> with arcades above and below. In the convent are the
> living rooms of the religious, the porters lodge, the din-
> ing-room, the kitchen, and the offices.[42]

If the structure Miss De Zavala was promoting resembled even remotely the original convento, it looked very little or next to nothing like the building had looked at the time of the 1836 Battle, nor did Miss De Zavala claim it was to be an exact reproduction of either of them. Her plan was to restore the building to a mission period style building to be used as a library and a museum, without disturbing evidence of the scars of the 1836 Battle on the "long barracks" which still stood underneath the false exterior of the Hugo-Schmeltzer Building.

Regardless of its authenticity, it was Miss De Zavala's idea of an appropriate kind of monument to be dedicated to the memory of the Alamo heroes. Anything less would have been unworthy of the noble cause, in her mind.

Up to the time Clara Driscoll had appeared on the scene, Miss De Zavala and her co-workers had worked for sixteen years according to their records to gain control of the "long barracks" building in the hope of saving it and restoring it, both before the DRT was organized and afterward. As its local chapter, once the purchase had been accomplished, they expected, and in fact, to some extent, had been led to believe, they would be in charge of the restoration plan. For them the major building to be featured would be the old "long barracks". The Chapel building would be honored, too, of course, but it would be secondary to the restored convento/ "long barracks", because this latter building was where so much of the fighting had occurred and where so many had died, not in the Chapel which was an open ruin at the time of the battle. This was something that many of the Daughters did not believe, or possibly understand, through ignorance of historical fact.

Dr. L. Robert Ables expressed it well in his account of the "Second Battle" by quoting one of the most knowledgeable of the Daughters:

> Adele B. Looscan [A founding member of the DRT] of Houston, the most capable historian in the DRT at that time [1904] and recognized as such by her regular re-election to the post of historian-general, wrote that "an unfortunate and inexcusable ignorance" existed concerning the Alamo, with the chapel "accepted by many who ought to know better, as the whole and only theatre of the siege, defense, and holocaust . . . this

grand old pile [chapel] has been made the medium for
the perpetration of the false accounts, until people who
do not read history, accept such teaching as true . . ."[43]

Incredible as it seems, there are some who still "accept" today that
the Alamo Chapel was the site of the entire battle.

Miss De Zavala was obsessed with the idea of preventing
the removal or changing of even one stone from what had remained
of the original convento and "long barracks", and which she
believed to still be there in spite of its alterations since the Battle of
1836. In her plan, the Alamo Chapel was to be a part of the museum display complex, but the building would be used just as it had
been rebuilt by the U. S. Army. As she well knew, it was only a
roofless shell piled with rocks and rubble inside its jagged walls
even during the mission period, and of course, it was even worse
during the 1836 Battle, and afterward for the eleven year period
that followed, before the U. S. Army moved in and rebuilt it.

Her research had revealed details that convinced her 'she
was right' about the history of the "long barracks" building and her
convictions about its fate during the Battle were based on such
accounts as the following:

It was impossible for the few men of the Alamo to
defend the outer walls long; and the most of them soon
retreated into the long two-story building which was
well fortified. . . . .
. . . .

"The bloodiest spot about the Fort was the long barrack [sic - originally written in singular form] and the
ground in front of it where the enemy fell in heaps."
(This is a quotation from Capt. Reuben M. Potter,
U.S.A., who was a resident of Matamoros at the time of
the fall of the Alamo.)

A Mexican soldier gave his testimony as follows:

"The Texans fought like tigers . . . The last moments of
the conflict were terrible. The darkness of the rooms, the
smoke of the battle and the shrieks of the wounded and
dying all added to the terror of the scene. Unable to distinguish friend from foe, Mexicans actually brained
each other in their mad fury. After the battle was over
and all were dead, the scene beggared description. The
floor [of the long barrack] was nearly shoe deep in
blood, and weltering there were hundreds of dead men,
many still clenched together with one hand while the
other hand held the sword, pistol or knife which told
how they had died in that last terrible struggle. And
thus, the curtain went down in darkness and blood on
the saddest and sublimest event in the world's history."[44]

Is it any wonder Miss Adina was so passionate in her
defense of this site and so convinced its memory was sacred and
should be preserved as a reminder of this tragic moment in Texas
history?

To further substantiate her claims about the historical significance of the old building that was considered such an "eyesore",
she quotes from the respected early historian John Henry Brown:

In Vol. I., Page 576, of Brown's History of Texas,
referring to Bowie is the following: "When the attack
came on, (Bowie) was confined to his bed in the upper
room of the barrack marked (P.) [the "long barracks"].
He was there killed on his couch, but not without resistance; for he is said to have shot down with his pistols
one or more of the enemy as they entered the chamber."
Again on page 587 is found: "Col. Fulton says:
"About the first of August, 1857, I first visited the
Alamo, in company with Judge Baker, then Chief
Justice of Bexar county, who directed my attention to
the room I have marked (B) [in the "long barracks"] as
the one occupied by Bowie on his sick bed, when bayoneted by Santa Anna's minions." [45]

Miss De Zavala tried continually through pamphlets she

published and magazine articles she wrote to correct the "mistaken idea" that the battle had all taken place in the Chapel, and to make plain that the chief struggle was in the "long barracks", including the room on the "upper floor" where James Bowie died as stated in John Henry Brown's *History of Texas*.

And what about Miss Driscoll's position on the matter of the "mistaken idea" of where the major part of the battle had occurred? During the year and a half they had been working to raise money to save the property, Adina De Zavala had been led to believe that she and Clara Driscoll were in agreement on the matter regarding the significance of the "long barracks". But did Miss Driscoll really agree with her? Or had she privately held another point of view all along?

In a letter written earlier upon her return from Europe in 1900, before meeting Miss De Zavala and joining the DRT, she had stated her dismay concerning the condition of the historic site:

> It is our Alamo . . . how do we treat it? We leave it hemmed in on one side by a hideous looking barracks-like looking building, and on the other by two saloons. Listen to what strangers say upon seeing the Alamo with such surroundings: 'Is that the Alamo? . . .' Today the Alamo should stand out free and clear. All unsightly obstructions that hide it away should be torn down and the space utilized for a park.[46]

Even after she met Miss De Zavala and had made plans to join the DRT, Clara Driscoll's attitude does not appear to be vastly different. In her own words she expresses her intentions about the property next to the Alamo in a letter dated Feb. 5th, 1903, to one of the owners, Mr. Charles Hugo:

Mr. Hugo:

Dear Sir—
While in San Antonio a few days ago I saw Mr. Schmeltzer in regard to the property adjoining the Alamo. He said it was for sale. The Daughters of the Republic are anxious to procure it in order to make a park about the old ruins . . . . [47]

It was on February 9, 1903, four days after writing this letter, that Clara Driscoll joined the Daughters of the Republic.

These statements of Miss Driscoll's would suggest that she seemed to have no intention of promoting the restoration of a building where the present building stood, even though she seemingly was supporting Miss De Zavala's position for such a plan. Did she, like so many others, really believe that the fighting had occurred in the Chapel, and that most, if not all, of the defenders had died within the walls of that building itself? This was in fact a position in which the DRT persisted for many years as recorded in their history, *Fifty Years of Achievement,* a publication printed 106 years later in 1942, wherein it is stated:

The Alamo, the Shrine [Chapel] itself, was now properly protected, [referring to the time when the State had taken possession and the De Zavala faction would no longer be allowed to control it] and the Chapter's [the later formed Alamo Chapter, which replaced the De Zavala Chapter] thoughts turned to the 185 heroes who died within its precincts. It was proposed that bronze tablets be placed on the walls commemorating the men who died there.[48]

There are 16 bronze tablets on the interior walls of the Chapel today containing the names of 217 men. They were placed there in 1936. Of those names, 199 are identified as "Heroes", 2 who "died of illness during the siege", and 16 who were couriers. This would tend to suggest to first-time, uninformed visitors that the remaining 199 "Heroes" died <u>there</u>, or in that building, which is not true, and the marker therefore is misleading. Quoting again from Dr. Ables:

> . . . A newspaper article related her [Clara Driscoll's] opinion that Texans during the battle defended the outer walls before retreating to the monastery and finally to the chapel.

> "Of the original buildings only the Chapel remains standing. The monastery fell to pieces long ago, and on the ground it occupied, a grocery store stands today. Even the Chapel for many years was used as a market . . . Whether the Alamo purchase bill passes the legisture or not the grocery store will come down and the hotel which it was proposed at one time to build there will not be erected. In their place will be a replica of the old monastery, built from the ancient ruins to serve as a Valhalla for Texas." [49]

Miss Driscoll is quoted here as saying there will be "a replica of the old monastery, built from the ancient ruins" which she claimed "fell to pieces long ago", as though that had happened long before the battle in all probability. But then a surprising and marked change soon begins to appear more and more in her attitude toward the idea of "a replica of the old monastery . . . to serve as a Valhalla for Texas" which would be used as a museum.

In an interview in January of 1905, a *San Antonio Express* reporter quoted her as saying:

> While no definite plan has been outlined, the idea of the Daughters is to beautify the place . . . I believe that the idea . . . is to lend more prominence to the Chapel, which of course is the main feature in the Alamo mission. [50]

Judging from these various statements made of how she felt

about the "long barracks", one begins to question whether she was interested in restoring or preserving anything except the Chapel.

The conflicting expressions of her statements concerning where the major part of the battle took place and what should be done with the "long barracks" site make one wonder if she intended to support Miss De Zavala's plan when she joined her in 1903. Or was she simply just as ill informed as the other Daughters who were under the misconception that the final moments of the battle occurred in the Chapel itself and all the heroes had retreated to it and were killed there, thereby believing the "long barracks" to be inconsequential to the history of the battle.

The answer to these questions will never be known, but her position certainly had changed from what it appeared to have been during the fund raising campaign she had shared with Miss De Zavala at the beginning of their relationship and the forerunner of that other Alamo conflict to come. The separation between them which began as a disagreement eventually escalated into what became open warfare. When it was all over, the only common link left between them personally was that the name of each one would be forever associated with the name of the Alamo, and they would go to their graves as bitter enemies.

The life of Adina De Zavala had been an intensive and sometimes turbulent struggle up to now to achieve her goals of historic preservation, but nothing could compare with what was ahead of her for the next several years.

She was forty-four years old by now and had been engaged in her efforts to preserve the history of Texas one way or another for at least twenty of those years. She had had successes and failures, triumphs and disappointments, but she did not hesitate to take on the challenge that arose now of saving the old Alamo convento/ "long barracks", which she knew to be one of the major sites of the Battle of the Alamo in 1836. The struggle to save it from destruction was to occupy her intensively for the next several years and it has become known as the "Second Battle for the Alamo".

Initially, however, the spark that ignited the fire that erupted into the "second battle" was a disagreement over the Chapel, not the "long barracks". The De Zavala Chapter had expected to take charge of the entire Alamo complex once the legislature had acted, since they had worked constantly toward the purchase of the remainder of the site and were the local chapter at its location. Under this assumption they had begun to put their plan for the complex into operation soon after the legislature said they were purchasing the "long barracks". While this assumption may have seemed logical to the De Zavala Chapter, that feeling was not shared by other members of the DRT, and it very soon began to rankle the executive committee and in short order other chapters as well.

As the feeling spread, the seemingly solid foundation of the unity of the organization began to crack, and before it was all over the Daughters of the Republic of Texas had split into two very separate and competitive factions. There was bitter infighting between them that was slow to die, and unfortunately some of the residual misinformation that was disseminated at the time still exists, causing an undercurrent of disharmony that appears occasionally to this day. Some of the Daughters today still seem to be surprisingly ignorant of the facts and "won't read history" as that founding Daughter, Adele Looscan, said of those so many years ago in 1904. Either that ignorance or possibly fear of reprisal or criticism still results in their not taking a public stand and admitting the error of some of those early Daughters who declared so vehemently that the Chapel was the real site of the Battle. There are those today who were told this was a fact by their mothers before them as members of the DRT and they persist in believing it and they continue to passionately defend it.

The first public evidence of an actual split in the DRT occurred at the next annual convention following the convened session of the legislature in January of 1905, when they voted to purchase the Alamo "long barracks" property.

The Daughters of the Republic of Texas annual convention was held three months later in April at the town of La Grange. Miss Driscoll was not recorded as present though she was still living in the state at the time. Her absence was not unusual, however, for she did not always attend executive committee meetings or state conventions. Miss De Zavala on the other hand never missed attending one throughout the years of her membership.

The friction that surfaced at this convention was over the fact that, according to the DRT's *Fifty Years of Achievement,* Miss De Zavala had attempted to take possession and control of the Alamo property, and in particular the Chapel, and had removed some artifacts from it immediately after the vote of the legislature had been taken[51] in January. This was, of course, before the bill was actually signed into law officially eight months later on August 31, 1905.

Since the De Zavala Chapter had felt from the beginning they should be in charge of the restoration and interpretation of the property, undoubtedly Adina De Zavala and her co-workers had begun trying to execute their long planned goals as promptly as possible which included their plans for the Alamo Chapel, and she had removed some artifacts she claimed were to be placed in the "long barracks" museum once it was built. As talk began to spread about plans for the total destruction of the Hugo-Schmeltzer building and converting the area into a park, leaving just the Chapel to be featured as the only site of the Battle, they set about trying to carry out their plans for the entire complex without delay to offset the possible destruction of the building. According to Miss De Zavala any artifacts removed from the Chapel were removed "for safe keeping" and were to be placed in the "long barracks" museum building later. Moreover, she claimed some of the items had been given to her personally and were hers to do with as she chose. No matter what may or may not have happened regarding any artifacts or anything else, Miss De Zavala had not endured years of waiting for this moment only to see it slip away without a struggle.

The assumption of control by the De Zavala Chapter had not only irritated the opposing group, it set them to work. At the 1905 La Grange convention, their first move was the use of a delaying tactic of saying the transfer of custodianship of the property had not been signed into law, and, therefore, it was premature and illegal for the De Zavala Chapter to attempt to take control of the property yet.

Using the legality of the matter as a reason to delay the decision on control of the site was merely an excuse, in the eyes of the De Zavala Chapter. The fact was many of the other DRT members did not agree with the De Zavala Chapter's plans for restoration and interpretive use of the two buildings and they were seeking a way to out-maneuver them. While the De Zavala Daughters, now the De Zavala Chapter of the DRT, had worked on their plans for these buildings for years, other DRT members had just begun to think about what should be done with the buildings in the last year.

The La Grange convention got underway, and since there was no official policy yet on the custody of the property, the subject was promptly addressed. A vote was taken and passed to defer the matter of custody of the Alamo until after the deed to the state of the "long barracks" was properly executed. But a counter move was quickly introduced by the De Zavala Chapter and others who supported them and voted in the affirmative which called for "immediately upon turning over of the Alamo property by the State to the Daughters . . a meeting of the executive board be called with regard to placing custodianship of the same in the hands of the De Zavala Chapter." [52]

The DRT membership in general seemed to favor a position that the custodian of a historic property chosen to manage it should be a member of a chapter in the locality of that historic site, and, therefore, the member would logically live at the locality of the site. This was to be proposed as an amendment to the constitution at the next convention in 1906, but in the meantime, a very divisive and bitterly unpleasant situation was developing over the matter, and the chasm between the two evolving groups began to widen irrevocably. The convention ended in an air of public politeness but not without growing private animosities.

The followers of Clara Driscoll, the young woman who by now had become nationally famous as the "Savior of the Alamo", were beginning to gain in strength and numbers, and they would soon emerge as the 'power group'. They felt the Chapel should be the major feature of the Alamo property, because they believed that was where the heroes had died, and they further felt Miss Driscoll should be the custodian of it since she had "saved the Alamo". The post might be temporary, until next year's convention possibly, but it would be a much deserved 'reward' for her and, not just incidentally, a way of their obtaining immediate control of the site.

There was just one thing wrong with this idea. Even before the vote on the matter the following year would make it a requirement, the majority of the members, regardless of following, still were known to feel that custodianship should be in the hands of someone who lived in the locality of the Alamo property for obvious reasons. While Miss Driscoll as a member of the appropriate chapter had lived in the general locality of the site, she did not live there now. In fact, she no longer even lived in Texas.

The bill making the state the official owners of the Alamo property and the DRT the custodians of it had barely been signed when Clara Driscoll left Texas. Final settlements were made on August 31st and just two days later on September 2nd she was bound for New York City and "the great white way". She was to pursue her new fledgling career as a novelist and a playwright of dramas and operettas, leaving the future of the Hugo-Schmeltzer Building and the entire Alamo property in the hands of the DRT hierarchy.

Except for occasional return trips, Clara Driscoll made her home in New York City for the next ten years and spent most of her time there. Her interests and energy were devoted to her life there in pursuit of her literary and theatrical career at first. Before very long, however, that rather tenuous career ended, but it was followed by several years of social activities that surrounded her marriage there to Henry Hulme "Hal" Sevier, which kept her in New York for several more years. It was not until the death of her father in 1914 that she returned to Texas to live.

In the meantime, while still a resident of New York City, her trips home were usually initiated by business or family matters, but oftentimes they were combined with current matters concerning the Alamo during those turbulent years of the "Second Battle". It appears that during the first year or so she returned fairly often for both family and Alamo interests, but as time passed she seems to have handled the Alamo by long distance more and more, or left things in the hands of others on the local scene.

When Miss Driscoll had left town so promptly after the signing of the Alamo property bill, she left without being named officially as custodian of the Alamo. She quickly took care of the problem though by telegraphing Mrs. Anson Jones, the President of the DRT, asking for temporary control until the next meeting of the executive committee. The executive committee responded for the president making Miss Driscoll custodian, but since plans called for her to be away for the next three to four months until Christmas, someone needed to fill the job immediately in her absence. Miss Driscoll took it upon herself to appoint her closest friend in San Antonio, Miss Florence Eager, to represent her. As it happened, Miss Eager unfortunately was not even a member of the DRT at this time. This did not alter Miss Driscoll's decision, however.

Miss De Zavala took quick advantage of the situation. The city up to now had been charged by the state with the management of the Alamo Chapel museum, and Adina De Zavala called on the mayor and requested she be given the key to the Chapel since it was now under control of the DRT. The mayor, knowing of her long years of work on the property, granted her the requested key and she promptly locked the door saying she would surrender the key to no one but Miss Driscoll herself.

The Driscoll group of the DRT reacted by threatening to take her to court. After considerable exchange between the two opposing groups, the De Zavala Chapter voted to surrender the key (by now Miss Eager was a bona fide DRT member), and the matter appeared to have ended or at least subsided for the time being.

But greater problems than this were ahead for the DRT. On April 18th, immediately prior to the 1906 annual convention, nine members of the De Zavala Chapter withdrew and formed a new chapter which they named the Alamo Mission Chapter. This chapter ultimately replaced the De Zavala Chapter and this was the beginning of the San Antonio chapter that exists today under that same name. One of the main purposes of the group of nine was the hope of gaining control of the Alamo Chapel and the rest of the complex surrounding it. The formation of the Alamo Mission Chapter took place just two days before the 1906 convention which was held on April 20-21 at another famous site of the Texas Revolution, the town of Goliad which is about 100 miles southeast of San Antonio.

The feud that had been brewing within the Daughters of the Republic of Texas for some time erupted at this convention in full bloom and the press had a gleeful time with it. One account in a St. Louis paper reported of the ladies that "some screamed, others yelled . . . [there were] many men who went to watch . . ." A cartoon accompanied the article which depicted ladies brandishing rolling pins at one another, others fencing with umbrellas, and some pulling hair, while others were hurling pies from the rooftop of the Alamo at the ladies battling it out below in front of the famous facade of the shrine.[53]

The cartoon was a thorough "put-down" and a gross exaggeration, of course, and the article itself was replete with inaccuracies, some of a serious nature. The public was beginning to hold the organization up to ridicule (with more yet to come, unfortunately) and was losing sight of its real purpose.

The convention did become a noisy one filled with some quite heated debates, and at one time it almost went out of control according to the DRT Report, but no one came away bloodied or bald. Clara Driscoll was in attendance at this convention. She arrived late, however, which she frequently seemed to do, but her entrance did not go unnoticed. A discussion was underway at the time regarding the purchase of a portrait of David Crockett.

The Executive Committee announced it had purchased a Crockett portrait with funds from the rental money collected from the Hugo-Schmeltzer Building, which was now being rented from the DRT by its former owners as a storage facility. The Committee stated it had learned of the portrait and recognized it as an opportunity to purchase a rare painting and had made the purchase without prior membership approval because the option deadline for purchase was to expire before the Convention would meet. They were now seeking ratification for the expenditure.

Adina De Zavala took a position which was something of an anomaly for her since she was such an admirer of Crockett. She stated she felt any available funds should have gone to restoring the old "long barracks" building, not to buy a portrait no matter whose. Miss Driscoll rose to say that "if the General Association fails to ratify the action of the Executive Committee in purchasing the David Crockett picture, she would buy it and present it to the Alamo."[54] The De Zavala supporters prevailed on the matter, however, with a vote of thirty-five to sixteen opposed to buying the portrait. This would seem to put the De Zavala group in control of the Convention, but the victory was meaningless apparently.

The offer of Miss Driscoll to purchase the portrait was declined with gratitude by the Executive Committee as being unnecessary since they had paid for the painting on February 23, 1906, and they considered the DRT as already the owners of the Crockett portrait painted by John Gadsby Chapman, celebrated artist of the day. The certificate of purchase was filed in New York County and recorded and was ". . . signed by Mrs. C. B. Stone, in Proceedings, 15th Annual Convention, Daughters of the Republic of Texas, April 20-21, 1906 (p. 19)." [55]

The Crockett painting was ultimately hung in the Alamo,but was later removed from the wall because of moisture collecting under it. It was placed in a protective vault.

The decision to purchase the Crockett portrait when they did was a wise one it seems because it was one of the very few portraits of David Crockett painted from life which is still extant. The value is said to be many times that of the $1,000 they paid for it.

A second vote in the favor of the De Zavala group came soon after their victory on the vote regarding the purchase of the Crockett portrait. This time it was in a motion which called for giving custody of the Alamo to the De Zavala Chapter, which would be a real triumph for them if it passed. The opposing group which supported Clara Driscoll, and as yet was still small, quickly followed up with a motion to amend the previous motion by substituting the name of Clara Driscoll for the De Zavala Chapter as custodian. The motion lost. At this point "the noise and confusion became and continued so great . . . that it was impossible for . . . one person to take accurate notes." [56]

When order was restored and the meeting resumed, the original motion was voted on and the result was thirty-three to sixteen in favor of giving custody of the Alamo to the De Zavala Chapter.

As a result of the failure of the motion to give her custody, Miss Driscoll soon rose and stated that since she was being thrust out of the custodianship she "tendered her resignation of both the custody of the Alamo and of her membership in the society, and asked that it be accepted." [57]

The DRT did not in actual fact accept her resignation, needless to say. But she was to write a letter to them a year later dated May 8, 1907, expressing her extreme displeasure over this incident wherein she said, ". . . since I am no longer a member of your organization . . .", etc., so, obviously it appears she did not consider herself a member any longer, whether they did or not. She still had not gotten over her rejection as custodian of the Alamo, and her bitterness seems to have grown as her letter suggests:

> When the purchase of the Alamo property by the State was completed my committee and myself were told by the de [sic] Zavala Chapter that our services were no longer needed, in other words the committee was only tolerated so long as its work aided in the accomplishment of the purchase, and my eligibility as a member of this chapter ceased when my money was no longer necessary . . . [58]

When the noisy upheaval that followed Miss Driscoll's resignation had subsided, the Convention resumed and continued with the anticipated amendment to the Constitution regarding the matter that had begun to divide the organization. The amendment required that monuments or buildings of "historic character" must be placed in the charge of the chapter in which such monuments are located.[59] This motion passed with a big majority, also, of thirty-six to fourteen. This vote assured the De Zavala Chapter of being custodian of the Alamo, since they were still recognized as the original chapter where the historic site was located.

Another constitutional amendment which passed was one requiring that vice presidents preside in their numerical order "in the event of death, resignation, disability, or absence of the president."[60] This amendment was to become a point of great contention at the next convention one year later in Austin and would be the critical point that resulted in finally tearing the organization apart.

After two days of some major disagreements and disrup-

tions, the convention ended without any actual hair-pulling or spar-
ring with umbrellas as the cartoon suggested. Although the women
adjourned in what appeared to be a quasi-civilized atmosphere,
more trouble was brewing under the surface.

Three weeks after the convention, the executive committee
called a meeting in Houston without Miss De Zavala, although she
was an official member of that committee. At this meeting they
made a decision to replace Miss Driscoll as custodian with another
member, in view of her announced resignation which they actually
never accepted. This decision was in direct opposition to the position they had just taken at the convention, which declared the DRT
"had acted in violation of Texas laws governing incorporated asso-
ciations" by amending the constitution. It had done this earlier
when it made Miss Driscoll custodian of the Alamo originally. The
fact was the act of the Twenty-Ninth Legislature gave care and custody to the general association anyway, no matter what amend-
ments to their constitution they might vote on to the contrary. In
deciding to replace Miss Driscoll with someone else of their choice
now, they were in violation of their own motion, not to mention the
legislative act.

Proceedings of the DRT conventions ordinarily were printed and distributed as soon after the convention ended as possible.
The Report of the 1906 Goliad Convention that had just ended, was
not delivered until almost one year later, however, according to the
De Zavala Chapter's records. It was delayed until just before the
1907 convention in Austin. This delay prevented the De Zavala
Chapter from taking any counter action since they could not be sure
of any official position on the matter of custody until just before
that next convention assembled.

Long before that convention was to meet, another crisis of
a more immediate nature arose, and this time it was over the "long
barracks", not the Chapel. A St. Louis hotel firm had purchased the
piece of property behind the Hugo-Schmeltzer Building and they

wished to "improve" the area by razing the Hugo-Schmeltzer Building completely and converting the area into a park. They sent Miss De Zavala a letter to this effect and implied that the state or the DRT or both had agreed to this.[61] The St. Louis firm could not have known what an alarming effect this would have on this champion of historic sites. This was like sending additional fuel to her with which to feed the fire that was already smoldering and ready to burst into flames beyond control.

With remarkable restraint, Miss De Zavala replied in polite terms and explained that the Hugo-Schmeltzer Building and the original building were one and the same. She told them that underneath the Hugo-Schmeltzer Building facade, which the hotel entrepreneur had characterized as a "common nuisance", stood the original convento/"long barracks" with its blood-stained walls which were the real heart of the Alamo proper, not the Alamo Chapel. She further described her plans for making a museum of the original building and this sacred spot, once the false exterior had been removed.[62]

Of course, the business man who had written the letter for the hotel company in St. Louis could not appreciate her idea at all, and the matter went from bad to worse when he scorned it in a semi-polite way and threatened to invest elsewhere if compliance was not to be obtained.

At the same time, the DRT executive committee also received a letter regarding removal of the building and making a park around the grounds of the Alamo. The board met and agreed to negotiate with the hotel company regarding the removal of the Hugo-Schmeltzer Building but with the stipulation that the hotel company "shall carefully preserve all of said original walls, and shall plant and train vines thereon . . ."[63]

The Houston and San Antonio newspapers carried stories concerning the board meetings with the DRT's proposed park plans. The stories as printed claimed that many San Antonio business men were also in accord with the hotel and DRT park plan and had started a petition to destroy the walls of the dilapidated building totally.

All of this was too much for Miss De Zavala. She immediately called a mass meeting of her supporters to discuss possible ways of trying to compete with what were becoming overwhelming odds.

To further weaken the De Zavala Chapter's ever diminishing position, another article soon appeared in the February 22, 1907 edition of the *San Antonio Express* newspaper quoting a local businessman's reference to Clara Driscoll as being in support of the plan, if not the initiator of it:

> The idea of making the Alamo more conspicuous by removing the unsightly bulletin board known as the Hugo-Schmeltzer Building is not new with us. The idea of Miss Driscoll and the Daughters . . . was to remove the old . . . walls and to beautify the grounds adjacent to the Alamo. In fact . . . [Miss Driscoll] stated to me when she was here recently that her idea was to act as I have said, and she authorized me to give public expression to her sentiments.[64]

Miss Driscoll's popularity and fame by now as the "Savior of the Alamo" gave her great credibility as far as her wishes about the Alamo property went, even though she was still living in New York at this time, far removed from the scene. The above statement, regarding her attitude about the Alamo property, expressed her position clearly as did the one expressing the position of the DRT executive committee which appeared in the *San Antonio Express* just days before the upcoming Convention in Austin:

> The preservation of the old walls, even the foundation of the Presidio, is the keynote to all efforts of the society today—not the destruction of any part. But the idea of remodeling on those foundations a monastery is entirely impracticable and chimerical. Those walls are gone and their stones forgotten . . . [65]

HUGO-SCHMELTZER BUILDING, CA.1910
(Institute of Texan Cultures at San Antonio, Courtesy of the Robert M. Ayers Estate.)

The term "unsightly bulletin board known as the Hugo-Schmeltzer Building" was coined no doubt from the appearance of the unoccupied building at a time when it was used as a storage facility with advertising billboards on its outer walls.

The rift between the followers of Miss De Zavala and those of Miss Driscoll had grown wider and deeper and more bitter by the day in the year that followed the 1906 Goliad convention. The climax came at the next annual convention in April of 1907. This one was held in the Senate Chambers of the State Capitol in Austin, an unusual meeting place for their convention to say the least. In a tumultuous session the two opposing groups erupted in a situation that ultimately went out of control and it brought about a dramatic change in the DRT.

"Protests and bickering filled the morning session", in the words of Dr. Ables. As the word spread, several visitors came to witness the afternoon session, including at least seven state senators.

The newspapers had a fine time with this convention, too, as a few excerpts from the *Austin Statesman* show:

> Mrs. Dibrell rose to read from Robert's "Rules of Order" but opened at the wrong place and sat down amid laughter.
> A motion to adjourn was made and an attempt to take the vote failed for the noise.
> Mrs. Dibrell said, "I move we pin badges on all new daughters, no matter what sex."
> Mrs. Fisher took the gavel and ruled that the convention stand adjourned sine die.[66]

Clearly, the male dominated press of 1907 regarded what they termed "ladies clubs" as a bit of a farce, regardless of the seriousness of the organization's purpose. Some accounts did reflect more than these ridiculous moments, but to learn what actually took place in the proceedings, the records and minutes kept by the DRT members would be one of the sources to which to turn.

The two major DRT accounts of the convention that were reviewed were the printed record of the Sixteenth Annual Meeting of the DRT at Austin,[67] and *Fifty Years of Achievement, History of the Daughters of the Republic of Texas.*[68] In addition to these DRT documents, the account of the convention proceedings as recorded by the De Zavala group[69] was the only other source available. It was found the two accounts of the DRT actually have conflicting statements with one another in some specific instances, but are in agreement with one another generally, as well as the De Zavala account in most areas. However, the accounts of the two groups differed completely on certain major points, as shown in some of the quotes on the following pages.

The Austin Convention was opened by Mrs. Rebecca Fisher, First Vice President of the DRT, in the absence of the President, Mrs. Anson Jones. Mrs. Jones was the widow of the last President of the Republic of Texas, and she had been named "honorary president for life" of the DRT. She rarely attended meetings as time passed, but would send a written message to be read to the assembly. She was absent more and more now because of her frail health and advancing years. She was 87 years old at the time of the Austin convention in April of 1907. She died eight months later on December 31st of that same year.

At the opening of the Convention, Mrs. Jones' letter was read and Mrs. Fisher as First Vice President then proceeded to conduct the meeting as chairman according to correct parliamentary rules and the rules of their own Constitution. She immediately announced that she did not feel well and she called on Mrs. L. B. Alford to preside in her place. Miss De Zavala rose at once and objected, stating that since the elected Second Vice President, Mrs. Wharton Bates, was in the hall she should preside. Mrs. Fisher replied that she had been told that as long as she remained in the hall herself she could call on whom she chose to chair the meeting as stated in the By-Laws. Miss De Zavala and other members

270

objected again and called the attention of the chair to the fact that the Constitution said Vice Presidents must preside in their numerical order if present. To which Mrs. Fisher still maintained she could invite whom she chose to chair the meeting and she would not yield her right. This exchange went back and forth for several minutes with various members joining in the objection. The fact was, Mrs. Fisher was not only the First Vice President of the organization, but she was also one of the members of the group who opposed thoroughly the De Zavala followers. It was apparent Mrs. Fisher had no intention of allowing the Second Vice President, Mrs. Bates, to chair the convention, since Mrs. Bates was the defacto leader of the opposing group, the De Zavala followers.

The appointed substitute chairman, Mrs. Alford, continued to attempt to run the meeting in spite of repeated interruptions and objections. When she was reminded twice by the De Zavala group of the Constitutional requirement that vice presidents present must preside in their numerical order, she finally responded sharply, "I do not care what the Constitution says, while I am in the chair there shall be no appeal."[70]

Another point of objection by the opposition was that according to the record, Mrs. Alford, the temporary chair, was not a member of any specific DRT Chapter and therefore was not entitled to the privilege of even a vote according to the Constitution, much less chairing the Convention. There was very noisy vocal objection to the matter of the handling of the chairing of the convention, and the De Zavala group apparently was being supported on the point by the senators and the pages who were observing the proceedings and their loud "no's" could be heard coming from the galleries. The De Zavala supporters objections continued to be ignored by the chair according to the De Zavala group's account of the proceedings.[71]

Because of the confusion that reigned over the De Zavala group's continued efforts to have Mrs. Bates chair the meeting,

Mrs. Fisher finally stepped forward and adjourned the meeting "sine die" legally according to the DRT report. The De Zavala group's claim differs completely with the DRT report, however, on this important and critical point.

The proceedings report by the DRT states that "Noise and confusion continued to such an extent". . . that Mrs. Fisher asked for a motion to adjourn the meeting. She called for a voice vote asking that all in favor stand and say "aye", and the account further reports fully two-thirds present were standing. The conclusion of the meeting is then described as follows by the Driscoll followers:

> The President then said: "Those opposed will say "No". Those seated, including the gentlemen [senators] and pages, shouted "No!" Not once but several times. As soon as there was sufficient quiet, Mrs. Fisher said firmly and distinctly: "The ayes have it. I now declare this convention adjourned sine die." She then walked out, followed by all those who had voted aye and remained standing.[72]

This "sine die" adjournment scene is described quite differently, by the De Zavala group. Their report claimed each time someone in their group rose and tried to request that Mrs. Wharton Bates chair the meeting, Mrs. Fisher continued to insist that Mrs. Alford do so, totally ignoring the De Zavala group's efforts to be recognized. After repeatedly going through this fruitless exercise with disturbances continually arising from both groups, the De Zavala group's report of those final moments describes them as follows:

> Mrs. Fisher for the third time stepped up to the front of the rostrum and in an impatient manner struck the desk before her several times, saying, "I declare this Convention adjourned sine die." She then left the rostrum, and started to leave the Senate Chamber. Some of her party were already on the outside, when Mrs. Fisher

must have been informed by some parliamentarian that way of leaving the hall did not constitute a legal adjournment, for she came back, and endeavored to repair the error, but it was too late, as a Secretary pro tem had already been elected, and the work of the Convention was in progress under its legally constituted officers [Those elected meantime by the De Zavala group.], and no attention was paid to her return. Mrs. Fisher and her following finally left the hall and the work of the Convention was carried on uninterruptedly, thereafter, to its adjournment.[73]

Following the disputed "sine die" adjournment, the "Driscollites", as they were called, had left the Senate Chamber, and Mrs. Wharton Bates, Second Vice President, who was next in line as presiding officer according to the DRT Constitution, remained on the rostrum and with gavel in hand assumed the chairmanship of the meeting. The De Zavala group then continued the meeting and immediately elected Miss Mary Briscoe as secretary pro-tem to record the minutes of the meeting. This was followed by the election of officers to fill the slots left vacant by those who had left the meeting before what this group considered was a legal adjournment. Mrs. Anson Jones was re-elected President (she declared later in a written statement that she was not the president of this group but of the opposing group), Mrs. Wharton Bates was elected First Vice President, and other officers were duly elected in sequence and Miss De Zavala was elected Chairman of the Executive Committee. The group continued to do business in an orderly manner and adjourned the meeting at its end without further incident.

With intuitive foresight or by direction, or both, Mrs. Wharton Bates, collected statements from some of the senators present as outside witnesses to the proceedings of the meeting and the adjournment in particular.

Four of these testimonials are quoted here:

SENATE CHAMBER
AUSTIN, TEXAS

In the afternoon Mrs. Alford took the chair and called the meeting to order. Miss DeZavalla [sic] moved that Mrs. Fisher, the President [First Vice President actually, who should preside in absence of President, Mrs. Anson Jones.] was present, and that she take the chair. Mrs. Alford refused to put the motion; and then it was stated that Mrs. Fisher was not well and was unable to preside; Mrs. Alford still refusing to put said motion of Miss De Zavalla [sic]; then Mrs. Bates, who was the second vice president and next in order to Mrs. Fisher, and who was sitting on the rostrum, took up the gavel and attempted to put said motion of Miss De Zavalla; and Mrs. Fisher stepped forward and said that she declared the meeting was adjourned "sine die" and left the rostrum. At the time Miss De Zavalla had the floor and was talking, and Mrs. Bates was still standing with gavel in hand presiding. No motion to adjourn had been made and no one had been recognized for said purpose by Mrs. Fisher or any body else. When Mrs. Fisher and Mrs. Alford left the rostrum Mrs. Bates was standing on the rostrum at the President's stand with gavel in hand presiding, and Miss De Zavalla still had the floor. Miss De Zavalla then moved to elect a secretary and Mrs. Bates had put the motion to the body, and just then Mrs. Fisher returned to the rostrum, and without having Mrs. Bates surrender the gavel, put the sine die adjournment and declared it carried, though no motion had ever been made, and Mrs. Bates had not yielded the chair.
(In Senator Grinnan's writing A.D.Z.)[74]

[Followed by other handwritten details of testimonial by Senator Grinnan. Author's note.]

SENATE CHAMBER
AUSTIN, TEXAS   April 26, 1907

To Whom it May concern:

This is to certify that I was in the Senate Chamber of the Capitol of Texas Friday April 19, 1907 while the Sixteenth Annual Convention of the Daughters of the Republic was in session. I watched the proceedings and state positively that the convention was declared adjourned by Mrs. Rebecca J. Fisher, the first vice president of her own motion without the question ever being put to a vote of the convention, and Mrs. Fisher and some of those left the hall. I witnessed the further proceedings with Mrs. Bates presiding and there was never a break in the conduct of a regularly organized convention, those of the membership remaining continuing the business without even hesitation during the time Mrs. Fisher and those with her were leaving the hall.

I make this statement voluntarily.

(Signed) H. C. McMillan[75]

Austin, Texas April 22, 1907

This is to certify that we the undersigned were present in the Senate Chamber in the Capitol of Texas Friday April 19 1907, and witnessed the action of Mrs. Fisher, first vice president, who took the gavel in hand and declared the convention adjourned sine die, without a vote being taken or motion put.

(Signed) E. G. Kellis
Senator 14th Dist.[76]

The above statement is correct if any motion to adjourning was made I did not hear it and was in position to have heard it.

(Signed) Thos. P. Stone
Senator 11th Dist.[77]

Hopefully, statements such as these would be useful in determining whether the meeting was legally adjourned, according to parliamentary law. Upon this point, the decision as to which of the two groups was the official DRT body might hinge.

After leaving the meeting in the Senate Chamber, the other group, the "Driscollites", convened later that day at the Driskill Hotel in Austin. They voted to put the matter of the Alamo property in the hands of their executive committee and follow the wishes of Mrs. Clara Driscoll Sevier to create a park around the Alamo. They agreed with her plan of not encouraging the building of a museum or hall of fame, preferring to leave the area an open space with grass and "trailing vines" , and other appropriate plantings. They further agreed that Mrs. Anson Jones' authority to appoint Clara Driscoll as custodian of the Alamo should be respected.

The day after the convention, the Driscoll group asked the governor and the Attorney General to advise them as to which of the two groups was the legal representative of the DRT. The Attorney General rendered the opinion that the Driscoll group was the legitimate authority.

Shortly thereafter, Miss Driscoll's followers called on the Governor and told him Miss Driscoll had stated she would be glad to buy the Hugo-Schmeltzer property back from the State and devote it to some patriotic purpose. The Governor said this would be impossible without the consent of the Legislature.[78]

The other group, known as the "De Zavalans", continued to consider themselves the official and legal DRT body, however, regardless of the "opinion" of the Attorney General, and the "Driscollites" did the same. As a result, each group was carrying on official business in the name of the Daughters of the Republic of Texas.

On July 8, 1907, two and a half months after this chaos began, the "Driscollites" obtained a temporary injunction against the "De Zavalans" to bring an end to this impossible situation. Suit was to be brought to court in Houston, the county seat of Harris County.[79] The "De Zavalans" countered with a plea of abatement soon after and "the second battle" was on in earnest. At the bottom of the whole thing, of course, was the disagreement over the Hugo-Schmeltzer Building.

Like most cases with critical issues at stake, this one seemed to have an interminably long wait coming to trial. This one was unusually long, though, and possibly for at least one very good reason. What male judge would want to get between two such angry and determined groups of women? While the judge may have been able to delay the trial date, things did not stand still for the Daughters during the first eleven months of that long wait. The usual controversies and personal animosities continued to fester, but one unexpected dramatic situation was to occur several months later which enlivened the wait and brought it closer to conclusion very quickly.

The De Zavala group had set about at once to defend their claim as the true and rightful Daughters by seeking legal help. Since they had no treasury, this help had to be sought on a volunteer basis. The response was quick and positive. Within days, lawyers who were in sympathy with their position came to their aid *pro bono*.

The following letter, a copy of which, along with several others to be found in Miss De Zavala's Papers, is one of several exchanged between Mr. John T. Duncan, an attorney in La Grange, who turned out to be one of their staunchest supporters to the end, and his friend and colleague, another lawyer, Mr. W. G. Love of Houston, who became a strong ally, also.

JOHN T. DUNCAN
ATTORNEY AT LAW
LAGRANGE, TEXAS

Aug. 14, 1907.

Hon. W. G. Love,
    Houston, Texas.

Dear Sir and Friend:—
  I understand that the Daughters of the Republic, headed by Miss Adina De Zavala, have called for volunteers
to aid them in maintaining their rights as the true Board
of Directors or managers of the Order for the ensuing
year. I understand that you have offered your services
and I am glad that you have done so. I have offered my
services to be rendered without fee or reward, and I suppose there will be others who will join our ranks. . . .[80]

The letter continues with a statement of his general understanding of what took place at the April 1907 convention in
Austin, with specific reference to the "sine die" adjournment, of
what brought it about, and what happened afterward. He sums up
the situation by saying:

  There was a stampede of some kind at Austin . . . In my
  judgment, there was a bolt rather than an adjournment.
  Please give me your views and I suppose the duty will
  devolve upon you to prepare all the pleading and to take
  the necessary depositions of such witnesses as are
  unable to attend in person.
  Hoping to hear from you, I remain as ever,

                            Your friend,
                            /S/John T. Duncan [81]

Upon receipt of a reply from Mr. Love, Mr. Duncan sends
him the following response:

JOHN T. DUNCAN
ATTORNEY AT LAW
LAGRANGE, TEXAS

Aug. 30, 1907.

Hon. W. G. Love,
    Houston, Texas.

Dear Sir and Friend:—

I am in receipt of your letter, this morning advising me that you have agreed with Jake, to try the case before Judge Moore. I have just advised Judge Moore of the honor that has been thrust upon him. He says that he will be "dad-gast" if he is going to let Kittrell throw off this job on him. He believes that suicide would be preferable. I told him that Kittrell would exchange with him and try any case that he may have, if Judge Moore's court should be in session at the time this case is set for trial. [Because of prior involvement with parties of the Driscoll group, Judge Kittrell had been disqualified from serving as judge in the case.]

Please give me a copy of your answer, and a brief of the authorities upon which you rely, and also let me know the legal question involved in the case, so that I may read up on it. My knowledge of the facts in the case is such as I obtained through the columns of the press at the time the meeting at Austin was held, and in my judgment, . . . the chief question involved was one of parliamentary law, as to whether a First Vice President, who had declined to act as presiding officer, and, while another Vice President was wielding the gavel, could, without any motion of adjournment being before the House, arise and order the meeting adjourned sine die . .

Please let me hear from you at your earliest convenience.
I remain as ever,

Your sincere friend,
/S/John T. Duncan[82]

Adina De Zavala was provided with copies of letters such as these between her attorneys and, thus, was kept informed as they tried to move matters forward. Things remained at a standstill on a trial date, however, regardless of how much pressure their legal advisors might put on the trial judge. Six months had dragged by and the date still had not been set.

The strain of the situation was becoming almost more than Miss Adina could bear, though. It was just at this time she received a most needed letter of encouragement from her chief attorney, Mr. John T. Duncan:

January 28, 1908

My dear Miss Adina:
Mrs. Tuttle was in my office this morning and showed me a letter from you in which you state that you are almost on the eve of nervous prostration and that if this trouble is not ended soon, your patriotic friends will have to bury you.
I write this letter to revive your courage. Never give up the ship.[83]

The letter continues with explanations regarding still further delays in the trial date, stating that "Judge Moore has been idle for the last two and one-half weeks, and could have tried the case at anytime, . . ." that he will soon begin spring courts in New Braunfels and so on, and so on, with delaying excuses . . . "that he could have tried it a dozen times over . . ." at earlier dates.

Mr. Duncan had become quite disappointed and frustrated over Judge Moore's lack of action it seems. He tells Miss Adina he thinks "it is now almost out of the question to get Judge Moore to try this case and I believe we will have to look for another Judge somewhere else and I have written to Mr. Love to this effect." It appears as though he was beginning to wonder whether they could ever get a fair trial with him anyway.

The letter concludes with these words of encouragement:

Do not become pessimistic; do not become despon-
dent, but nerve yourself for the contest and be ready for
any fate that thc Power above may send. I remain,

Sincerely your friend,
/S/ John T. Duncan[84]

Mr. Duncan remained "sincerely her friend" and her strong
ally until the very last of the long ordeal and even beyond.

A new and dramatic crisis arose at this time, however, that
would further complicate the situation and bring national attention
to it once more. It was not another threat of demolition, but one of
quite a different nature. Under the present arrangement, after selling the old converted "long barracks" building to the State and
moving to their new store, the Hugo-Schmeltzer Company as
reported earlier had rented the old building as a storage facility, and
their rental lease was to expire on February 10, 1908. On January
27th, just two weeks prior to the expiration date of the lease, a San
Antonio newspaper published a story saying "numerous proposi-
tions" had been submitted to the Driscoll executive committee asking for a lease of the property, one of "which contemplates the
installation of a vaudeville and variety show within the walls. . . .
It was rumored last night that the structure had been rented . . ."[85]

Miss De Zavala was stunned when this "rumor" she had
been hearing about now appeared in print, and she issued a statement of her own the next day saying "the Alamo has not been and
never would be rented for any such purpose by the DRT."[86] Her reference to the DRT meant her group, of course, since she considered
them the official group until the court might decide otherwise. In
referring to the "Alamo", she meant the "long barracks", a.k.a. the
Hugo-Schmeltzer Building. To her the entire property was "The
Alamo" actually, but the "long barracks" was the significant build-

ing. Untold numbers had died in the "long barracks", including one of the best known of the heroes, Jim Bowie, according to Miss De Zavala's belief, whereas only a handful of defenders had died within the jagged-walled ruins and rubble of the Chapel. While it was certainly an honored site of the battle, it by no means was the sacred site the other building was in her mind.

Just as this "rumor" of leasing the Alamo ("long barracks") for a "vaudeville show" appeared in print, Miss De Zavala received a letter dated January 27, 1908, from her attorney, Mr. Love, from Houston with the following advice:

> . . . As I wrote you before I think if Hugo Schmeltzer
> and Co. will turn the keys over to you as President of the
> De Zavala Chapter you had better get them to do it . . .[87]

This time Miss De Zavala wasted no time in calling on Mr. Charles Heuermann, the employee of Hugo-Schmeltzer cited earlier, with a request for the keys to the building in order 'to protect it' in the name of the De Zavala Chapter of the DRT. He willingly complied with her request for reasons he gave in his testimonial quoted earlier on pages 226 and 227.[88]

Upon obtaining the keys, she hired three watchmen to guard the building. She felt certain her opponents or "their allies" (business men seeking to rent the premises) intended to take possession of it and she was determined to prevent them from doing so in any way she could. Just how she was going to do that she did not know yet, but in no time the opportunity presented itself in an event that was to make Adina De Zavala the one to become famous throughout the country this time in connection with the Alamo—it was the highly publicized "barricade" of herself inside the Hugo-Schmeltzer Building.

Because of repeated misrepresentation as to what actually happened on that occasion, she described the entire episode in a

282

"Statement by Miss De Zavala" she published soon afterward.[89]

Since that time the story has been told, re-told and "miss-told" by writers and self-proclaimed "historians" over the years. The DRT account as they recorded it is on file at the DRT Library. To have the most complete and accurate account of what happened, however, the rule is always go to the primary source first if at all possible, and get the story from one who experienced it. Miss De Zavala's account was consulted for this purpose.

The "Statement by Miss De Zavala", describing her experience, opens by saying, "I did not surrender nor retreat", which is an echo of the same positive statement made by William Barret Travis in his letter from the Alamo, pleading for help to come to their aid. Travis did not surrender nor retreat. Neither did Adina De Zavala. A copy of Miss De Zavala's entire "Statement" is included in Chapter Eight, pages 301-303. A condensed description of the "barricade" incident itself, based on that statement, follows.

According to Miss De Zavala, she established her watchmen at the building and had gone home for the evening, but she returned shortly afterward to take care of a weak door she had forgotten "to have properly strengthened." She went inside the building, locking the door behind her, and discussed the matter of reinforcing the door with the watchmen. As she was just starting to leave to return home, she noticed a carriage near the front entrance of the building. She decided to wait to see what might develop.

Soon a loud knock sounded at the main entrance to the building, and a voice then demanded that the door be opened. When it was not opened immediately, the knock sounded again and then several more times. Then the loud voice announced that if the door was not opened they would break it down. When the door still was not opened, several rushes were made against it, glass panes were shattered, and finally the heavy double-doors burst open.

Upon entering, the intruders saw the watchmen and demanded to know by what right they were there. The watchmen were informed by the intruders that they represented the sheriff and they had a court injunction ordering that the premises be vacated at once. When the watchmen did not comply, the "lawmen" threw them out "bodily".

Having disposed of the guards, the intruders returned to confront Miss De Zavala herself. After a moment of hesitation, they stepped outside to have what she described as a "whispered consultation", no doubt regarding what they should do about her now.

Miss De Zavala had been completely dumfounded by their bold tactics with such a forcible entry, but even though she was in a state of shock, she made a bold decision of her own and a firm resolve to stand by it. The instant the men stepped outside the building this time she closed the door and barred it. And there she remained, unmovable for three days and nights, refusing to open the door or come out unless she had assurances that the building would remain in status quo until it had been decided by the court who would have legal control of the future plans for it.

The Sheriff announced that no food or drink could be brought in to her, in the hope, as she stated, she would be "starved out". Further, she could have no communication with outside visitors—only official contacts would be allowed as determined by him.

Negotiations were attempted, but all failed until Miss De Zavala was assured by no one less than the Governor himself that neither of the opposing groups would have control of the building until the court decision had been made. Until that time came she refused to open the door voluntarily and come out. She said she would stay there "if she had to starve" if necessary.

When the representative of the Governor, the Superintendent of Buildings and Grounds, Mr. W. C. Day, arrived on the third day and stated that Governor Campbell would negotiate with the official group on the future plans for the building only after the court had decided which one that would be, Miss De Zavala opened the door and came out. She then proceeded to show

Mr. Day around the grounds in what was her normal gracious manner, as though nothing unusual had taken place and this might be something she did every day.

The story of this famous barricade would not be complete, however, without accounts from some other sources as to what happened to her during those three days and three nights. How did she fare with no food and no water? No creature comforts of any kind?

The information and descriptions of that, found in the words of the newspaper stories of the day, whether they can be believed or not, far surpass what any present day writers could offer. The audacity of a small wisp of a woman doing such a thing naturally captured the imagination, and the admiration, of people everywhere, and Miss De Zavala received numerous letters and telegrams of support from all over the country. But the story was one made in heaven for the press. As Dr. L. Robert Ables put it, they "saw the action as excellent copy and thousands of words crackled over the wires."

The farther away the newspaper, the more colorful the story it would seem. One out-of-state account from the *Courier-Herald* of Saginaw, Michigan reported the story in fine dramatic style:

DAUGHTER HOLDS ALAMO; DEFIES STATE OFFICERS

Descendant of Vice President of Republic
of Texas Takes Possession
of Historical Building.

San Antonio, Texas, Feb. 12.

Without food and water for over thirty hours, Miss Adina Desavala, [sic] president of the Desavala Chapter, Daughters of the Republic, is in prison at the Alamo where she defies Judge Norman K. Kittrell of Houston, who has ordered her to leave, and dares the officers of the law to put her out of the historic building.

She says she will remain in the building until she starves before she will surrender it.

The transfer of the property was to have been made last night. Miss Desavala took possession yesterday afternoon and refused to give up the property. She locked the doors in the face of the sheriff, who tried to serve the injunction. He broke down the doors, but Miss Desavala took refuge on the second floor in the room in which Bowie was killed, and she has remained there ever since. She held the fort all last night despite the fact that she was in absolute darkness, and that rats scampered over her feet. The sheriff has refused to permit food to be carried to her, and although faint from hunger she is still standing firm. She says she will hold her position indefinitely. Her grandfather was Vice President Desavala [sic] of the Texas republic.[90]

A local San Antonio newspaper, the *Light,* carried a story that appeared the next morning after the "barricade" had begun which presented a somewhat more accurate account:

Within the walls of the Alamo again is strife being waged. This time it is a silent battle. The combating forces are Miss Adina DeZavala on the one side and the strong arm of the law, represented by a shamed looking deputy sheriff on the other. Miss DeZavala holds the fort and so does the deputy. Miss DeZavala has the keys to the locks on the doors and the deputy has the means of freeing the bolts and bars that are held in place by means of common padlocks. To talk to either you must use the port holes in the wooden doors.

"I'll stay here forever if needs be," says Miss DeZavala.

"You can't get anything to eat," says the sheriff's assistant.

Miss DeZavala was on the ground last night and entered the property. Sheriff John Tobin also was there, flanked by a couple of deputies, and so was J. E. Webb, the attorney representing Alamo chapter, Daughters of the Republic of Texas. Victor [sic, correct name is Charles Hugo] Hugo was there as the representative of the company that has been paying rental for the property. Mr. Hugo was not particular as to whose possession the property passes into, but the others were. Sheriff Tobin was armed with a court injunction, issued by Judge Noman [sic] G. Kittrell in the Harris county court house at Houston. This injunction forbids Miss DeZavala and any and all members of DeZavala chapter from seeking to interfere with the Alamo property.

An attempt was made to serve the injunction upon Miss DeZavala by the sheriff, but the decrees of a court brought no fear to the grand-daughter of the Castillian general who threw his fortunes with the young republic in the struggle for freedom. She refused to accept a copy of the document and when an attempt was made to read it to her, she stopped up her ears.[91]

Adina De Zavala had not only "stopped up her ears", she had put the large placard shown in a visible spot discouraging in no uncertain terms any attempt to communicate with her whatsoever. A copy of the fragment of the handwritten message found in the De Zavala Collection is shown on the preceding page.

Two days after her voluntary incarceration, the following account appeared in the *Galveston News:*

ALAMO OVERTURES
WERE BROKEN OFF

FACTIONS ALMOST AGREED TO TURN
PROPERTY OVER TO THE GOVERNOR.

MISS DE ZAVALA GETS FOOD

Friend Sent Her an Oil Stove—Received
Congratulatory Telegrams—Willing
to Turn Property Over.

SPECIAL TO THE NEWS.
San Antonio, Tex., Feb. 12—After it seemed that all points of difference in the dispute over the possession of the Alamo Property and the Mission San Antonio had been settled a sensation was sprung late this afternoon, when all negotiations between the attorneys were broken off and the matter referred to the attorneys at Houston for settlement.

Although Miss Adina de Zavala has already been in the Alamo for forty-eight hours, with practically no food, and until early today, no water, she is still defiant and refuses to surrender the property.

The break in the negotiations came from the anti-De Zavala faction of the Daughters of the Republic, at the head of which is Mrs. Rebecca J. Fisher of Austin, represented here by Attorneys Webb and Goeth and Miss Jennie Burleson, sister of Congressman Burleson.

Superintendent of Buildings and Grounds Day, representing Governor Campbell, arrived this morning. A
conference was held at which were present those named
above, Judge Don A. Bliss, Judge J. D. Guinn, and
Nelson Lyttle, attorneys for Miss de Zavala, and Mrs.
Wharton Bates of Houston, president of the De Zavala
faction of the Daughters of the Republic.

Both sides were willing to turn over the property to
the representative of the governor without prejudice to
the rights of either party pending the settlement of all
litigation.

Split on court Decision.

The De Zavala attorneys, however, wanted a provi-
sion that in case the injunction suit at Houston could not
be brought to a speedy trial that a similar suit pending in
Bexar County be brought to trial, and that all parties
abide by the result of the suit which should be decided
first. Both suits are of the same nature, and involve the
question of the legal possession of the Alamo and the
adjoining property.

Suit is Delayed.

The attorneys for Miss De Zavala stated that frequent
efforts had been made to have the case at Houston
brought to trial but all efforts had failed. They claimed
that the suit here could be brought to trial on its merits
at once, if the Houston case was again postponed.

This agreement was satisfactory to Superintendent
Day and Gov. Campbell and the De Zavala faction, but
the other faction would not agree to it. Attorneys Webb
and Goeth claim that they had no authority to go beyond
the terms of the agreement reached by the attorneys at
Houston, and which has already been published in *The
News.*

It was therefore agreed to refer the whole matter to the
attorneys representing both sides in Houston and if the
attorneys for Mrs. Fisher in Houston would agree to the
terms proposed by Miss De Zavala's attorneys the property would be turned over to Superintendent Day.

The papers were mailed to Houston tonight and
Superintendent Day will remain here pending a decision

at Houston tomorrow. [93]

As the article continues, the matter of no food or water is played up to the fullest in this one, too, but that obstacle was overcome, as the article explains:

Miss De Zavala Remains Firm

In the meantime, Miss De Zavala will maintain possession of the property and will refuse to remove the barricades from the door. The rule prohibiting food being sent to her is still in force. However, strong friends have outwitted the Deputy sheriffs and smuggled food to her.

Several packages of chocolates were smuggled into her in newspapers through the small aperture in the door. A paper bag full of sandwiches was also smuggled to her by a friend, who was in the street and who attracted the attention of Miss De Zavala, who was standing on the gallery of the second floor and she let down a long cord, to which she tied the paper bag. She pulled this up and feasted.[94]

Food for the hungry heroine of the Alamo from "strong friends"!

Two well-known San Antonio women who are the granddaughters of two of those faithful friends who took food to Miss De Zavala still reside in San Antonio today, and they recall the stories of each respective grandmother smuggling food in to that lone defender of the Alamo, who had said she would "starve before she would surrender." Those ladies who took food to Adina De Zavala were two sisters who were members of the well known Bowen family of San Antonio.

Writer and historian, Mary Ann Noonan Guerra (Mrs. Henry Guerra), is a granddaughter of one of the sisters, Cornelia Bowen Noonan, who was the wife of Judge George Henry Noonan. Cornelia and her sister Isabella had been staunch supporters of Miss Adina from the beginning of her crusade and now they stood by her throughout her ordeal. When Cornelia Bowen Noonan learned of the unbelievable fact that the sheriff had refused to allow food to be sent in to Miss De Zavala, she determined to do something about it. She prepared a "paper bag full of sandwiches" and set off to deliver them. But, since no one was allowed to take food in to her, how would she get them in? She arrived at the "long barracks" and stood across the street wondering what to do. She spotted Miss De Zavala out on the upper gallery and managed to get her attention. When Adina De Zavala saw her friend with her paper bag in hand, the solution was suddenly clear. Her resourceful and practical nature came to the fore, and the story has a happy and successful conclusion at the end of "a long cord", as the newspaper account relates. Miss De Zavala simply lowered the cord and pulled up her friend's offering. That story of how Mary Ann Noonan Guerra's "grandmother took sandwiches to Adina De Zavala when she was barricaded in the Alamo" has come down through the family over the years.[95]

The other granddaughter who has a story to add to this one, is a well known historic preservationist and activist, Wanda Ford. Wanda Graham Ford (Mrs. O'Neil Ford), is the daughter of Elizabeth Graham, who was also an active historic preservationist, and the granddaughter of Isabella Bowen Orynski, Mrs. Leonard Orynski. Wanda is a first cousin to Mary Ann Noonan Guerra. Wanda's grandmother, Isabella, the other resourceful Bowen sister, did her part to help sustain Miss De Zavala, too. As always told in family lore, the story tells how Isabella Bowen wrapped her offering inside some newspapers which she passed through an opening in the door in full view of the deputy sheriffs on guard. Wanda said she had never heard that it was chocolates that her grandmother had smuggled in to her inside the newspapers as the account says, but she did know her grandmother loved chocolates (as does her granddaughter today!) and that would have been a logical choice for her.[96]

Sandwiches for the starving lone defender of the Alamo to

"feast on" and chocolates for dessert! It appears that not only was Adina De Zavala resourceful, but so were her friends.

The article continues with stories of other comforts, some provided by more of her resourceful and "strong friends". A statement from Miss De Zavala and the attorneys for the opposing group concludes story of the incident with the following:

> She is now also supplied with water. She found a hydrant in the yard, which had been used for watering horses, and is drinking from this.
>
> She has no cup and has to use primitive methods. Since she has been in the Alamo, she has had no coffee. As she is addicted to the coffee habit she is suffering from a very bad headache. She has slept but little for two nights, having no place in which to lie down and having nothing to keep her warm but the clothes she wore into the Alamo.
>
> ### Gets Oil Stove
>
> She will fare better tonight, however. By means of a rope she let down from the second story gallery she pulled up an oil stove a friend in the street tied to the end of it, and that will keep her warm. She does not seem to be suffering much from her privations and is as firm and defiant as ever.
>
> In explanation of his orders that the deputies shall not permit any food to be brought to the Alamo, Sheriff Tobin says:
>
> "Miss de [sic] Zavala is at liberty to leave the building and get meals at any time she sees fit. Two deputies are on duty. They spell each other, so they are suffering no privations."
>
> ### Miss de Zavala said tonight:
>
> "I am perfectly willing to turn the property over to Gov. Campbell. I have every faith in his honor and integrity. I am perfectly willing to submit my rights to the courts. All I want is to keep the property out of the hands of people who have no right to it. I will starve before I will turn the building over to them."
>
> "The two days and nights spent in the Alamo were

very trying. I hardly slept at all and got only such food as was smuggled to me by friends who outwitted the deputies. I had no place to sleep and suffered some from the cold, but I did not mind that. I am simply fighting to hold what I believe I have a right to hold."

Miss de Zavala received many telegrams from over the State yesterday and today urging her to stand firm. Among them was the following from Mrs. Wharton Bates of Houston, president of the Daughters of the Republic of Texas: "You are a true daughter; call for reinforcements if needed." Mrs. Bates also sent the following telegram to Mayor Callaghan:

"Miss de Zavala is in possession of the Alamo as authorized agent of the Daughters of the Republic of Texas. See that she is treated right."

This telegram was conveyed to Miss de Zavala in a letter by the City Clerk, which was written at the direction of Mayor Callaghan. He took no action in the matter.

The following telegram was also received from Goliad, Texas:

"Congratulations. Success to your bravery. With you heart and hand."

This telegram was signed by Miss Kate Davis, president, and Mrs. C. Derring, treasurer, of the Labalia [La Bahia] Chapter, Daughters of the Republic.

Attorney Webb said tonight:

"We are willing to turn the property over to the Government under the agreement arrived at in Houston. We have no authority to go further." [97]

This last statement by the "Driscollites" attorneys seems to say they now accepted the fact they had no authority to put Miss De Zavala out of the building in the first place, nor to take possession of it. They now seemed to accept that they must wait for the trial ahead of them before attempting further action of any kind.

The next morning, February 13th, three days after she had

entered the Hugo-Schmeltzer Building and "barricaded" herself inside, was the day she voluntarily walked out and surrendered the property to the representative of the governor, the State Superintendent of Public Buildings, upon assurance that the governor would not negotiate with either side until a court decision had been made as to which group would be the official DRT group.

The following day, a San Antonio newspaper carried a subdued and almost sad account of the end of the dramatic incident in one small, forlorn paragraph, almost like an obituary:

> A lone watchman is all there is today as a reminder of the second Alamo warfare. Miss Adina De Zavala, who for three days remained in possession, jointly with one of Sheriff Tobin's deputies, last night surrendered her part of the property to W. C. Day, who was sent by Gov. Campbell to take possession. Miss De Zavala acted upon advice of her attorneys after an agreement had been reached. Mr. Day was pleasantly greeted when he arrived and he was shown around over the property by Miss De Zavala. Miss Sarah Eager remains as custodian of the Alamo Mission Chapel.[98]

In her judgment, Adina De Zavala had done nothing more than what she felt a patriotic Texan should do. Nothing else she had done in the forty-six years of her life thus far, or would do in the remaining forty-seven, would surpass it. She accomplished many significant things toward the preservation of Texas history, both before and after this that ended with success, but all those things put together would not even come close to this one event in the memory of the public to this day.

She dismissed it, however, as simply her duty. In the interview several years later with Pearl Howard, cited earlier, she said:

> . . . There was nothing else for me to do but hold the fort. I did.[99]

Nothing else for her to do? As Pearl Howard said, "she could have washed her hands of the whole affair," as others might have done, but that was not the nature of Adina De Zavala.

Further reassurance, beyond that offered by the public came a few days later in a letter from her attorney, John T. Duncan. In it he states he and others fully approved of what she had done regarding her "barricade" and assured her it was quite legal in his opinion. His letter gives the legal basis for what she did as he viewed it.

JOHN T. DUNCAN,
ATTORNEY AT LAW
OFFICE OVER FIRST NATIONAL BANK
LAGRANGE, TEXAS

Feb. 15, 1908.

Miss Adina DeZavalla, [sic]
San Antonio, Texas

My dear Miss Adina:—
We have been watching, with great interest, the stand which you took with reference to the Alamo buildings, and we all fully approve of your patriotic and unselfish stand.

The only thing that astonishes me is that the manhood of Bexar County could have stood silently by and have you treated as the public print claims that you were treated. There are some legal aspects to this matter, to which I desire to briefly submit to you.

1st: Judge Kittrell being disqualified to try this case, he was disqualified from making any order in it. He was disqualified from granting the preliminary injunction, therefore the preliminary injunction was absolutely null and void, and you are in no contempt of court for disregarding said order.

2nd: When the Sheriff served the writ of injunction upon you in the Alamo, that gave him no power or right to take possession of the building, no more than he would have had the right to have held possession of your private residence, if he had served a writ of injunction or a citation upon you at that place.

3rd: If you disobeyed this writ of injunction, even if it had been a valid writ, the Sheriff could not have punished you for holding the writ in contempt, nor could he have taken you into custody. His function was performed, when he served this writ upon you and the act of contempt, if any, not having been done in the presence of the court, you could only have been proceeded against for contempt, by a motion having been filed in the District Court at Houston and had you cited to show cause why you should not be punished for contempt.

4th: It was reported here in the papers that the Deputy Sheriff prevented persons from giving you food or water and that you had to get water by having it poured to you through a hole. Now I believe this act of the Deputy Sheriff was tantamount to false imprisonment, and I believe that something ought to be done by you against the Sheriff for this indignity. The Sheriff had no more right to prevent people from bringing you food or water, while you were in the Alamo, than any other private citizen would have had to have prevented your friends from thus ministering to you.

Now these are my views. I intended to prepare them as an interview for Mrs. Tuttle, but we heard of your release before anything was done along this line.

Mrs. Tuttle tells me that she has had a fever for the last two days on account of the manner in which you have been treated. I am satisfied that if she had been in San Antonio, there would have been war.

Please excuse me for this short note, but I feel it my duty to write to you and approve of your patriotic course.

I salute you with esteem and respect.

Sincerely your friend,
/S/ John T. Duncan

JTD[100]

Two weeks after her "barricade" of the Alamo ended, Miss De Zavala went to Austin to visit her sister Mary who was working and living there at that time. The local newspaper, *The Austin Daily Statesman*, sent a reporter over to interview her and on February 29, 1908, an article appeared from which the following excerpts are taken:

HEROINE OF THE ALAMO
MISS ADINA DE ZAVALA TELLS OF HER RECENT
STRUGGLE TO KEEP SACRED MEMORY OF THE
HISTORIC BUILDING.
CERTAIN OF VICTORY

. . . . that Miss Adina recently prevented the serving of an injunction regarding the possession of the Alamo by taking possession of that historic building and holding it against all comers for about a week.

A Statesman reporter called on Miss de Zavala last night and learned a new version of the incident which has attracted so much attention recently. Miss de Zavala stated that she did not take possession of the Alamo to prevent the serving of the injunction, as has been stated, but that her presence in the building was due to an accident, she having gone there to attend to a minor matter.

"The other side had spies watching the building," said Miss de Zavala, "and I was seen to enter the building early in the afternoon. I went there to give instructions to the men there with regard to the building, but soon got through and left. After I had gotten home I thought of a door which was weak and needed attention and decided to return, which I did, ending a march on the other side. I had the weak door strengthened and was at the door, just about to leave, when the sheriff appeared to serve the injunction.

"He called to the men on the inside, but they did not answer, and he then broke through the large double doors and entered the building. When he came in one of the men spoke to him and asked him what he wanted. He replied and told the men to get out, that he had an injunction against their being in the building. They refused to come out saying they were there by my authority, and he then started to read the injunction. It was about six pages long and full of legal phrases and took him awfully long to read it. I stepped out before he had finished and asked him what he wanted. He answered that he had an injunction forcing my side to leave the building. I told him the injunction was void, that it was issued by a judge who had no right to issue it and was being served by a sheriff who was known to be on the other side. He took the men out of the building and went away, leaving me there."

"Did you suffer much while in the Alamo?" was asked.

"Well, the sheriff wouldn't let them bring me any supper and there was no place to sleep and not a particle of water in the building. But when my friends learned where I was they saw that I was made comfortable in spite of the sheriff. I had an orange for breakfast the next morning and had plenty to eat after that. But I would have stayed there without anything. I didn't care."

"Do you consider that your leaving the Alamo was a victory or merely a compromise?"

"I consider it a victory, and so do my friends over the state, from whom I have received dozens of congratulatory telegrams."

"What will be the next step of your side in the present controversy?"

"We can't do anything until the matter is settled in the courts. The other side has kept postponing and postponing until it seems as if we never will get it on trial. Judge Kittrell has been disqualified as judge, and we will have to have a special judge. If we lose we will just retire gracefully. Our position has been on the defensive, and the others have brought all the suits and haven't kept their agreements. I feel sure that we will win, for we are certainly on the right side." [101]

When they had asked her indirectly what she would do if she lost, Adina De Zavala had said, "If we lose we will just retire gracefully." Prophetic words were those, but she didn't realize it at the time, nor did she believe the trial would be decided that way.

Miss De Zavala still believed unshakably that her side would win, and she continued to believe that until the final moment, because, as she maintained, "we are on the right side." Her motto had always been David Crockett's motto: "Be always sure you're right-then go ahead!", and that is what she had done.

Adina De Zavala's determined stand had brought her great satisfaction in one sense, but it had been a tremendous emotional and physical strain on her. It had won her the admiration of a great many people, not only all the Texans who agreed with her position historically, but also many other Americans throughout the country, for standing up for the courage of her convictions. Letters continued to come in to her from near and far.

In a letter four months later dated June 14, 1908, from her friend Adele Looscan, however, she says:

> I have come to the point of agreeing with your sister, Mary, that all the relics and old buildings in Texas are not worth the trouble that this matter has caused.[102]

The dramatic episode had become immediate fodder for the opposing DRT group. They began a campaign to discredit her even further by saying she had done this for publicity for herself and that the Hugo-Schmeltzer Building was not a part of the Alamo complex; that she was interested in gaining selfish control of the building so she could 'create an imitation of an old mission style museum building without any historical significance, built to her own liking.'

After all her conscientious efforts to spread accurate historical information regarding the building, the "Driscollites" still insisted that the Hugo-Schmeltzer Building had nothing to do with the Battle of the Alamo and that this whole affair had been misguided and completely unnecessary.

The Executive Committee of the Driscoll group issued a public statement of its version of some details of the incident:

In this connection, the Committee begs to state that Miss De Zavala did not occupy "the room where Bowie died" but did take up her abode in the old Hugo-Schmeltzer Warehouse, a dilapidated wooden structure in no sense part of the Alamo or the old Mission de Valero.[103]

A newspaper account had made this statement regarding Bowie, but Miss De Zavala herself did not claim she had occupied "the room where Bowie died". She did claim, however, he had died in a former hospital room on the second floor of the building where she had barricaded herself. She based this on historical sources quoted earlier.

In answer to the claim by the De Zavala Chapter that the Driscoll group had intended to tear the building down or rent it to a vaudeville company, the Vice President of the Driscoll group, Mrs. Fisher, wrote a letter to the *Houston Chronicle* on March 1st stating:

The executive committee were on the eve of renting it to a reliable business gentleman of San Antonio . . . She [Miss De Zavala] was not in the Alamo, but in the Hugo-Schmeltzer Building, erected during the war of 1846-48, between the United States and Mexico. The building was constructed by military authorities at that time and used for a commissary and other purposes. . ."[104]

While this was a denial that the Driscoll group had any intention of tearing down the building under question, it was clear evidence that they intended to take possession of it and rent it without court authorization to do so yet.

Statements such as those made by the Driscoll followers angered and upset Miss De Zavala almost beyond control and kept her in a state of intense frustration. She and her group felt there was ample proof that the original two-story "long barracks" building, site of the final assault on the Alamo, was still there under cover of the commercial wooden structure. They contended and rightly so, as would be proven later, the building was indeed a part of both the Alamo battle and the old mission. She and her group were determined to continue their fight to save it in any way possible, for as Miss De Zavala was quoted as saying:

> Would it be reasonable to suppose De Zavala Chapter would labor for sixteen years to save a building and then, when they believed their work ended and the building secured, submit to its demolishment without . . . a murmur?[105]

It was because of such continuing claims made, not only by the DRT opposition group, but by the public in general by now, that Adina De Zavala took every opportunity to make statements regarding what she felt were the true historical facts about the building, and to publish her own "Statement" referred to previously and reprinted here in full:

STATEMENT BY MISS De ZAVALA

> I did not surrender nor retreat. It is not a fight for power, but principle.
> It is a fight by the Daughters of the Republic of Texas, to keep intact the most priceless treasure of Texas, and one of the most historic and noted buildings on the American Continent - the Alamo. To prevent its desecration by sacrilegious hands, and its demolition by those now insensible to its value as a precious heritage.
> It is not generally known, but there is a combine of men who have determined to destroy the usefulness of the Association of the Daughters of the Republic of Texas, because it has dared to stand for the truth of Texas history, and the preservation of the sacred landmarks, and refused to grant the request of a hotel syndicate and some property owners, adjacent to the Alamo, that it agree to the tearing down of that part of the Alamo, recently purchased, and graciously permit these parties to make a park of its site; in order that the prop-

erty of said parties, now on a back or side street might front the proposed park, and incidentally become several times more valuable.

These people or their allies had planned to capture this part of the Alamo, and knowing that once they obtained possession, the Alamo was doomed, I determined to be there before them, and to take possession. I had full authority to do this, as President of De Zavala Chapter, and agent of the General Association of the Daughters of the Republic of Texas.

I left the Alamo building late on the afternoon of February 10th, after instructing the guards I had placed there for the night. I returned soon afterwards, as I had forgotten to have a certain weak door properly strengthened; I had the door reinforced and started to go home again, when I noticed a carriage near the front entrance, and I awaited developments. In a short time there came a loud knock, and a voice demanded admission in the name of the Law. I knew that no Court had given anyone else a right to the property and no reply was vouchsafed. A second time, a third time, and several more times the voice was heard: "Open the door; if you do not open the door, I will burst it open." Still no reply. The glass was then shattered, and a rush made on the large, heavy double glass doors, with outside wooden shutters. They were then asked what they wanted and by what authority they dared attempt to invade the premises. A number of rushes were made on the doors by the party, and they finally broke in. Of course I was amazed and rather stunned at this bold course. I knew that the enemy had planned to capture the building gentecly or otherwise, and that they were at their wit's end when they found that I had possession, but neither I, nor any of us, could have imagined such high-handed action as actually occurred in utter disregard of the rights of property or the laws of the State. They took into consideration the somewhat isolated position of the Alamo, and expected to trade, and did trade on the want of accurate knowledge of people in general as to the laws; for the man who thus forced entrance was a Sheriff, and he announced that he was acting as such, serving a citation or some court paper relative to an injunction that had been brought by his party.

Providentially, and to their great dismay, I was there, and the possession so ardently coveted could not be obtained. I positively refused to leave the building though they deprived me of my servitors, and like brave(?) men hoping to frighten a timid woman into beating a retreat, and at any cost secure possession, they cut my telephone and electric light wires, and thus deprived me of communication with my friends for the night, and in addition, prevented my watchman from bringing me supper.

Seeking to avoid publicity, I kept the matter as quiet as possible, and few learned of the trouble until the afternoon papers appeared on Tuesday. I was too tired and exhausted from my vigil to make plans, but hourly expected a legal settlement of the outrageous situation. To add to the unpleasantness and delay, it happened that none of my regular attorneys were in the city, and no one seemed able to grasp the real situation, as it was almost unthinkable. One of the enemy's guards was placed at the door to see that nothing to eat came in, in the hope, as the Sheriff expressed it that I should be "starved out."

My attorneys saw at once on their return, that the enemy were attempting to take something to which they had no right. The enemy withdrew their guard, and I agreed to have the Governor of Texas, as a disinterested party, who was worthy of trust, to hold the property in status quo until the question as to the case now pending in the Courts be settled.

(Signed) ADINA De ZAVALA

Chairman, Executive Committee, Daughters of the Republic of Texas, and President of De Zavala Chapter, Daughters of the Republic of Texas.
117 Fourth Street, San Antonio, Texas[106]

Her purpose and decision not to leave the building without assurance that the other group would neither rent it nor have it demolished, had been stated very clearly. At the same time, she also gave the same assurance that her group would not do anything further until that court decision had been made. And so the waiting game continued.

The Driscoll group persisted in their erroneous claims regarding the Hugo-Schmeltzer Building. They would not accept historical evidence contrary to their misconceptions. The following "Supplemental Statement" submitted for their case is further example of their continuing error.

> The public at large do not understand that the major portion of the ground which was originally purchased by Miss Clara Driscoll from Hugo & Schmeltzer . . . is not occupied by any portion of the original Alamo building or mission, but that same is occupied by a building built long after the fall of the Alamo . . . That many people not familiar with the facts believe . . . that this building is a part of the building that was hallowed by the blood of the heroes of Texas, when in truth and in fact it has never been hallowed except by good, bad and indifferent whiskey. [This refers to the Grenet and then Hugo-Schmeltzer use of the building as a whiskey sales and warehousing facility.] It was the intention of the plaintiff's [Driscollites] Executive Committee . . . to remove this unsightly building and place in lieu thereof a park, museum or something else.[107]

The tumult over the "barricade" did succeed in accomplishing one thing, though, if nothing else. It apparently caused the court authorities to realize at last that this was not just a 'tempest in a teapot' carried on over the tea-cups of a ladies club, and the trial was scheduled soon afterward.

On May 14th, Miss De Zavala's attorney, John T. Duncan, wrote her from LaGrange a hasty, handwritten letter (because his "stenographer was on vacation"), with great news at last! He had seen Judge Moore and he said he could "try the case any day between the 21st and 28th of the month of May in Houston". Duncan urged Miss Adina to get behind Mr. Love and "Jake", and the other attorneys in Houston, to set the date.[108]

The date was set and the trial finally took place in May at Harris County Courthouse in Houston with Judge Moore presiding. After such a long wait, it was a very short trial, and when it concluded, the court found in favor of the plaintiff, the Driscoll group.

Miss De Zavala was completely devastated. She and her group were in a state of shock and disbelief, it was all over so quickly.

She had a letter almost immediately though, from one of her supporting lawyers, a judge in San Antonio, Don A. Bliss, which must have restored her courage somewhat and given her a ray of hope.

DON A. BLISS,
ATTORNEY-AT-LAW.
SAN ANTONIO, TEXAS.
May 31st., 1908.
Dear Miss DeZavala:

You will doubtless be surprised at receiving a letter so soon from me; but there is a matter concerning which I desire to be more thoroughly informed and to get the information at once, as upon the nature of this information depends my opinion as to the proper course for you individually to pursue in the case that has just been decided against you.

You will remember that I did not reach Houston until after the trial had been begun and the pleadings all settled. One of the first questions I asked Mr. Love was whether there was any sworn plea denying the authority of the parties who brought the suit. Mr. Love informed that there was such a plea, and I suppose that there is and that it is in proper shape. But I was never able to find our answer in the case. It seems that it was misplaced. We were so rushed in the trial of the case that we hardly had time "to turn around", and I shall be uneasy about the pleading mentioned until I see it or a true copy. Can you not get some one to send me a copy of our pleading?

More mature reflection has only confirmed me in the opinion that I gave you all last night, and that was that if you expected to maintain your connection with the organization and preserve any standing therein, you should appeal. If our pleading is in proper shape, I am absolutely confident that the judgment will be reversed at least as to you, and that the higher court will hold that the Executive Committee could not override the will of the organization as expressed by it in a corporate meeting (the Goliad meeting) and take the custody of the Alamo from those whom the Association had by a solemn act in a corporate meeting had made the agents to hold the property.

The truth about it is that for you to submit without an appeal to this shameless decision of Judge Moore would be an act of almost if not quite pusillanimity on your part. It would certainly be so construed by your adversaries, and your continued connection with the organization would be rendered intolerable. My opinion is that a conflict should always be avoided if possible consistent with honor and self-respect, but if a conflict is forced upon one, then the fight should be to the death.

With my respects to Mrs. Looscan and family, and thanks for her hospitality, I remain

Yours sincerely,
/S/ Don A. Bliss[109]

The decision was appealed, but once again there was a long wait before the appellate court met, and so the waiting game was on again.

During all this rancor surrounding the turmoil of this whole episode, Clara Driscoll Sevier [as she signed her name at that time] had not been visible or publicly involved. In fact, the Executive Committee of her followers stated that she was not associated with the Alamo disagreement in any way.

Apparently she still felt a strong possessiveness regarding the place she had "saved," though, because she wrote a letter to the President, Mrs. Fisher, on March 9, 1909, from New York, in which she "outlined what she always wanted to do, had her work not been so rudely interrupted at Goliad." She asks "for the privilege, once more of enlisting in the ranks of the DRT and continuing her work with them", with her new plan for the Hugo-Schmeltzer Building and the park with which she planned to replace it. She enclosed a copy of a letter she had written to the Governor and the Legislature of Texas with her offer to the state. The following excerpt from the letter describes her "proposition":

> . . . . . I will at once, at my own expense, without cost to the State, cause the immediate removal of the unsightly modern structure now known as the Hugo-Schmeltzer Building, surround the property with an appropriate stone or mortar fence with one or more iron gates and convert the interior into a park where in the future monuments may be erected to the memory of the heroes of the magnificent struggle or such evidences of recognition of their valor as the people of Texas may in the future decide as fitting.[110] . . . . . .

Nothing more was pursued on the matter at the moment, so apparently nothing came of Mrs. Sevier's offer.

It is a well known fact that delay is a legal tactic used in many cases to favor the party with the most to lose. And money (and position) do talk in most cases. Finally, after another incredible wait, this time of one and one half years, the case was scheduled for the appellate court that met in November of 1909. Again Miss De Zavala's cause met defeat. The district court's decision in favor of the Driscoll group was upheld by the appelate court and the Driscoll group were now in control of the Alamo Chapel and the Hugo-Schmeltzer Building and grounds officially.

The court system of appeals was different than that of today. Mr. Duncan filed an application for writ of error in the Texas Supreme Court asking that court to reverse the court of civil appeals. However, the supreme court refused the application, thereby making the court of civil appeals final. [111]

Miss De Zavala could not bring herself to give up her fight for what she knew was right and was the truth—that the "long barracks" was underneath the wooden exterior of the Hugo-Schmeltzer Building and that it was the major site of the final tragic moment of the fall of the Alamo and it must not be destroyed.

Even though the application for writ of error had been refused, she wrote John Duncan proposing they make another appeal to the higher court.

Mr. Duncan wrote Miss De Zavala as follows concerning the advisability of filing a motion for rehearing.

JOHN T. DUNCAN,
ATTORNEY AT LAW
  OFFICE OVER
FIRST NATIONAL BANK
                LAGRANGE, TEXAS, Jan. 25, 1910.
Miss Adina DeZavalla, [sic]
  San Antonio, Texas.

My dear Miss Adina:—
I was just on the eve of writing to you, when I received your letter. I had seen where the Supreme Court had refused our Writ of Error. I have just had a note from Mr. Love asking me to file a Motion for Rehearing. I have just written to him to the effect that I had made the application for Writ of Error and had made it as strong if not stronger than I could make the Motion for Re-hearing and if the Application for Writ of Error was insufficient and did not and could not move the court, I did not think a Motion for Re-hearing would be able to accomplish anything.
I regret that the Court did not decide this matter right,

but we were placed at this disadvantage. The Courts and it seemed that nearly everybody else, was anxious to have the litigation brought to an end and I think the Court concluded that it was better to end the litigation, wehter [sic] the principles of law were violated or not. Now I would advise against making a Motion for Re-hearing for the reasons above stated. It will accomplish no good and will involve some costs and possibly a compromise of our dignity.

I send you under separate cover, a copy of the evening's brief and a copy of the opinion of the Court of Appeals. The Supreme Court in refusing the Writ of Error, rendered no opinion. The opinion of the Court of Civil Appeals was very disappointing to me. It looks to me that they decided everything in our favor except just one little matter, to wit, that Mrs. Fisher was the legal presiding officer for about half a minute during the time that she took the gavel from Mrs. Alford and put the motion and put an end to the existence of the conven-tion. I haven't a copy of my application for Writ of Error, but if you would like to see it, you might write to the clerk of the Supreme Court at Austin and ask him to send you a copy.

Mrs. Tuttle is well, but I think her strength, on account of increasing age, is perceptibly lessening.

Mrs. Duncan and family all join in love to you.

The next time I go to San Antonio and have time, you will certainly be the recipient of a visit from me. I want to shake your hand and take off my hat to the Queen Bee of the Daughters of the Republic of Texas.

Sincerely your friend,
/S/ John T. Duncan[112]

Mr. Duncan may have been thinking, and saying indirectly, that there is a potential for a backlash when a case has dragged on and on, and appears to have been lost. If the inevitable is not acknowledged, even people sympathetic or neutral begin to feel like enough is enough.

And thus Mr. Duncan accepted the fact that Adina De Zavala had lost her battle for the Alamo with the DRT. On May 4, 1910, a final letter on the matter brought an end to the long painful ordeal for him. The case had dragged out from July 1907 to March 1910—almost three years.

> My dear Miss Adina:—
> The litigation is over. We have lost, and our defeat is another verification of a well known truth, that the right does not always prevail.
> . . . .
> I hope this will find you well and that you may continue to enjoy your usual good health. I wish you much joy in the future.
>
> > Sincerely your friend
> > /S/ John T. Duncan[113]

The opposition group was jubilant but Miss De Zavala's group never really recovered. Others expressed their disappointment to her, including Pompeo Coppini who had joined her at the beginning of her fight to save the "long barracks". He was moved to say:

> I thought it was a shameful and ungrateful decision against a poor woman who had worked so hard to save all that was a memento of sincere, true patriotism, and who had an almost fanatical devotion to all that was connected with the history of Texas.[114]

While this battle was over and she had lost, that was not all Adina De Zavala lost. She and her nucleus of supporters no longer could even claim membership in the organization they had worked so hard for. The Driscoll followers, who were now the legal DRT group and who had been formally awarded custody of the Alamo property on March 10, 1910,[115] now made a decision:

> In consequence of the Court injunction against Miss
> De Zavala and the twelve members that had mistakenly
> aided her in the controversy, these individuals could no
> longer claim to be members of the Daughters of the
> Republic of Texas . . . . [116]

And the names of these thirteen women were removed from the
membership list of the Daughters of the Republic of Texas.

The triumphant Driscoll group now embarked on their role
as custodian of the Alamo property. They persisted officially now
in the stand they had held from the outset of removing the "unsightly" Hugo-Schmeltzer building. Their president, Mrs. Fisher, having
been elected officially as their leader upon the death of Mrs. Anson
Jones in 1907, reiterated this position in a statement she made at the
1909 convention, even though the final court decision had not then
been made that would determine they were the official DRT group.
In that statement she urged the members to:

> Use your influence to have the Alamo [Chapel] protect-
> ed from the intrusion of other buildings. Insist that it
> must stand there alone, the sentinel of patriotic love and
> devotion, the tomb of martyred heroes, and that the
> Hugo-Schmeltzer building be removed at once, because
> of danger of fire which would ruin the Alamo. The
> stones of that building should be placed in a wall as near
> as possible to that left after the siege, with Texas vines
> gracefully twining over its rugged points, and Texas
> shrubs and flowers adorning the entire ground. No chap-
> ter should ever have control of the Alamo; it is State
> property, and under State authority. The Alamo must
> stand there alone in its silent and solemn grandeur, a
> monument of that tragic scene of suffering and death,
> whose ramparts were washed with the blood of heroes,
> men who sacrificed their precious lives for Texas free-
> dom. Any other building on that sacred soil would
> detract from the sanctity of that sacred shrine, and
> would be an insult to those blood stained walls and the
> patriotic fathers of Texas. Protect it from such an insult-

ing, sacrilegious spirit.

Dear Mrs. Clara Driscoll Sevier never ceases her patriotic work. Her liberal offer to fence and beautify those hallowed grounds at her own expense commends her to the love and admiration of all Texas. She is a grand woman; we all love her and are proud of her noble and patriotic worth.[117]

The next year at the 1910 convention, when the victory for her DRT group was final, Mrs. Fisher emphasized again that the Hugo-Schmeltzer Building "has no historic interest and its presence is an insult to that dear historic shrine—the hallowed Alamo."[118] Following her lead, the group voted again to remove the Hugo-Schmeltzer building and convert the area to "a sacred shrine" in the form of a park.

The state resisted this though, saying that the original official act gave the DRT custody of the building for remodeling or improvement but not destruction, and that a new legislative act would be required for that. While the court decision had made this particular group the official DRT body, it had not solved the matter of what was to be done with the building itself. And the battle over that critical point was on once more.

It was at this fortuitous time, at least for the Driscoll group it would appear, that the architect Harvey Page entered the scene again with a new plan for the area. In this plan being distributed to local San Antonio businessmen dated July 14, 1910, he was selling shares in a project under the name of Alamo Amusement Company. The company's plan was to purchase the property immediately behind the Hugo-Schmeltzer plot, and immediately adjacent to the DRT's "hallowed shrine", the Alamo Chapel. The plan included the erection of a building there to accommodate "an Ice Skating Rink in the basement, a high class Dance Hall on the first floor and a Roof Garden with a Vaudeville Stage, Cafe, etc., above."[119] All of this was to be behind the state owned Hugo-Schmeltzer property and adjoining the Alamo Chapel.

Accompanying this offer of shares in the property, he included the following description of details regarding his plan.[120]

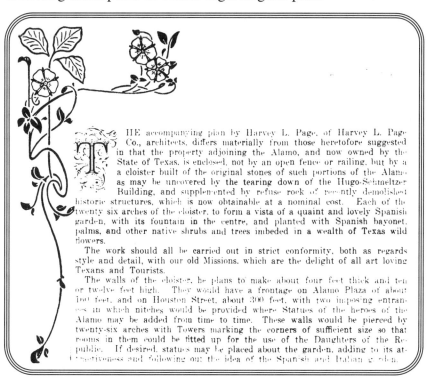

THE accompanying plan by Harvey L. Page, of Harvey L. Page Co., architects, differs materially from those heretofore suggested in that the property adjoining the Alamo, and now owned by the State of Texas, is enclosed, not by an open fence or railing, but by a cloister built of the original stones of such portions of the Alamo as may be uncovered by the tearing down of the Hugo-Schmeltzer Building, and supplemented by refuse rock of recently demolished historic structures, which is now obtainable at a nominal cost. Each of the twenty six arches of the cloister, to form a vista of a quaint and lovely Spanish garden, with its fountain in the centre, and planted with Spanish bayonet, palms, and other native shrubs and trees imbeded in a wealth of Texas wild flowers.

The work should all be carried out in strict conformity, both as regards style and detail, with our old Missions, which are the delight of all art loving Texans and Tourists.

The walls of the cloister, he plans to make about four feet thick and ten or twelve feet high. They would have a frontage on Alamo Plaza of about 100 feet, and on Houston Street, about 300 feet, with two imposing entrances in which nitches would be provided where Statues of the heroes of the Alamo may be added from time to time. These walls would be pierced by twenty-six arches with Towers marking the corners of sufficient size so that rooms in them could be fitted up for the use of the Daughters of the Republic. If desired, statues may be placed about the garden, adding to its attractiveness and following out the idea of the Spanish and Italian garden.

Accompanying his design, he had submitted three photographs, one showing the San José Mission, near San Antonio; one a view of the cloister at San Luis Rey Mission, California, and the third, a view of the Alcazar gardens, Seville, Spain. The picture taken at San Luis Rey Mission, shows the beauty of a cloister, such as Mr. Page designed for the Alamo, and gives an idea of the view that would be presented through one of the arches of the wall. The picture of San José Mission gives an idea of the style of architecture Mr. Page believed should be adhered to and the picture of the Alcazar gardens shows to good advantage how such buildings as he suggested for the adjoining property could add to the general effect and the style which would give individuality to San Antonio and also suggest the beauty of the garden he proposed. A comparison of the three pictures gave an idea of what could be accomplished around the Alamo at comparatively small expense.[121]

Mr. Page also showed site plans and drawings, including this conception of a visual overview of the plan as described. The Alamo can be seen adjacent to the planned cloistered garden.[122]

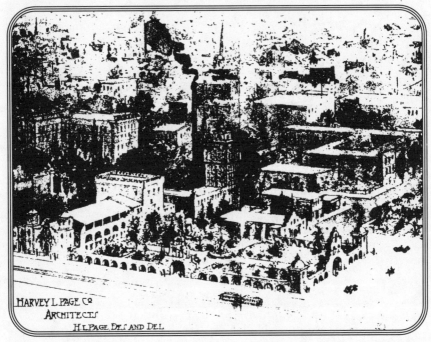

Naturally, plans such as this set Miss De Zavala off again. The small De Zavala group had not exactly "just retired gracefully." Although no longer members of the official DRT group, they remained quite unified and active in their own way, in continued efforts to save the building and the surrounding grounds. The new governor, Oscar B. Colquitt, who had followed in the aftermath of the height of the disagreement between the two groups, seemed to be in sympathy with the De Zavala followers on the basic idea of preserving the property or at least looking into the matter. Miss De Zavala had written the governor seeking his support.

DE ZAVALA CHAPTER
Daughters of the Republic of Texas
San Antonio, Texas,
August 21, 1911

O. B. Colquitt,
Governor of Texas:

Dear Mr. Colquitt:
   I have been informed that you have called for an
appropriation of $7,000, to repair and clean up the
Alamo. I thoroughly approve of the repair and the clean
up, and applaud the patriotism which prompted the
thought, as do all the members of the De Zavala Chapter,
in common with all true Texans, but, if the papers are
correct when they say that you intend to tear down the
"Hugo-Schmeltzer Building," or even that you intend to
tear down "one story" of it, then no patriotic Texan will
approve and we feel sure you have been grossly misin-
formed as to facts. What these "interested" property
owners, the syndicate and "interested" papers call the
"Hugo-Schmeltzer Building is the Alamo Proper, the
main building for the Fort, the building in which the
heroes died, the same "old two story building" that has
stood there since about 1718, and in whose upper story
in the south-west corner Bowie was killed. There is no
question about it, it is a fact-and all history proves it. All
deeds of property adjacent measure from this old stone
building, maps, drawings, plats of the city, all show it. It
was never torn down, nor even much injured, history
also makes that statement. Just give me time to show
you the proofs or look them up yourself, as you please.
Start with Potter who was in Monterey in 1836, he saw
the buildings in '41, described them in 1860, in an article he wrote in San Antonio and which was published in
the *San Antonio Herald* at the time, again in 1878 he
wrote of the Alamo. Also see Yoakum, Thrall, p. 239,
240; John Henry Brown, p. 576, 580, & 581 of Vol I, Vol
II, p. 206, 211, 212, Bancroft, Report to U. S.

Government in 1846, by Brig. Gen'l Wool [Woll], and Captain Hughes, contains plat of the Alamo as it was then; these all show the ancient two-story stone building, also various other documents and books too numerous to mention, that I can produce.

I am convinced that you wish to do the right thing for the Alamo and the honor and glory of Texas, and it would be a dreadful catastrophe were you to make such a mistake as to tear down The Alamo. The whole civilized world would deride us and point the finger of scorn. The criticism now is bad, but the papers do not publish as they are with the syndicate who wish a corner on the Alamo Plaza and Houston Streets.

The deed conveying the Church in the Alamo to the State begins its measurements at "the southwest corner of the old stone building." This was in 1883. This building, not the Church, is the Alamo Proper, and was the Fortified Building during the siege. The church was roofless and piled full of rocks, mortar and debris . . . [unclear] . . .

Governor, now please do nothing until you can look into the matter thoroughly. See Bolton's *With the Makers of Texas*. I regret so much I did not see you when you were here, as a glance at the histories and documents and the simple hearing of a few facts that I can place before you will give you the key to the whole situation so frightfully and shamefully ignored or distorted by the S. A. papers and "interested parties."

Are you coming over in the immediate future? If so, please let me know when I can see you.

Very sincerely
/S/ Adina De Zavala
141 Taylor St. corner of Fourth.[123]

O. B. Colquitt
Governor of Texas
Austin, Texas.

Dear Governor:

Your letter in reply to mine of the 22nd inst, is very much appreciated and I know that not only our own people of Texas, but the World will applaud your determination "to restore" the main building of The Alamo. Not only will that building whose thick stone walls re-echoed the last sighs of the martyred heroes, be the monument of the heroes of Texas - but yours as well. The governor <u>who restores the Alamo</u> will bind the hearts of the people to him indissolubly and historians will write his name high in the lists of those worthy of the Hall of Texas. Hearing that the same "interests" who have been endeavoring at each past session of the Legislature to accomplish the destruction of the Alamo were likely to succeed in having a measure introduced under the plea of "Civic Beauty," I prepared a Resume of the Story of the Alamo and some circulars ready to be distributed at the right time for the information of the public; this course being necessary as the San Antonio papers have, in the past, failed to publish any facts or history on the subject. Since the matter has taken the form it has been placed entirely in your hands, and you have "determined to restore," we feel so happy and encouraged, that the separate circulars, two of which were copied in the *Story of the Alamo,* will not be sent out, as was the intention, as we feel it will be unnecessary. The booklets we will present to our friends. I send you the very first copy published, and while it is not the full story, I hope you will find it of interest and <u>containing more</u> references of historical facts than have yet been brought together under one cover.

Hoping to see you when you come to San Antonio.

Very sincerely,
/S/ Adina De Zavala
Aug. 25, 1911[124]

𝔈𝔵𝔢𝔠𝔲𝔱𝔦𝔳𝔢 𝔒𝔣𝔣𝔦𝔠𝔢,
𝔖𝔱𝔞𝔱𝔢 𝔬𝔣 𝔗𝔢𝔵𝔞𝔰.
𝔄𝔲𝔰𝔱𝔦𝔫.

Sept. 20, 1911.

Miss Adina De Zavala,
    141 Taylor Street,
            San Antonio, Texas.

Dear Miss De Zavala:
    I acknowledge your letter of the 18th instant.
    I have not had time to read up on the Alamo but intend
to do so before I take any action. When I get ready to
proceed I shall come to San Antonio and invite those
having information concerning the Alamo to meet me
and discuss the matter.
                        Yours truly,
                        /S/ O. B. Colquitt
                        Governor.[125]

The governor's attitude seems to have given her new hope, and she
sent the following communication to all members of her group.

    . . . The day is brightening for the Alamo, I think. I hope
    and pray that Mr. Colquitt will realize our expectations
    for the Alamo, and believe that he will from what he has
    said and his intimate friends say.
        Did you get the booklet I sent you?
        With my best love and hoping to hear from you soon,
                        Lovingly,

                        /S/ Adina De Zavala, President
                        De Zavala Chapter

141 Taylor St.
San Antonio,
Sept. 28, 1910[126]

In a development that boosted their morale, the governor and the legislature upon convening in the fall, approved an appropriation of $5,000 for improvements of the property.[127]

Then 'the day brightencd' even more for the Alamo in the eyes of Miss De Zavala when she received the following letter from the governor:

**Executive Office,
State of Texas,
Austin**

October 1, 1911

Miss Adina De Zavala,
141 Taylor St., Corner Fourth,
San Antonio, Texas

Dear Madam:
   I shall give the women who are interested in this a hearing before I do anything, but I shall decline to become a partner to either faction of the Daughters of the Republic. After I hear them, I will act upon what I think is the best information in effort to restore the Alamo to its original appearance, as far as the small appropriation at my disposal will permit.

Yours truly,
/S/ O. B. Colquitt
Governor.[128]

On December 11, 1911, the governor called an open meeting in San Antonio for information "about the Alamo as it stood at the time of the butchery of Travis and his men." He was making a sincere effort to avoid taking an active part in the continuing disagreement while he was attempting to obtain the facts to be used as guidance in a decision on what should be done about the building.

The meeting the governor called was attended by a number

of interested parties on both sides of the argument. Miss De Zavala was there, of course, with her followers, as were members of the now official DRT group. Clara Driscoll Sevier, who thus far had not been involved in the Alamo affair, at least not publicly, came also. She arrived after the meeting had begun, making an impressive late entrance, and the governor repeated his opening remarks for her benefit regarding the facts on the building at the time of the battle and the condition of the area afterward.

According to the *Dallas Morning News,* in response to the governor's request for remarks from her then, Mrs. Driscoll Sevier replied:

> I have never sanctioned touching one of the original stones; but I don't think the Alamo should be disgraced by this whisky [sic] house, which obscures the most remarkable relic of the world.[129]

Adina De Zavala then stated that she had historical data supporting her claim that the building was a part of the battle site. She then proceeded to quote from some of it, including that which described the configuration of the compound just prior to the battle as shown in the plat and letter by an eyewitness, Green B. Jameson, just before the battle occurred. Jameson later died in the battle. The governor asked her to supply him with copies of this material, and she readily agreed to do so and she mailed him copies soon thereafter.[130]

A discussion of the actual location of the "long barracks" and how much of it, if any, was there at the time of the battle, lead to the following revealing exchange as reported in the same *Dallas Morning News* article:

> Mrs. Sevier—There is no objection to a standing wall, but why build a Franciscan monastery where there was none?
>
> The Governor—If anybody has evidence that it was

an eight-foot wall and not a building, let us have proof of it. It is asserted on the one hand that the outer wall of the Hugo-Schmeltzer building was two stories and was part of the monastery. On the other hand, it is contended that it was an eight-foot wall to protect the monastery which was in the rear. Now is there any objection to having that eight-foot wall stand as a part of the Alamo?

Mrs. Roach—We want it to stand as it was after the battle; they left it jagged and torn.

The Governor—You want the scars of the cannon balls to remain? How will you maintain ruins in that condition?

Mrs. O. M. Farnsworth—In Europe they maintain them by training ivy and vines over them.

The Governor—Suppose we adopt that plan; who will tell us where the holes are?[131]

The De Zavala group contended the eighteen-foot walls of the heavy masonry were the original walls of the two-story mission convento, later used as barracks by the Spanish soldiers, followed by the Mexican soldiers, and then by Travis and the Texians who defended the Alamo.

The DRT group had held that the original masonry walls were only eight feet high and if the wooden walls covering them were torn away and the upper part of the walls that were there were found to be of masonry, it would be proven that it was material from a later period.

The De Zavala group responded to that saying the historical data available would refute that. Further, it was believed the heavy masonry was so massive that it would preclude the idea of construction of it at a more recent time because of the cost of building with such material at a later period.

When the meeting ended, the governor and certain members of the group toured the Hugo-Schmeltzer building. The governor and the accompanying newspaper reporters described the building as having two stories with one long wall and two short end walls.

Each wall appeared to be of heavy stone masonry, about four feet thick and eighteen feet high. There was a three-foot extension of wood above this, and the roof and floors were of wood, also. The fourth side appeared to be of wood with some stone areas.[132]

All of the contentions by both sides as expressed in the meeting and the inspection trip following the meeting are described in the summary by Tom Finty, Jr., Editor of the *Dallas Morning News*.[133]

This summary was included in Governor Colquitt's Message to the Legislature referred to earlier and a copy of the portion that applies to this matter is reprinted here.[134]

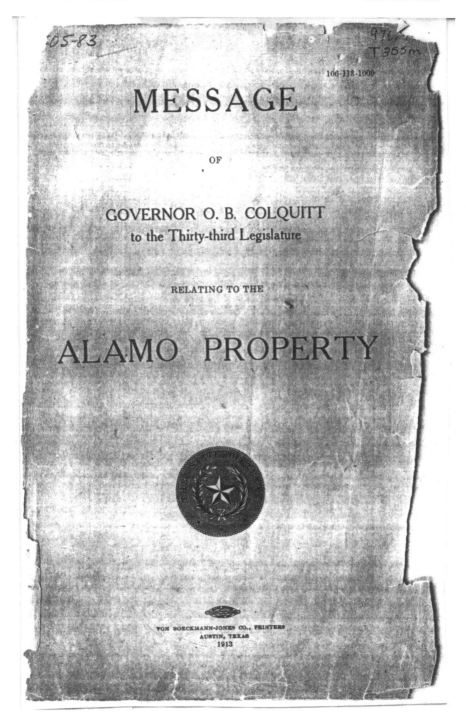

MESSAGE

OF

GOVERNOR O. B. COLQUITT
to the Thirty-third Legislature

RELATING TO THE

ALAMO PROPERTY

VON BOECKMANN-JONES CO., PRINTERS
AUSTIN, TEXAS
1913

he as the representative of all of the people of Texas desired information from the Daughters and all other persons competent to give it, and then purposed acting, not for either faction nor for both, but for the State of Texas.

Moreover, step by step, he brushed away such immaterial issues as to whether or not the property had been devoted to commercial purposes, and got his audience down to the one material issue, which is: How much of the existing buildings was there at the time of the battle?

The Governor intends to tear away all the frame part, which it is generally agreed is modern. He will be guided in determining what shall be done with the walls and as to restoration by what shall be disclosed by the uncovering of the masonry and by excavation; by historic data, and by such reports as may be obtained from the archives of the Republic of Texas and the Federal Government at Washington.

The opinion of this writer is that the frame part of the Hugo & Schmeltzer building ought not to be torn away until the Governor is prepared to act and act quickly in the work of restoration, to whatever extent that may be determined upon. The unprotected walls would suffer some from the weather, and there is some danger that they might be intentionally demolished. There was talk in San Antonio at one time of taking a mob and destroying the "shacks" on that ground.

Daughters' Dispute Outlined.

About a year ago, the writer published two articles explaining the dispute and collateral matters. It seems in order to brief a part of that report here.

One faction of the Daughters of the Republic, led by Miss Adina De Zavala, has contended that the walls of the Hugo & Schmeltzer building are original parts of the building in which the defenders of the Alamo made their last stand, being then referred to as the barracks or fortress, and originally the convent or monastery of the Alamo mission. They assert that these walls should be preserved and the building restored.

The other faction, led by Miss Clara Driscoll, now Mrs. Hal Sevier, contends that the Hugo & Schmeltzer building is not historically sacred; that of its wall only eight feet was a part of the Alamo, and that was simply a wall inclosing the grounds of the monastery, whereas the monastery itself was further back. They would tear all of this building down, take away all the commercial part, as they term it, and leave only the jagged remains of the eight foot wall. They would make the grounds into a park and erect upon it a monument to the heroes. They agree that the grounds are historically sacred, but they contend that the Alamo chapel is the real Alamo.

The De Zavala faction answers that historical data all identifies the so-called Hugo & Schmeltzer building as the fortress or monastery in which the heroes made their last stand; and in response to the contention that only jagged remains shall be left, they cite historic data to prove that the church itself was a ruin at the time of the battle, and ask if the restored portions of the church shall be torn away and its jagged remains left.

The Driscoll faction contends that the Hugo & Schmeltzer building was erected by the quartermaster's department of the United States army after annexation of Texas, and some suggest that Mr. Grenet, who subsequently owned the property, may have built a portion of the walls.

Governor Colquitt means to have the records ransacked to see if any such construction was done by the United States government.

Amusement Palace Project.

A project has been on foot in San Antonio for some time to erect an amusement palace on the lot immediately back of the Alamo tract. This lot fronts eighty nine feet on Houston street and is 168 feet deep. If the so called Hugo & Schmeltzer building shall be demolished and a park created, the aforesaid lot will have a frontage of 168 feet on said park and Alamo Plaza, and this is held out as a considerable advantage in the amusement company's prospectus. If the building shall be restored, that advantage will not accrue.

The writer still believes that the Hugo & Schmeltzer walls are a part of the original Alamo. The Daughters of the Republic, when they came to Austin with a united purpose, first convinced him of that fact. Their bill which the Legislature passed stands as mute evidence upon that point. It provides that the

— 135 —

property shall be "maintained in good order and repair," and shall be "remodeled and maintained." There isn't a word in it about demolition nor parking.

Benefit of Doubt.

Historical data verifies and strengthens that conclusion. Any doubt should be resolved in favor of the status quo. It would be better that a stone laid there by men in commerce (is commerce necessarily a crime?) should be suffered to remain than that the mistake should be made of removing a stone that was there when the heroes died. The error in favor of the status quo would not be fatal; the error against it would be beyond repair. It is well to remember, too, that Travis and his men did some restoring and building before the battle. The Alamo at that time was by no means entirely of Franciscan construction.

Moreover and lastly, the writer believes that in no event should the buildings be torn away before the Legislature has had a chance to enact a law protecting the site from undesirable occupancy of abutting premises. The writer does not object to people drinking beer if they feel so disposed, but does insist that the State ought not maintain a park as the front yard of an institution where beer is sold or in which dancing and other amusements are conducted.

Further than this the writer will not obtrude personal views. The remainder of this article will be devoted to a somewhat detailed report of the Governor's peace conference.

Participants in Conference.

Present at the conference were Mrs. W. P. Anderson of Amarillo and Mrs. Hal Sevier of New York City, nee Miss Clara Driscoll of Texas, and the following residents of San Antonio: Gustav Schramm, Mrs. E. W. King, Charles T. Boelhowse, Miss Eleanor Wilson, Mrs. F. R. Dunlap, Mrs. E. O. Spencer, Mrs. L. J. Northrup, Mrs. M. J. Keeran, Miss Marguerite Coleman, Mrs. T. A. Coleman, Mr. and Mrs. Pompeo Coppini, Miss Anne Brown, Mrs. D. J. Allen, F. F. Collins, Mrs. Nellie Jameson, Mrs. W. L. Bringhurst, Miss Miriam Winsor, Mrs. T. M. Winsor, A. B. Briscoe, Mrs. C. Briscoe West, Miss Adina De Zavala, Mrs. W. H. Beck, Mrs. F. W. Applewhite, Mrs. H. M. Newton, Mrs. Bettie Carnar, Mrs. Nat Mitchell, Mr. and Mrs. C. E. Channing, H. P. Drought, H. L. Page, Charles Merritt Barnes, Mrs. J. J. Stevens, Mrs. Frank Paschal, Mr. and Mrs. E. P. Jersig, Hal King, Mrs. Susan Roach, Mrs. O. M. Farnsworth, Miss Mary Elliott Howard and Mrs. Sarah Elizabeth Eager, custodian of the Alamo chapel for the Daughters of the Republic.

Governor Colquitt opened the proceedings by saying that the Legislature had appropriated $5000 to be expended under the direction of the Governor and the Superintendent of Public Buildings and Grounds for the purpose of remodeling and restoring the Alamo, and he had called the meeting for the purpose of receiving evidence tending to show the condition of the Alamo at the time the battle was fought or after the battle, and he invited submission of the same.

H. P. Drought read a communication from Mrs. Rebecca Fisher, president of the Daughters of the Republic, and the other officers and executive committee of that association, asking the Governor to sanction their plan for tearing down the Hugo & Schmeltzer building and for parking of the grounds.

Hal King informed the Governor that Miss Adina De Zavala was present to submit historical data and asked that she be heard.

Miss De Zavala said she would be glad to let the gentleman (Mr. Drought) present everything he had to say and then follow with a presentation of the "historical side."

Against Park Project.

"It might be well for me to state," said Governor Colquitt, "that I am not a party to any controversy between the descendants of those who established the independence of Texas, but am here for the purpose of learning facts. I have already declared myself upon this question. I do not believe there is any monument that can be erected on this spot of ground that can take the place of the buildings that constituted the fortifications of Travis and his men, and as long as I am Governor of the State I will not give my consent to use it as a park or for a monument to the valor of these men.

"I want information this afternoon upon which I can act, for I am going to assume all the responsibility for my action. If I can find out how this building looked when Travis lost his life, I will spend every dollar at my disposal to make it look like it looked then. I want information. Then I am going to assume the responsibility, and no power can budge me from my determination. (Applause.) I am not going to let this meeting be taken up with joint debates. I speak very plainly about it. I am going to tear down that fire trap in so far as additions have been made since the battle. I want to build a substantial stone wall along Houston street, and I want to clean out that ditch and make it look as it did at the time of the battle, and I want to put all of the commercial vandals out of the Alamo. (Applause.) I tried to do that on the first of September. If this State can not maintain the Alamo as a monument it shall not be used for commercial profit while I am Governor.

"I am not going to take part in the controversy between the Daughters of the Republic. The statute gives custody of the Alamo to the Daughters of the Republic, subject to the approval of the Governor, and as long as I am Governor, I am not going to let the proper supervision of that building pass out of my hands. I am not a Daughter of the Republic, but I am a Texan, and I am going to protect that monument. I had relatives who helped establish the Republic of Texas, and I have an interest in the Alamo. Also, while I am Governor I am going to see if we can take charge of the ground where Fannin and his men lost their lives at Goliad. (Applause.)

Governor Urges Unity.

"This is a proposition upon which we should be united. The Alamo as a park might be very pretty, but it would not be a monument." (Mr. Drought—We want to put up a monument in it.) "We can cultivate flowers elsewhere, but the flowers here would not be a monument. Therefore, we want to preserve the Alamo as a monument.

"I say this to save time; the only question I will listen to is as how we can spend this money to restore the Alamo to the condition in which it was when Travis and his men fell. We can not retain it in the form in which it was after the battle. That would be impracticable. You can not maintain the house as a ruin, but you can restore it and maintain it, and when people come here from all parts of the world you can point out the place where Santa Anna made his assault, the place where Travis fell, etc.

"I won't consent to tear down the Hugo & Schmeltzer building. (Applause.) It is a part of the Alamo. Not all of the Alamo is there now; but as long as I can exercise the authority now vested in me, I will not consent to the tearing down of the walls that were there as a part of the Alamo." (Applause.)

Republic Natives Applaud.

F. F. Collins said: "As an old Texan, I think the Governor has expressed the desire and wish of the organization known as the Natives of the Republic of Texas. That is the desire and wish of every member, with one or two possible exceptions, of the association of which I am president. I don't think there is a single man in that association but who is in favor of doing just about what the Governor has been talking about. I don't want to express my individual feelings because the Governor has cut that out, but I am willing to give $500 toward restoring the Alamo property as it stood (applause), and I believe I can make up sufficient money to restore it as it was before the battle of the Alamo. Five thousand dollars is not enough. There is no question but it can be shown historically how the Alamo looked, and there is patriotism in San Antonio to help the State restore the property."

Mrs. Sevier's Position.

Mrs. Hal Sevier had just entered, and had not heard the Governor's remarks. She asked: "Is this a proposition to restore the old mission, or what shall be done with this mercantile structure, the Hugo & Schmeltzer building, concerning which no one can feel any sentiment?"

Governor Colquitt repeated the substance of his remarks, saying he had committed himself against tearing down any part of the Hugo & Schmeltzer building that represents walls of the Alamo, and that he believed it was a part of the Alamo proper.

"I don't think any of us who are patriots should be mis-understood," said Mrs. Sevier. "I have never sanctioned touching one of the original stones, but I don't think the Alamo should be disgraced by this whisky house, which obscures the most remarkable relic of the world."

"I agree entirely with that sentiment," Governor Colquitt replied. "The fact that these walls have been used for commercial purposes is not the fault of the present Executive; the fact that they were used for a whisky house is not his fault. But the fact that they were used for such purposes is not a good reason why the walls used by Travis and his men in the defense of Texas should be demolished. The walls which were then standing, we want to preserve."

Mrs. Sevier- So do we, Governor.

Governor Colquitt repeated that it was his purpose to restore the building to the condition it was in at the time of the battle.

Mrs. Sevier- You don't mean to restore it as it was built by the Franciscan fathers before the battle?

The Governor- I am not going back of 1836. I want to restore it as it was before Travis defended it, and will do so if it takes $50,000, and I can get the money. If you have information as to how it looked then, I would like to have it. If not, this meeting will be adjourned.

Kinsman of Jemison.

Charles Merritt Barnes said that his kinsman, Green B. Jemison, who was killed in the battle of the Alamo, planned the defense of the Alamo and that there was present a lady who had a letter written by Jemison shortly before the battle, describing the Alamo. He further said he was glad to hear the lady who started the movement for the preservation of the Alamo (Mrs. Sevier) say she was in unison with the idea of preserving it. He further delivered a message from his aunt, Seramus Jemison of Marshall, a cousin of Green B. Jemison, saying she hoped the Governor would restore both the chapel and the convent as monuments to the heroes who fell there. He further said that one of the Maverick family was willing, if the buildings should be restored, to donate one of the original Alamo cannon, which is in his possession, to be placed upon the building. Mr. Barnes presented to Governor Colquitt a copy of his recently published book, "Combats and Conquests of Immortal Heroes," which contains an account of the battle of the Alamo, historic data as to the fortress and an argument in favor of restoring the buildings. Mr. Barnes devoted much of his time during thirty years to gathering the data and writing the book.

Miss De Zavala Submits Data.

Miss De Zavala was then heard. She submitted a number of histories of Texas. They all tell the same tale, she said. All the plats, maps and descriptive matters show that the walls now standing, and known as the Hugo & Schmeltzer building, the convent or the monastery, are the original walls of the fortress. She read from Yoakum's History of Texas, published in 1856, wherein it is stated that this building was a two-story stone building; that the Texans retreated into that building; that the chapel was a ruin at the time of the battle. It was impossible, she observed, that the battle could have been fought at the chapel. She further read from Yoakum his statement that before him was a letter from Green B. Jemison with a plat and description of the Alamo just before the battle.

Miss De Zavala said that she had this letter and plat, heretofore unpublished, with her, and she proceeded to read the former. The letter was directed to General Houston; refers to the plat; describes the condition of the buildings. Among other things it says: "The church of San Antonio is in the Alamo and adjoins the fortress." Miss De Zavala directed attention to the fact that the fortress as shown by Jemison corresponds with the so-called Hugo & Schmeltzer building. She also directed attention to Jemison's recommendation that the adobe quarters for the men be torn down and that houses of stone be erected, it being said that "there is plenty of stone in the old ruins of the church San Antonio."

The Governor- He describes the church as a ruin. If that were true, why was it necessary for Santa Anna's men to knock a hole in the walls to get into it?

Miss De Zavala said they did not. There were guns on the chapel, however. Some of the historians say the Mexicans came over the west wall; others say over

— 138 —

the south wall. It made little difference, she said. The undisputed historic fact is that the Texans retreated into the long building and made their last stand. She referred to the story of Mrs. Dickinson and others, and said she thought she had proved that the existing building was there in 1836. However, she had a map of the United States government and much other data.

Governor Colquitt asked her to send this to him at Austin.

"Will Preserve Both."

"I think," said Gustav Schramm, "the question is what constitutes the Alamo."

The Governor—No; don't waste any time on that. The chapel and the Hugo & Schmeltzer building are both the Alamo.

Mr. Schramm—That is correct. I think the question is which shall we preserve.

The Governor—We are going to preserve both.

Mr. Schramm—If that is the case I don't think it is necessary for me to say anything.

The Governor—It is of no use to ask me to tear down either one; I would use the militia, and the rangers, too, if necessary, to prevent it. Neither the chapel nor the Hugo & Schmeltzer building shall be destroyed. My reading of Texas history teaches me that they are both sacred.

Mr. Schramm declared that history showed the so-called Hugo & Schmeltzer building was standing at the time of the battle of the Alamo; it was not built by the United States army, but was in existence when Texas was annexed, and there were living witnesses who had seen the patches made by the United States army.

"Believe in One Alamo."

Mrs. Sarah Elizabeth Eager, custodian of the Alamo chapel for the Daughters of the Republic, said that her father came to San Antonio in 1839. She had been brought up to believe there was but one Alamo, "and that the one I am in today." She said the outer wall of the Hugo & Schmeltzer building was originally only eight feet high, and was put up as a fence, to protect the monastery.

The Governor—Do you think that wall ought to be torn down?

Mrs. Eager—I have no sentiment in the matter. I think the ground all around is sacred. If the Governor wants to leave that wall there I do not object. I have no love for the old eyesore. If a widow owned it, they would have compelled her to move it long ago.

The monastery, she declared, was on the other side of this wall. Several priests whom she had interrogated, she said, had told her she was right; that a monastery was never put in front of a church.

Governor Colquitt said he thought none of these arguments had any bearing whatever. If citizens let the building get into private use, it did not militate against restoration. "If it is a part of the Alamo we want to preserve it," he repeated.

Mrs. Eager—If that is true, we owe a debt of gratitude to Miss Clara Driscoll.

The Governor—I think so too.

Governor Congratulated.

At this juncture an elderly lady, Mrs. E. W. King, came forward and, grasping the Governor's hand, excitedly said: "Governor, I want to congratulate you. That is certainly a part of the Alamo. I wish I could talk about it, but I am too nervous." (Applause.)

Governor Colquitt welcomed her to a seat beside him.

Referring to the clause in the marriage ceremony, "Speak now, or forever after hold your peace," he declared that he wanted the necessary information to be presented at this time and not later, adding that when he had made up his mind he was about as stubborn as was Travis. He repeated what he had formerly said about tearing down the frame structures, and added that when that was done, architectural evidence as to the original walls might be disclosed.

"If anybody objects to this plan, I would like to hear the reasons. (Applause.) As there is no objection, it is understood that that part is unanimously agreed to. (Applause.) I take it that the wall that is there now is of the kind that was all around the Alamo. I have an idea, too, that the ditch is a part of the Alamo and we are going to move that fence on the opposite side of the ditch, unless

— 139 —

somebody stops us. (General applause.) We are going to claim all to the other side of the ditch as a part of the Alamo."

To Restore Monastery.

Mrs. Sevier—Is there anything in contemplation about restoring the roof of the chapel?

The Governor—Yes, the roofs of the monastery and the chapel both just as they were.

Mrs. Eager—You will have to build up a monastery, then, back there.

The Governor—It doesn't cut any figure whether Travis and his men were in the monastery or not; it was a part of the Alamo and we are going to rebuild it.

Mrs. King here took a part in the debate, saying the things which she had theretofore wanted to say.

"Why rebuild it?" she exclaimed. "Why rebuild it, when it is there now just as it has stood for many years? It has been there while I can remember. I am 77 years old today. My parents came to San Antonio when I was 9 years old. Many a time I have scaled the walls. This building was a two-story building then."

The Governor—Has anybody got any better evidence than that?

Mrs. Susan Roach said that she could not testify so far back, but her mother had lived within five blocks of the Alamo as early as 1827 and she never spoke of the walls as being two-story. She said that people differed in their recollection of buildings, just as they differ in their recollection of fights.

Governor Colquitt asked if it would be conceded that if the walls were built up by the United States government there would be some evidence of that fact in the archives of the Republic at Austin or of the government at Washington. He asked if anybody objected to that kind of evidence. None was heard, and the Governor declared it to be conceded that such evidence would be good.

What's the Difference?

Mrs. Roach—My mother never believed it was used as a convent.

The Governor—What difference does that make?

Mrs. O. M. Farnsworth—It was only a wall.

The Governor—What is the objection to it as a wall without a roof?

Mrs. Sevier—There is no objection to its standing as a wall, but why build a Franciscan monastery where there was none?

The Governor—If anybody has evidence that it was an eight foot wall and not a building, let us have proof of it. It is asserted on the one hand that the outer wall of the Hugo & Schmeltzer building was two stories and was part of the monastery. On the other hand, it is contended that it was an eight foot wall to protect the monastery which was in the rear. Now, is there any objection to having that eight foot wall stand as a part of the Alamo?

Mrs. Roach—We want it to stand as it was after the battle, they left it jagged and torn.

The Governor—You want the scars of the cannon balls to remain? How will you maintain ruins in that condition?

Mrs. Farnsworth—In Europe they maintain them by training ivy and vines over them.

The Governor—Suppose we adopt that plan; who will tell us where the holes were?

Mrs. Farnsworth—We can't do that, but architects can tell the old masonry from the new.

Mr. Collins—The building should be restored as it was before the battle—not afterward.

Best Kind of Monument.

The Governor—It has occurred to me that if we could ascertain the condition of the building as it was before Santa Anna assaulted it, restore it to that condition and then mark the spot where Travis fell, etc., it would be best. But I apprehend it would be very difficult to put it in the condition it was after the battle and maintain it.

Mrs. Eager renewed the suggestion that the building be torn down and a monument erected in the park.

— 140 —

"There is a monument in Austin to the heroes of the Alamo, but we have none here," she said.

The Governor—Texas could build a monument 7000 feet high, and it wouldn't commemorate their deeds like these buildings. (Applause.)

Mrs. Eager—But not a building that was a whisky house.

The Governor—Its use does not detract from the sacred character of the monument. We don't want to designate it as Hugo Schmeltzer's whisky house or grocery any more.

"Don't Call It Whisky House.

Mrs. King—Don't refer to it as the Hugo & Schmeltzer whisky shop any more. It hurts me! It hurts me! We can't help it.

The Governor—Now, I think we all understand each other, and I have gained about as much information as I had when I came. If there is anybody who knows more about the Alamo than I do, come up here and let us have the information. Now I want you to go with me to the Alamo. I am going to point out what I intend to tear down. You might talk to me a thousand years and you couldn't change my opinion about tearing those parts down.

Upon motion of Mr. Collins a resolution was passed thanking Governor Colquitt for the fair manner in which he had conducted the investigation.

Thereupon the meeting was adjourned, and the party went with Governor Colquitt to the Alamo. The inspection was confined to the tract bought from Hugo & Schmeltzer some six years ago. At the front of this, facing Alamo Plaza, is what is known as the Hugo & Schmeltzer store or warehouse. The front and the two ends of this are of heavy masonry, about four feet thick, two stories, or about eighteen feet in height. Above this masonry the walls are continued in wood for some three feet. The back wall of the storehouse is of wood, as is the roof and the floors. All of this woodwork the Governor intends to tear away.

One faction contends that these stone walls are, except for some repairs, as they were originally; that they were a part of the monastery, two stories in height, and that evidences of the rear wall of the monastery may be found by excavation.

The other faction contends that these walls were but eight feet in height, and constituted but a fence around the monastery, which they claim was further back. They declare that when the woodwork is torn away and the plaster removed from the walls it will be disclosed that the masonry above the eight-foot line was of a later period. Architects, they say, can determine the difference, as they have done in the ruins of Babylon and Nineveh.

The first mentioned faction deny that the judgment of the architects would be unerring or that it would constitute evidence to overcome the historical data, and they point to the fact that the masonry above the eight-foot line is so massive as to preclude the idea that it is recent and build for commercial purposes.

Back of the Hugo & Schmeltzer building there is another lone wall, to which have been tied a bunch of frame sheds of modern construction, which have been used as a livery stable, blacksmith shop, etc. This wall is of stone, some fourteen feet in height.

One of the men in the party declared that it was evidently of modern construction, as the arch in the central doorway is of brick.

"Evidently the old arch was torn away, and they built a new one of brick at a later period," said Governor Colquitt.

The stone above the other doorway is supported by wooden beams, seemingly of live oak. One lady remarked that this wall evidently was recent, as "they had no stone quarries when the mission was built." She did not explain upon what authority she made this statement.

All of these frame sheds are also to come down. It is Governor Colquitt's idea to award the contract for this wrecking to a San Antonio man who offered to do the work for the salvage and to pay the State $200 as a bonus.

The Bishop of San Antonio has promised Governor Colquitt that he will have an examination made for all of the records of the church pertaining to the Alamo, and will furnish him a translation of the same.

The following year, Governor Colquitt canceled the earlier orders giving custody of the property to the DRT because they had done nothing to improve the property during the time of their custodianship. The DRT countered with the claim that this was a clear usurpation of their authority and they obtained an injunction against the governor. The court decided in favor of the DRT, and the governor promptly appealed to the State Supreme Court, which ruled in this instance the State Executive Branch could make improvements. This seems to be the first and only court setback the Driscoll followers of the DRT experienced, from the beginning of this entire disagreement over the Hugo-Schmeltzer property to the end of it.

The governor began his restoration program in 1912, following the plans of a University of Texas Professor of Architecture, F. E. Giesecke. The first step was the removal of the wooden exterior structure of the building. When it was cleared away, there stood the heavy masonry of what clearly was a two-story building—the proof that Miss De Zavala's claims had been right all along.

THE ALAMO SHOWING WALLS OF CONVENTO, CA. 1912.
(Coppini Collection, Gift of Charles J. Long, Daughters of the Republic of Texas Library, CN95.39.)

There was one long wall and two short end walls of heavy stone masonry which were eighteen feet high and four feet thick, as the newspaper story reported, but most of the opposite long wall of masonry was missing. However, the footings that would have supported such a wall were there which indicated a long rectangular two story building of heavy masonry had stood there originally. From accounts written by various recorders after the battle, the building was there at the time of the Battle of the Alamo, and the missing wall must have collapsed afterward and the stones carried away during the following eleven year period before the U. S. Army remodeled the building.

After the removal work was completed, the missing long wall and the arched arcade as described in early records was restored and finished. The rest of the building, the roof, flooring, etc., was scheduled to be rebuilt, but by then the $5,000 that had been appropriated for the restoration project had run out. The governor applied for deficiency funds but the DRT again obtained an injunction to stop him. This time the Supreme Court upheld the DRT on grounds the governor did not have the power to create a deficiency fund for that purpose.[135]

Shortly thereafter the governor left on an official state trip to Panama, and the lieutenant governor allowed the San Antonio authorities to tear down both the rebuilt and the existing walls of the upper story.[136] All that remained then was the lower story of the heavy stone masonry walls of the original convento/"long barracks", along with the rebuilt arches of the arcade of the first floor,[137] and the project was abandoned there. To relieve the starkness of the scene, however, the DRT had those vines, which they were so anxious to have, planted to "gracefully trail . . ." over the walls that were still there. And the roofless ruin with a dirt floor remained that way for over fifty years until in 1967-68 it was finished off at last into the one story museum it is today.

The "second battle" finally came to an end except for that random echo which can be heard from time to time. It had never ended, however, for the two principal contestants, who remained bitter enemies until the day each drew her last breath.

~ ~ ~ ~ ~ ~ ~

~ ~ ~  ~ ~ ~

Epilogue

There is so much revision and myth associated with history as it is written sometimes today, that it is a relief to see something that comes from documented facts. There is an old saying which declares truth is stranger than fiction. It is also more interesting oftentimes when you know it is actually true.

This has been a very challenging and interesting experience, but I would never attempt it again. Writing about real people in an effort to make their stories as truthful as possible from the facts found, becomes obsessive. Mysticism has never held any fascination for me but I once read something a mystic said that seems appropriate here — "Bringing the dead back to life is a dangerous thing because it sometimes makes them become a part of you." The people get inside your mind, they dominate your conversation; and you are continually concerned you may write something about them that is not true. You write, rewrite, and rewrite again. You suffer with them and you feel their happiness. They fill your daytime thoughts and invade your sleep, your dreams, your restless, wakeful spells, and your efforts to go back to sleep. You get up and write down that thought you just had before you forget it.

These people who have possessed you absorb your life completely until you can divest yourself of their stories. At last you finish and you hope to be able to resume your own life and thoughts without their invasive spirits seeping into everything you think and do.

I hope I can do that now that I have written my final chapter on them, but somehow I suspect these women are a permanent part of me that is here to stay.

As I stroll the grounds of the place called The Alamo, and I pause in the old Chapel and in the "long barracks", I hear echoes of the voices of those women who were there, as well as anguished cries of the men who died there. I hear Susanna Dickinson and Ana Esparza and the others. And I hear the echoes of the voices of Adina

De Zavala and Clara Driscoll who came later.

Those women of courage and loyalty who lost their husbands in the nightmare of that battle fought there, and the women of vision and determination who worked to save this symbol of freedom later for future generations. Even as I move among the throngs of curious tourists and thoughtful visitors alike who come to see these buildings and grounds, I hear voices of those special women in my head. They rise above all the noise and din of the traffic as it drives over hallowed ground — echoes of voices from the past.

While we must always "Remember the Alamo" and the men who perished there, we must never forget the women who were there as well — both the survivors and the saviors later of this monument to humanities highest ideal, this shrine of liberty, The Alamo.

ENDNOTES

Endnotes for Chapter One: Susanna And Angelina Dickinson

1. Bond of Almeron Dickinson and B. D. Johnston for the marriage of Dickinson and Susanna Wilkerson. Hardeman County, Tennessee, May 24, 1829, Original Document, DRT Library. C. Richard King, *Susanna Dickinson: Messenger of the Alamo*, (Austin: Shoal Creek Publisher, Inc., 1976.), 4.

2. Ibid., 29.

3. Ibid., 30.

4. Dr. John Sutherland, "The Fall of the Alamo," 6, Daughters of the Republic of Texas Library.

5. *The Papers of the Texas Revolution, 1835-1836*, John H. Jenkins, General Editor, (Austin: Presidial Press, 1973), Vol. 4, 501; Walter Lord, *A Time to Stand*, (Lincoln and London: University of Nebraska Press, 1961), 95.

6. Ibid., 143.

7. Capt. John E. Elgin, "Reminiscences of the Story of the Alamo," from Collection in the Center for American History, University of Texas, Austin.

8. Evelyn Brogan, *James Bowie, A Hero of the Alamo*, (San Antonio: Theodore Kunzman, Printer and Publisher, 1922), 38.

9. King, *Susanna Dickinson*, 42.

10. Brogan, *James Bowie, A Hero of the Alamo*, 38.

11. Adjutant General's Letters Concerning the Alamo, 1875-1878, Texas State Archives, DRT Library.

12. Brogan, *James Bowie, A Hero of the Alamo*, 38.

13. King, *Susanna Dickinson*, 51.

14. Ibid., 56.

15. Ibid., 57.

16. Ibid., 63.

17. Ibid., 64.

18. Ibid., 68.

19. Ibid., 69.

20. Susanna Dickinson File, DRT Library.

21. King, *Susanna Dickinson*, 70.

22. Susanna Dickinson File, DRT Library.

23. King, *Susanna Dickinson*, 78.

24. Ibid., 71.

25. Ibid., 72.

26. Ibid., 75.

27. Ibid.

28. Ibid., 119.

29. Susanna Dickinson File, DRT Library.

30. B. J. Benefiel, interview by author, Luling, TX., 1994.

31. Susanna Dickinson File, DRT Library.

32. Ibid.

33. King, *Susanna Dickinson*, 119.

34. Angelina Dickinson File, DRT Library.

35. King, *Susanna Dickinson*, 122.

36. Ibid., 122.

37. Ibid., 84; Angelina Dickinson File, DRT Library.

38. John Bartlett, *Bartlett's Familiar Quotations,* Thirteenth Centennial Edition, (Boston, Toronto, Little Brown and Company, 1955), 306a.

39. Ibid., 637b.

40. King, *Susanna Dickinson*, XVI.

Endnotes for Chapter Two: The Incredible Journey Of The Travis Ring

1. Angelina Dickinson File, DRT Library.

2. Adina De Zavala File, DRT Library.

3. Angelina Dickinson File, DRT Library.

Endnotes for Chapter Three: Ana Esparza

1. "Another Child of the Alamo," *San Antonio Light*, Nov. 10, 1901, Enrique Esparza File, DRT Library.

2. Kay Thompson Hindes, "A Historical Study and Archaeological Notes on the Esparza Site, the Esparza Farms, The San Augustine Mission Church and San Augustine School, with Relevant Character Histories and Biographical Information," unpublished paper, 8. University of Texas at San Antonio.

3. "The Story of Enrique Esparza," *San Antonio Express*, Nov. 22, 1902, Enrique Esparza File, DRT Library.

4. "Alamo's Only Survivor," by Charles Merrit Barnes, *San Antonio Express*, May 12, 1907, Enrique

Esparza File, DRT Library.

5. Howard R. Driggs and Sarah S. King, *Rise of the Lone Star,* (New York: Frederick A. Stokes & Co., 1936.), 214.

6. "The Story of Enrique Esparza", Enrique Esparza File, DRT Library.

7. "Remembering," *Today's Catholic*, April 21, 1989, 13. Courtesy Ray Esparza private collection.

8. "The Story of Enrique Esparza", Enrique Esparza File, DRT Library.

9. Ibid.

10. "Remembering," *Today's Catholic*, Enrique Esparza File, DRT Library.

11. "The Story of Enrique Esparza," Enrique Esparza File, DRT Library.

12. Barnes, "Alamo's Only Survivor."

13. "The Story of Enrique Esparza", Enrique Esparza File, DRT Library.

14. Barnes, "Alamo's Only Survivor.".

15. Ibid.

16. Lt. A. B. Hannum, "A Thrilling Adventure of Mrs. Rebecca Fisher," Austin, Texas, March 15, 1906, DRT Library.

17. "Rebecca Jane Gilliland Fisher," *The New Handbook of Texas, Vol. 2.*, (Austin: The Texas Historical Association, 1996), 1012.

18. Hindes, "A Historical Study and Archaeological Notes on the Esparza Site," 6.

19. Reynaldo Esparza, "Esparza Family History," 1970, unpublished paper, Esparza Private Collection.

20. Hindes, "A Historical Study and Archaeological Notes," 7.

21. "Esparza Family History," Reynaldo Esparza.

Endnotes for Chapter Four: Juana Navarro And Gertrudis Navarro

1. John S. Ford, *Memoirs of John S. Ford, 1815-1836*, MS. 122-124, "Mrs. Alsbury's Recollections of the Fall of the Alamo," Juana Alsbury File, DRT Library.

2. "Petition of Juana N. Alsbury to the State of Texas," dated Nov. 1st, 1857, Holdings of the Texas State Archives, Juana Alsbury File, DRT Library.

3. "Champions of the Tejanos," Mary Love Bigony, *Texas Parks and Wildlife*, Feb., 1995, Vol. 53, No.2, Austin, 4.

4. Cecilia Steinfeldt, *San Antonio Was* (San Antonio: Museum Association, 1978), 70.

5. Ford, *Memoirs of John S. Ford.*

6. Letter Leonardo de la Garza, San Antonio to Miss L. L. Bowie, Wash., D.C., July 27, 1923, De Zavala (Adina Emilia) Papers, Center for American History, University of Texas at Austin.

ENDNOTES

7. San Fernando Church Records, Marriage of Juana Navarro and Alejo Peres [sic].

8. San Fernando Church Records, Baptismal record of Alejo Peres, Jr. [sic]. Courtesy of Dorothy Perez (descendant), San Antonio.

9. San Fernando Church Records, Baptismal record of Gertrudis Navarro. Courtesy of Dorothy Perez, San Antonio.

10. Ford, *Memoirs of John S. Ford.*

11. Amelia Williams, "A Critical Study of the Siege of the Alamo and of the Personnel of Its Defenders," Thesis, University of Texas Austin, 1931, 260, DRT Library.

12. Richard C. King, *Susanna Dickinson: Messenger of the Alamo*, (Austin: Shoal Creek Publishers, Inc., 1976), 105.

13. Williams, "A Critical Study of the Siege of the Alamo and of the Personnel of Its Defenders," 152.

14. Ibid., 264.

15. Barnes, "Alamo's Only Survivor, Interview With Enrique Esparza".

16. "Noncupative" Will and Distribution of the Estate of Angel Navarro, 1837. Courtesy of Dorothy Perez, San Antonio.

17. Texas Centennial Gravestone Marker for Y. Alsbury and Wife, *San Antonio Light*, Aug. 16, 1991.

18. "First Officials of Villa de San Fernando de Bejar," Elton Cude, San Antonio Public Records. Courtesy Mr. and Mrs. Horace Alsbury (descendants), San Antonio.

19. Petition of Juana Alsbury to the State of Texas, Nov. 1, 1857. Courtesy Mr. and Mrs. Horace Alsbury, San Antonio.

20. Petition of Juana Alsbury to the State of Texas, Mar. 3, 1855. Courtesy Mr. and Mrs. Horace Alsbury, San Antonio.

21. "Noncupative" Will and Distribution of the Estate of Angel Navarro, 1837. Courtesy of Dorothy Perez, San Antonio.

22. Mary A Maverick, *Memoirs of Mary A. Maverick*, (San Antonio: Alamo Printing Co. 1921),54.

23. Williams, "A Critical Study of the Siege of the Alamo and of the Personnel of Its Defenders," 261.

24. *San Antonio Light*, July 25, 1888, Courtesy of Dorothy Perez, San Antonio.

25. San Fernando Church Records, Baptismal record of Juana Navarro. Courtesy of Dorothy Perez, San Antonio.

26. Copy of Handwritten Death Announcement of Juana Navarro y Alsbury by Alejo Perez, Jr., July 23, 1888. Courtesy of Dorothy Perez, San Antonio.

340

27. *San Antonio Daily Express*, July 25, 1888. Courtesy of Dorothy Perez, San Antonio.

28. Williams, "A Critical Study of the Siege of the Alamo and of the Personnel of Its Defenders," 260.

29. Dorothy Perez correspondence to the author, 1996, San Antonio.

30. Maverick, *Memoirs*, 33-35.

31. San Fernando Church Records, Marriage record of Gertrudis Navarro to Miguel Cantu. Courtesy of Dorothy Perez, San Antonio.

32. Death Notice of Gertrudis Navarro Cantu, *San Antonio Daily Express*, April 8, 1893. Courtesy of Dorothy Perez, San Antonio.

33. Standard Certificate of Death, Oct. 19, 1918, Texas Dept. of Health, Bureau of Vital Statistics. Courtesy of Dorothy Perez, San Antonio.

34. Dorothy Perez, interview by author, 1996, San Antonio.

Endnotes for Chapter Five: Others

1. Walter Lord, *A Time to Stand*, (Lincoln and London: University of Nebraska Press, 1961) 208.

2. "Another Child of the Alamo," *San Antonio Light*, November 10, 1901, San Antonio Conservation Society Library.

3. Randell G. Tarin, "Toribio Lasoya", *The New Handbook of Texas, Vol. 4,* (Austin: The Texas Historical Association, 1996.) 296-297.

4. "The Story of Enrique Esparza," *Enrique Esparza File*, DRT Library.

5. Bill Groneman,"Eliel Melton", *The New Handbook of Texas, Vol. 4*, 609.

6. Charles Merritt Barnes, "Alamo's Only Survivor," *San Antonio Light*, May 10, 1907.

7. "The Story of Enrique Esparza," *Enrique Esparza File*, DRT Library.

8. Ibid.

9. William Corner, *San Antonio de Bexar, A Guide and History*, (San Antonio: Bainbridge and Corner, 1890), Facsimile Reproduction Printed by Graphic Arts, San Antonio, 1977.

10. "Another Child of the Alamo," *Enrique Esparza File*, San Antonio Consevation Society Library.

11. Barnes, "Alamo's Only Survivor".

12. Lord, *A Time To Stand*, 208.

Endnotes for Chapter Six: Adina De Zavala

1. Original in Archives Division, Texas State Library, Austin.

2. Adina De Zavala, "Statement by Miss De Zavala," De Zavala (Adina Emilia) Papers, Box 2M 134, Center for American History, University of Texas at Austin.

3. Luther Robert Ables, "The Work of Adina De Zavala,"A Thesis Presented in Partial Fulfillment of the Requirements for the Degree of Master of Art, Universitarios of Mexico City College, Mexico D. F.,

Mexico, August,1955, 127.

4. Winnie Allen, Archivist, The Mirabeau B. Lamar Library, University of Texas Library at Austin, Letter to Judge B. P. Matocha, 15 Mar. 1955, De Zavala Papers, Holding Record.

5. Senate Resolution No. 132, "In Memory of Miss Adina De Zavala," Texas State Senate, March 22, 1955, Austin, Texas, Adina De Zavala File, San Antonio Conservation Society Library.

6. Ables, "The Work of Adina De Zavala," 3.

7. Margaret Swett Henson, *Lorenzo de Zavala, The Pragmatic Idealist*, (Fort Worth: Texas Christian University, 1996), 121; Ables, "Adina Emilia De Zavala," *The New Handbook of Texas, Vol. 6*, (Austin: The Texas State Historical Association, 1996), 1147.

8. Henson, *Lorenzo de Zavala*, 55.

9. Ibid.

10. Ibid., 67.

11. Henson, telephone interview with author, June 27, 1997.

12. Henson, Lorenzo De Zavala, 77.

13. Henson, telephone interview with author, June 27, 1997; *Newsletter*, Texas Conservation Council, November, 1964; De Zavala Family File, S.A.C.S. Library; *The New Handbook of Texas, Vol. 6*, 1148.

14. Ibid.

15. Lorenzo De Zavala, Jr., Letter to Adina De Zavala, June 19, 1895, Merida, Yucatan, Mexico, De Zavala Papers, Box 2M 127.

16. Lorenzo De Zavala, Jr., Letters to Adina De Zavala and H. A. McArdle, De Zavala Papers, Box 2M 127.

17. Henson, telephone interview with author, June 27, 1997.

18. "Pioneer Woman Is Claimed by Death," *San Antonio Express*, December 15, 1918, Adina De Zavala File, DRT Library.

19. Ables, "The Work of Adina De Zavala," 19, Endnote 24: "Miss De Zavala would never reveal her age to friends and her correct age was often a point of conjecture. However, shortly before she died she revealed that she was born on the above date (Nov. 28, 1861). Neither the Bureau of Vital Statistics in Austin nor offices of the County Clerk in Harris or Galveston counties have any record of her birth. In Texas such information was not recorded until 1903, the official said."

20. L. Robert Ables, "The Second Battle for the Alamo," *The Southwestern Historical Quarterly*, Vol. LXX, July 1966 to April 1967, Austin, 373.

21. Pearl Howard, "Southern Personalities, Adina De Zavala . . . Texas Patriot-Historian," *Holland's,*

The Magazine of the South, December, 1935, 7.

22. Lois Johnson, "Miss De Zavala Continues Shrine Fight," San Antonio Light, February, 1947, Adina De Zavala File, DRT Library.

23. Howard, "Southern Personalities, Adina De Zavala," 36.

24. Ables, "The Work of Adina De Zavala", 8.

25. Henson, *Lorenzo De Zavala*, 121.

26. Ables, "The Work of Adina De Zavala," 10.

27. Henson, *Lorenzo De Zavala*, 121.

28. Adina De Zavala, "Grandmother's Old Garden", *San Antonio Express*, September 2, 1934, S.A.C.S. Library.

29. Ables, "The Work of Adina De Zavala," 10.

30. Ibid., 11.

31. De Zavala Papers, Box 2M 128, Holding Record.

32. Ables, "The Work of Adina De Zavala," 23.

33. Ibid., iv.

34. Adina De Zavala, *The Alamo, Where the Last Man Died*, (San Antonio: The Naylor Company, 1956, Reprint,) 47.

35. Ables, "The Work of Adina De Zavala," 80.

36. De Zavala Papers, Box 2M 131.

37. Ables, "The Work of Adina De Zavala," 119, from Frances Donecker, "A Journal of Our Trip Through East Texas and West Louisiana, July 2-19, 1935", 30.

38. De Zavala Papers, Holding Papers; Ables, "The Work of Adina De Zavala," 105.

39. Ibid., Box 2M 163.

40. Ables, "The Work of Adina De Zavala," 89, from Donecker personal interview with Ables.

41. Elizabeth Graham, "A Letter to My Congressman," (undated), S.A.C.S. Library.

42. Lewis Fisher, *Saving San Antonio*, (Lubbock: San Antonio Conservation Society, Texas Tech University Press, 1996), 97, from "A Message from Emily Edwards," undated typescript in S.A.C.S. Library.

43. Ables, "The Work of Adina De Zavala," 91, Mrs. Elizabeth Graham, personal interview with Ables.

44. Harvey P. Smith, "Architect Who Restored Palace Appeals to San Antonio To Keep Individuality All Its Own," *San Antonio Express*, March 1, 1931, S.A.C.S. Library.

45. Adina De Zavala, *The Alamo, Where the Last Man Died*, Foreword by Col. Harry M. Henderson.

46. Adina De Zavala, *History and Legends of the Alamo and Other Missions In and Around San Antonio*, edited by Richard Flores, (Houston: Arte Publico Press, 1996), lii.

47. Ibid., from book cover statement.

48. Fisher, *Saving San Antonio*, 63-64.

49. De Zavala Papers, Holding Record.

50. Ibid., Box 2M 131.

51. Ibid., Holding Papers.

52. Ables, "The Work of Adina De Zavala," 127-130.

53. *Last Will and Testament of Adina De Zavala*, Bexar County Archives, San Antonio, Texas, February 12, 1953, Filed March 7, 1955, No. 463, Page 277-279.

54. Sister Margaret Patrice Slattery, Chancellor, University of the Incarnate Word, San Antonio, personal interview with the author, September, 1998.

55. Sister Margaret Patrice Slattery, personal interview with the author, May 7, 1999.

56. Sister Margaret Patrice Slattery, C.C.V.I., *Promises to Keep*, Vol. Two, (San Antonio: Privately Published, 1995), 399, Endnote 70.

57. Ables, "The Work of Adina De Zavala," 5.

58. Ables, "The Second Battle for the Alamo," 413, from Butterfield, "Clara Driscoll Rescued the Alamo."

59. *The Medallion*, "Who Really "saved" the Alamo?", Texas Historical Commission, March, 1990, 5.

60. Ibid., March 1991, 5.

Endnotes for Chapter Seven: Clara Driscoll

1. Ables, "The Work of Adina De Zavala," 66, from the *Dallas Morning News*, December 31, 1911.

2. Martha Anne Turner, Clara Driscoll, An American Tradition, (Austin: Madrona Press, 1979), 2.

3. Ibid.

4. Ibid., 8 and 10.

5. Margaret Elizabeth Goodson, *"Clara Driscoll, Philanthropist-Politician,"* A Thesis Presented in Partial Fulfillment of the Requirement for the Degree of Master of Science, Texas College of Arts and Industries, Kingsville, Tx., August 1950, 8.

6. Turner, *Clara Driscoll*, 10.

7. Frank Wagner, "Robert, Driscoll, Jr.," *The New Handbook of Texas, Vol. 2*, 703.

8. Turner, *Clara Driscoll*, 10.

9. Goodson, "Clara Driscoll," 11.

10. Ibid.

11. *San Antonio Express*, December 3, 1899, 8, San Antonio Public Library, Texana-Genealogy File.

12. *Fifty Years of Achievement, History of the Daughters of the Republic of Texas*, (Dallas: Banks Upshaw and Company, 1942), 184-185, from an article in the *San Antonio Express*, January 14, 1901, DRT Library.

13. Turner, *Clara Driscoll*, 114.

14. Ibid., 115.

15. Ibid., 23.

16. Goodson, "Clara Driscoll," 15.

17. Ables, "The Work of Adina De Zavala," A Thesis, 31.

18. Ables "Adina De Zavala," *The New Handbook of Texas, Vol. 6*, 1146.

19. DRT Records, DRT Library.

20. *Message of Governor O. B. Colquitt to the Thirty-third Legislature Relating to the Alamo Property*, (Austin, Texas: Von Boekmann-Jones Co., Printers, 1913), 91; Goodson, "Clara Driscoll," 16.

21. *Message of Governor O. B. Colquitt*, 91-93; Turner, Clara Driscoll, 24, 44-45 (Photocopy of dated check written in this amount and signed by R. Driscoll); Goodson, "Clara Driscoll," 16.

22. Ibid.

23. Turner, *Clara Driscoll*, 25.

24. Ibid., 44-45 (Photocopy of dated check written in this amount and signed by Clara Driscoll).

25. Turner, *Clara Driscoll*, 26.

26. Goodson, "Clara Driscoll," 18.

27. *Fifty Years of Achievement*, 181-182; Turner, Clara Driscoll, 26-27; Goodson, "Clara Driscoll," 18.

28. Ibid.

29. Turner, *Clara Driscoll*, 28-29.

30. Ables, "The Second Battle for the Alamo," 390.

31. *The Victoria Advocate*, May 13, 1906, Clara Driscoll File, DRT Library.

32. Ibid.

33. Turner, *Clara Driscoll*, 33.

34. Clara Driscoll, *In The Shadow of the Alamo*, (New York-London:G. P. Putnam's Sons, The Knickerbocker Press, 1906, 41.

35. Ibid., 44.

36. Ibid., 44-45.

37. Turner, *Clara Driscoll*, 40.

38. De Zavala Papers, Box 2M 134.

39. Ibid.; Ables, "The Second Battle", 388.

40. De Zavala Papers, Box2M163.

41. Ibid.

42. Turner, *Clara Driscoll*, 43.

43. Dorothy De Moss, "Henry Hulme Sevier," *The New Handbook of Texas, Vol. 5*, 981.

44. Turner, *Clara Driscoll*, 45.

45. Ibid.

46. Goodson, "Clara Driscoll," 39.

47. Turner, *Clara Driscoll*, 47.

48. Ibid., 50; Goodson, "Clara Driscoll," 39.

49. De Moss, "Henry Hulme Sevier," *The New Handbook of Texas, Vol. 5*, 981.

50. "The History of Laguna Gloria," An Information Brochure, 1, Austin Museum of Art, Austin, Texas.

51. Ibid.

52. Turner, *Clara Driscoll*, 57.

53. De Moss, "Henry Hulme Sevier," *The New Handbook of Texas*, Vol. 5, 981.

54. "The History of Laguna Gloria," 2.

55. Turner, *Clara Driscoll*, 66, from *Corpus Christi Caller Times*, July 18, 1945.

56. Goodson, "Clara Driscoll," 48.

57. Ibid., 50, from "Their Excellencies, Our Ambassadors," *Fortune Magazine*, IX, April 1934, 120-122; also, Turner, *Clara Driscoll*, 75.

58. Turner, *Clara Driscoll*, 75.

59. Goodson, "Clara Driscoll," 50.

60. Ibid., 51, from "Mrs. Clara Driscoll is Seeking a Divorce," San Antonio (Texas) *Evening News*, May 21, 1937, p. 3.

61. Ibid.

62. Ibid., 52.

63. Turner, *Clara Driscoll*, 77.

64. Goodson, "Clara Driscoll," 52

65. Turner, *Clara Driscoll*, 77.

66. Ibid., 78.

67. Ibid., 81.

68. Goodson, "Clara Driscoll," 89, from *History of the Tezas Federation of Women's Clubs, 1918-1939*, 387.

69. Turner, *Clara Driscoll*, 110.

70. Ibid.

71. Goodson, "Clara Driscoll," 58-59.

72. Ibid., 65, from "Mrs. Driscoll Active in State Democratic Politics and Many Philanthropies," *Corpus Christi (Texas) Caller Times*, July 18, 1945, p. 1; Turner, Clara Driscoll, 105, from *Austin American*, July 17, 1945.

73. Goodson, "Clara Driscoll," 65.

74. "Empress Clara," *Time Magazine*, July 30, 1945, 23, Clara Driscoll File, DRT Library.

75. Turner, *Clara Driscoll*, 111.

76. Goodson, "Clara Driscoll," 107.

77. Ibid.

78. Turner, Clara Driscoll, 148.

79. Goodson, "Clara Driscoll," 105.

80. Turner, Clara Driscoll, 14, from Jack C. Butterfield, *Clara Driscoll Rescued the Alamo-A Brief Biography*, (San Antonio, 1961), pamphlet, np.

Endnotes for Chapter Eight: "The Second Battle" — Echoes Are Still Heard

1. *Eighteenth Annual Meeting of the Daughters of the Republic of Texas*, Held at San Antonio, Texas, April 20-22, 1909, (Houston: Gray, Dillaye & Company, 1909), 44, DRT Library

2. John Q. Anderson, *The New Handbook of Texas, Vol. 1*, 737; Clipping File on Antoinette Houston Bringhurst, DRT Library.

3. William Corner, *San Antonio de Bexar*, (San Antonio: Bainbridge and Corner, 1890), Reprint by Graphic Arts of San Antonio, 1977, 9.

4. Father Marion A. Habig, *The Alamo Chain of Missions*, (Chicago: Franciscan Herald Press, 1968), 56.

5. Ibid., 62.

6. Steinfeldt, *San Antonio Was*, 28.

7. Ibid., 28-30, from Footnote 30, "H. Grenet," *San Antonio Daily Express Supplement*, ND., (c.a. 1879).

8. Adina De Zavala, *The Story of the Siege and Fall of the Alamo, A Resumé*, (San Antonio, Texas: 1911), and De Zavala, *The Alamo, Where The Last Man Died*, (San Antonio: The Naylor company,

1956), 47.

9. Steinfeldt, *San Antonio Was*, 30.

10. Turner, *Clara Driscoll,* An American Tradition, 20.

11. Chas. Heuermann, "Notarized Statement," September 20, 1937, De Zavala Papers, Box 2M 163 and Box 2N 151.

12. Corner, *San Antonio de Bexar*, 9.

13. *Message of Governor O. B. Colquitt*, 131.

14. De Zavala, *The Alamo, Where The Last Man Died*, 48-50.

15. Heuermann, "Notarized Statement."

16. Ibid.

17. Ibid.

18. Pompeo Coppini, *From Dawn to Sunset*, (San Antonio: The Naylor Company, 1949), 86-87.

19. Ibid., 105-106.

20. Ibid., 107.

21. Ibid.

22. Ibid., 108.

23. Ables, "The Second Battle for the Alamo," 379, from Jack C. Butterfield, *Clara Driscoll Rescued the Alamo* (San Antonio, 1961), unp. pamphlet.

24. *Message of Governor O. B. Colquitt*, 131; De Zavala, *The Alamo, Where the Last Man Died*, 48-49.

25. De Zavala, *The Alamo, Where The Last Man Died*, 49; "Testimony of Mr. Gustav Schmeltzer."

26. *Fifty Years of Achievement*, 186; Message of Governor O. B. Colquitt, 91.

27. *Fifty Years of Achievement*, 187.

28. Ibid., 188.

29. Ables, "The Second Battle for the Alamo," 379, from *San Antonio Express*, April 29, 1900.

30. *Fifty Years of Achievement*, 190-191.

31. De Zavala Papers, Box 129.

32. *Fifty Years of Achievement*, 184.

33. Turner, *Clara Driscoll*, 23.

34. Ibid., 16.

35. *Message of Governor O. B. Colquitt*, 131; Robert Ables, *The New Handbook of Texas, Vol. 6*, 1146.

36. Pearl Howard, "Southern Personalities, Adina De Zavala . . . Texas Patriot-Historian," *Holland's,*

The Magazine of the South, December, 1935, 36, Adina De Zavala file, DRT Library.

37. *Message of Governor O. B. Colquitt*, 137; Ables, "The Second Battle for the Alamo," 409, from *Dallas Morning News*, December 31, 1911.

38. De Zavala Papers, Box 2M 134.

39. Ibid.

40. Ibid., Box 2M 135.

41. Susan Prendergast Schoelwer, *Alamo Images, Changing Perceptions of a Texas Experience*, (Dallas: De Golyer Library and Southern Methodist University Press, 1985), 24.

42. De Zavala Papers, Box 2M 164.

43. Ables, "The Second Battle for the Alamo," 383,

44. Adina De Zavala, *The Story of the Siege and Fall of the Alamo, A Resumé, The Alamo, Where the Last Man Died*, 30-31.

45. De Zavala, *The Alamo, Where the Last Man Died*, 17, from John Henry Brown's *History of Texas*.

46. Ables, "The Second Battle for the Alamo," 379, from *San Antonio Express*, April 29, 1900; Fisher, *Saving San Antonio*, 54.

47. Turner, *Clara Driscoll*, 23.

48. *Fifty Years of Achievement*, 218.

49. Ables, "The Second Battle for the Alamo," 383-384.

50. Ibid., 384, from *San Antonio Express*, January 29, 1905.

51. *Fifty Years of Achievement*, 198.

52. Ables, "The Second Battle for the Alamo," 385, from *DRT Report*, 1905, 46.

53. "Alamo's Women Saviors Are Now Fighting Among Themselves For Its Control," *St. Louis Post Dispatch*, May 6, 1906, 3B.

54. Ables, "The Second Battle for the Alamo," 389, from *DRT Report*, 1906, 41.

55. Curtis Carroll Davis, "A Legend at Full Length, Mr. Chapman Paints Colonel Crockett and Tells About It," Reprinted from Proceedings of the American Antiquarian Society for October 1959, Worcester, Massachusetts, Published by the Society, 1960, Footnote 20, 164.

56. Ibid., 389-390.

57. Ibid., 390.

58. Clara Driscoll File, DRT Library.

59. Ables, "The Second Battle for the Alamo," 391.

60. Ibid.

61. Ibid., 395, from De Zavala Papers, B-5/33, Charles M. Reaves to Adina De Zavala August 30, 1906.

62. Ables, "The Second Battle for the Alamo," 395-396.

63. Ibid., 397.

64. Ibid., 398.

65. Ibid., 399.

66. Ibid., 400, from *Austin Statesman*, April 20, 1907.

67. *Sixteenth Annual Meeting of the Daughters of the Republic of Texas, April 19th, 1907, Austin*, (Houston: Gray, Dillay, and Company, 1907).

68. *Fifty Years of Achievement.*

69. "Report of Convention," De Zavala Papers, Box 2M 163.

70. Ibid., 4.

71. Ibid.

72. *Sixteenth Annual Meeting of the Daughters of the Republic of Texas, April 19th, 1907, Austin*, 17-18.

73. "Report of Proceedings of 16th Annual Convention," 6, De Zavala Papers, Box 2M 163.

74. De Zavala Papers, Box 2M 163.

75. Ibid.

76. Ibid.

77. Ibid.

78. Ables, "The Second Battle for the Alamo," 402, from *San Antonio Express*, April 28, 1907.

79. Ables, "The Second Battle for the Alamo," 402, from "Plaintiff's Petition," DRT vs. Adina De Zavala, docket No. 43344, Sixty-First District Court of Texas, Harris County (District Clerk's Office, Houston).

80. De Zavala Papers, Box 2M 129.

81. Ibid.

82. Ibid.

83. Ibid., Box 2M 130.

84. Ibid.

85. Ables, "The Second Battle for the Alamo," 403, from *San Antonio Express*, January 27, 1908.

86. Ibid., from *San Antonio Express*, January 28, 1908.

87. De Zavala Papers, Box 2M 129.

88. Ibid., Box 2M 163.

89. Ibid., Box 2M 134

90. Ibid., Box 2M 129, *The Courier Herald*, Saginaw, Michigan, February 12, 1908.

91. Ibid., *The San Antonio Light*, February 11, 1908.

92. Ibid., Box 2M 130.

93. Ibid., Box 2M 129. *Galveston, Texas News*, February 12, 1908.

94. Ibid.

95. Mary Ann Noonan Guerra, personal interview with author, April 23, 1998.

96. Wanda Ford, personal interview with author, April 24, 1998.

97. De Zavala Papers, Box 2M 129.

98. Adina De Zavala File, DRT Library.

99. Howard, "Southern Personalities . . . Adina De Zavala."

100. De Zavala Papers, Box 2M 127.

101. Ibid., Box 2M 130, *The Austin Statesman*, February 29, 1908.

102. Ibid., Box 2M 131.

103. Ibid., Box 2M 164, Executive Committee of the DRT, "Statement of the Situation."

104. Ables, "The Second Battle for the Alamo," 405, from the Houston *Chronicle*, March 14, 1908.

105. Ibid., 405, from the *Weatherford Herald*, May 16, 1908.

106. De Zavala Papers, Box 2M164.

107. Ibid., 406, from "Supplemental Petition," Daughters of the Republic of Texas vs. Adina De Zavala, Docket No. 43344.

108. De Zavala Papers, Box 2M 130.

109. Ibid., Box 2M 131.

110. Clara Driscoll File, DRT Library.

111. De Zavala et al. vs Daughters of the Republic of Texas, 124 SW, 160 (1909,writ refused), *Sounthwestern Reporter, West Publishing Co.*

112. De Zavala Papers, Box 2M 131.

113. Ibid., Pocket #3.

114. Coppini, *From Dawn to Sunset*, 181.

115. *Fifty Years of Achievement*, 211.

116. Ibid., 212.

117. *Eighteenth Annual Meeting of the DRT*, 11.

118. Ables, "The Second Battle for the Alamo," 407-408, from *San Antonio Express*, April 20, 1910.

119. De Zavala Papers, Box 2M 131, Harvey L. Page, Plans and Drawings for Alamo Amusement

Company, July 14th, 1910.

120. Ibid.

121. Ibid.

122. Ibid.

123. Ibid.

124. Ibid.

125. Ibid.

126. Ibid.

127. Ables, "The Second Battle for the Alamo," 409, from General Laws of the State of Texas, 32nd Legislature, 1st Called Session, 6.

128. De Zavala Papers, Box 2M 131.

129. *Message of Governor O. B. Colquitt*, 137; De Zavala Papers, Box 2M164; Ables, "The Second Battle for the Alamo," 409, from *Dallas Morning News,* December 11, 1911.

130. *Message of Governor O. B. Colquitt*, 138; De Zavala Papers, Box 2M 164.

131. *Message of Governor O. B. Colquitt*, 139; De Zavala Papers, Ables, "The Second Battle for the Alamo," 409-410, from *Dallas Morning News,* December 11, 1911.

132. *Message of Governor O. B. Colquitt*, 140; Ables, "The Second Battle for the Alamo," 410.

133. *Message of Governor O. B. Colquitt*, 133. De Zavala Papers, Box 2M164.

134. Ibid, 134-140; DRT Library.

135. Ables, "The Second Battle for the Alamo," 412, from A. V. Conley vs. DRT, 156, S.W. 199 *(1913)*.

136. Ibid., 412, from Oscar B. Colquitt to James T. De Shields, July 7, 1938, in *Message of Governor Colquitt in Relating to the Alamo*.

137. Ibid.

Selected Bibliography

Ables, Luther Robert, "The Work of Adina De Zavala," A Thesis Presented in Partial Fulfillment of the Requirements for the Degree of Master of Arts, Universitarios of Mexico City College, Mexico D. F., Mexico, August,1955), Our Lady of the Lake University Library, San Antonio.

"The Second Battle for the Alamo"; The Southwestern Historical Quarterly, Vol. LXX, July 1966 to April 1967, Austin, 375-413.

Adjutant General's Letters Concerning the Alamo, 1875-78; Texas State Archives, DRT Library.

Ahlborn, Richard Eighime, *The San Antonio Missions: Edward Everett and the American Occupation,* 1847, Fort Worth: Amon Carter Museum/Los Compadres de San Antonio Missions National Historical Park, 1985.

Alsbury, Juana Navarro File, DRT Library.

Brogan, Evelyn, *James Bowie, A Hero of the Alamo,* San Antonio: Theodore Kunzman, Printer and Publisher, 1922.

Carrington, Evelyn M., ed., *Women in Early Texas,* AAUW-Austin Branch, Austin: Jenkins Publishing Co., The Pemberton Press, 1975.

Coppini, Pompeo, *From Dawn to Sunset,* San Antonio: The Naylor Company, 1949.

Corner, William, *San Antonio de Bexar, A Guide and History,* San Antonio: Bainbridge and Corner, 1890, Facsimile Reproduction Printed by Graphic Arts, San Antonio, 1977.

Crawford, Ann Fears and Crystal Sasse Ragsdale, *Women in Texas,* Austin: Eakin Press, 1982.

De Zavala, Adina File, DRT Library and San Antonio Conservation Society Library.

De Zavala, (Adina Emilia) Papers, Center for American History, University of Texas at Austin.

De Zavala, Adina, *The Alamo, Where the Last Man Died,* San Antonio: The Naylor Company, 1956 Reprint.

Dickinson, Angelina File, DRT Library.

Dickinson, Susanna File, DRT Library.

Driggs, Howard R. and Sarah S. King, *Rise of the Lone Star,* New York: Frederick A. Stokes & Co., 1936.

Driscoll, Clara File, DRT Library.

Driscoll, Clara, *In The Shadow of the Alamo,* New York-London: G. P. Putnam's Sons, The Knickerbocker Press, 1906.

Eighteenth Annual Meeting of the Daughters of the Republic of Texas, Held at San Antonio, April 20-22, 1909, Houston: Gray, Dillaye & Company, 1909, DRT Library.

Elgin, Capt. John E., "Reminiscences of the Story of the Alamo," Center for American History, University of Texas, Austin.

Esparza, Enrique File, DRT Library.

Fifty Years of Achievement, History of the Daughters of the Republic of Texas, Dallas: Banks Upshaw and Company, 1942, DRT Library.

Fisher, Lewis, *Saving San Antonio,* Lubbock: San Antonio Conservation Society, Texas Tech University Press, 1996.

Flores, Richard, ed., *History and Legends of the Alamo and Other Missions In and Around San Antonio,* by Adina De Zavala, Houston: Arte Publico Press, 1996).

Gambrell, Herbert, *Anson Jones, The Last President of Texas,* Austin: University of Texas Press, 1947.

Goodson, Margaret Elizabeth, "Clara Driscoll, Philanthropist-Politician," A Thesis Presented in Partial Fulfillment of the Requirement for the Degree of Master of Arts, Texas College of Arts and Industries, Kingsville, TX., August 1950.

Guerra, Mary Ann Noonan, *Heroes of the Alamo and Goliad,* San Antonio: The Alamo Press, 1987.
_____The Alamo, San Antonio, The Alamo Press, 1983.

Habig, Father Marion A., *The Alamo Chain of Missions,* Chicago: Franciscan Herald Press, 1968.

Henson, Margaret Swett, *Lorenzo de Zavala, The Pragmatic Idealist,* Fort Worth: Texas Christian University, 1996.

Hindes, Kay Thompson, "A Historical Study and Archaeological Notes on the Esparza Site," University of Texas at San Antonio, unpub.

Jenkins, John H., *The Papers of the Texas Revolution, 1835-1836,* Austin: Presidial Press, 1973.

King, Richard C., *Susanna Dickinson: Messenger of the Alamo,* Austin: Shoal Creek Publisher, Inc. 1967.

Lord, Walter, *A Time to Stand,* Lincoln and London: University of Nebraska Press, 1961.

Maverick, Mary A., *Memoirs of Mary A. Maverick,* Rena Maverick Green, ed., San Antonio: Alamo Printing Co., 1921.

Ragsdale, Crystal Sasse, *Women and Children of the Alamo,* Austin: State House Press, 1994.

Ramsdell, Charles, *San Antonio: A Historical and Pictorial Guide,* Austin: University of Texas Press, 1959.

Schoelwer, Susan Prendergast, *Alamo Images, Changing Perceptions of a Texas Experience,* Dallas: De Golyer and Southern Methodist University Press, 1985.

Sixteenth Annual Meeting of the Daughters of the Republic of Texas, April 19th, 1907, Austin, Houston: Gray, Dillay, and Company, 1907

Slattery, Sister Margaret Patrice, C.C.V.I., *Promises to Keep,* Vol. Two, San Antonio: Privately Published, 1995.

Steinfeldt, Cecilia, *San Antonio Was, Seen Through A Magic Lantern,* San Antonio: San Antonio Museum Association, 1978.

Sutherland, John, "The Fall of the Alamo," DRT Library.

Williams, Amelia, "A Critical Study of the Siege of the Alamo and of the Personnel of Its Defenders," Thesis, University of Texas at Austin, 1931, DRT Library.